S0-AUB-159

# SUICIDE

*by*

Mark William Viner, M.D.

**DORRANCE PUBLISHING CO., INC.**
**PITTSBURGH, PENNSYLVANIA 15222**

The opinions expressed herein are those of the author, who assumes complete and sole responsibility for them, and do not necessarily represent the views of the publisher or its agents.

*All Rights Reserved*
Copyright © 2005 by Mark William Viner, M.D.
No part of this book may be reproduced or transmitted
in any form or by any means, electronic or mechanical,
including photocopying, recording, or by any information
storage and retrieval system without permission in
writing from the publisher.

ISBN 0-8059-6829-6
Printed in the United States of America

*First Printing*

For information or to order additional books, pleased write:
Dorrance Publishing Co., Inc.
701 Smithfield Street
Third Floor
Pittsburgh, Pennsylvania 15222
U.S.A.
1-800-788-7654
or visit our web site and on-line catalog at www.dorrancepublishing.com

To Bonnie Eloise

# CONTENTS

# PREFACE

THE READER OF this book should be primarily post-graduate students in psychiatry and behavioral sciences. Medical students, residents-in-training, junior and senior faculty, practicing physicians including general practitioners, obstetricians and gynecologists, pediatricians, surgeons, and emergency room staff also may gain insight into recognizing suicidal patients. In addition, nurses, pharmacists, psychologists, mental health technicians, service coordinators, social workers, recreational therapists, clergy, law enforcement, school counselors, medical first responders, educators, and community gatekeepers will appreciate suicidality from this medical perspective. Legislatures, federal, state, and local agencies, organizations, families, and survivors of suicide will gain important insights into suicidality.

Chapter 1 includes the neurobiological aspects of suicidality, and the biochemical changes observed in the suicidal patient are illustrated. Localizing suicidal thoughts and suicidal acts using PET scans of the brain as guidance are introduced. Peripheral biological markers of suicide are compared with recent findings in the central nervous system tissue and the nerve cell changes in the brains of suicidal victims. Central serotonergic pathways in the brain, serotonin binding in depressed and suicidal patients, and intraneuronal cellular changes involved in suicide are described. Greater DNA and mRNA synthesis of the 5HT2 type of serotonin receptor in the pyramidal layer of the prefrontal cortex in suicide victims is independent of the psychiatric diagnosis. In addition, a candidate gene is hypothesized to play a role in the pathophysiology of suicide. This basic science knowledge forms the foundation into understanding suicidality.

Chapter 2 covers the clinical characteristics of suicidality among patients suffering from all the major primary psychiatric disorders. Suicidality is presented in the context of each major primary psychiatric disorder. This chapter highlights suicide in patients with substance related disorders including alcohol, benzodiazepines, and cocaine, as well as inhalants, ecstasy, heroin, combinations of drugs, and prescription drugs. With each DSM-IV psychiatric diagnosis, the characteristics of suicidality are methodically described. It describes suicidality among patients suffering from major psychiatric disorders including dementia, psychotic, mood, anxiety, eating, sexual, sleeping, and impulse control disorders; also mental retardation and personality disorders are highlighted. There is an emphasis on mood disorders and suicide. It delineates a relationship between psychosocial stressors and the timing of suicide.

Chapter 3 is an advanced illustration of the psychopharmacologic treatment options for suicidality. The psychopharmacologic treatment of suicidality is presented in depth with numerous case examples. Medication options are outlined for clinical consideration, and they include the use of atypical antipsychotics. A practical classification of atypical antipsychotics is reviewed to help the clinician choose the most effective one for the suicidal patient with psychotic or mood disorders. The use of clozapine as a first line agent for suicidal schizophrenia is discussed. Detailed and illustrative case examples using clozapine in suicidal schizophrenic patients review the safety and efficacy when prescribing this medication. It then details various types of antidepressants used to treat depression and reduce suicidality. There is an outline of the controversy about antidepressants and suicide. It emphasizes the use of lithium as an "anti-suicidal agent," comparing anticonvulsants for suicide risk reduction in bipolar patients. It outlines strategies when encountering a patient who fails to respond to standard antidepressant treatment. Novel augmentation strategies as treatment options for the more resistant, depressed, suicidal patients are presented as numerous case examples in clinical practice with reports of outcome measures. One novel approach emphasized is the use low dose atypical antipsychotic combination therapy with antidepressant medication for imminent suicide threat.

Chapter 4 describes suicide across the entire life span. Teen suicide is covered. There is a review of the diagnosis and treatment of suicidality in children and adolescents. There is a review of pediatric mood disorders, personality disorders, and risk factors for girls compared with boys. Psychosocial stressors such as physical abuse, childhood sexual traumatization, homelessness, dating violence, sexuality, guns and violence, peer pressure and interpersonal relationships in teenagers in high school and college age students are also discussed. Emphasis on treatment approaches to the suicidal teen, a discussion about the controversial use of antidepressants and suicidality in children, and a review of treatment options for suicidal teens with bipolar disorder are described. There are clinical considerations of suicide in women in relation to menarche, menstrual cycle, pregnancy, miscarriage, and the postpartum, peri- and postmenopausal periods. Women's issues are compared and contrasted with suicidal tendencies among men. Adult patients suffering from general medical conditions and the relationship to suicide in primary care are explored. Suicidal patients with neurological, cardiac, respiratory, and endocrine disorders have illnesses associated with increased risk of suicide. The specific disorders and their relationship to suicide are revealed. There is a section on the use of selective serotonin reuptake inhibitors and hormone replacement therapy. There is consideration of rheumatological disorders, infectious diseases, and renal disorders, as well as medications in the treatment of dermatological disorders and gastrointestinal diseases as they relate to suicide. Cancer and suicide is also discussed.

Late-life suicide, an increasing clinical concern, is discussed, and the treatment of suicidality in elderly patients is reviewed. Epidemiological considerations and risk factors, common psychiatric disorders and clinical presentations, and treatment and outcomes with case examples of treating late life depression are presented. Special psychopharmacologic considerations when treating elderly patients with depression are emphasized. Emergency medicine/surgery and trauma in its relation to suicide is reviewed. Suicides can present themselves as homicides, motor vehicle accidents, drug overdoses, accidents, gunshot wounds, or murder. Patterns of injury in suicide attempts and completions as well as types of trauma and emergency procedures frequently performed involve suicidal patients.

Finally, throughout the handbook, there are compilations of many case examples I have remembered over ten years of clinical practice as a Board Certified Psychiatrist treating suicidal patients. This clinical experience is interwoven with the latest reports in literature on this important topic of suicide. There is an extensive reference list. I hope this Handbook of suicide prevention is useful for you. I can be contacted at MVMD@prodigy.net for live educational programs.

# CHAPTER 1

## Neurobiological Aspects of Suicide

## Neuroimaging of Suicidality

RECENTLY, OUR MEDICAL technology is becoming more sophisticated, to the point that we can image real time brain activity of a person[1].

The PET scan picture is generated by injecting a form of radioactive glucose, flurodeoxyglucose (FDG), into a patient. FDG is fluorinated glucose which is actually made in a cyclotron. This radioactive glucose then travels to the brain through the blood stream. Glucose is normally the brain's fuel. The more active a part of the brain is during a task, the more glucose it uses. Where the brain is active, radiation detectors in the scanner locate the radioactivity and send it to a computer that produces two-dimensional, color-coded images. The brighter colors, red, orange, and yellow indicate more activity. A PET scan is a brain imaging technique that uses a radioactive tracer to show chemical activity of the brain[2]. The PET scan allows one to look at many brain functions by measuring levels of activity in specific areas of the brain[3]. PET scans generate pictures of the working brain, providing maps of learning, vision, hearing, emotions, memory, thinking, and acting.

Localizing in the brain where thoughts and actions, including suicidal thoughts and suicidal acts, originate is an important step in the understanding of suicidality. What areas of the brain are activated in a suicidal patient? Since suicide is unique to the human race, and the prefrontal cortex, part of the frontal lobe, is the most human part of the brain, this is a good place to start. The prefrontal cortex is the most human part of the brain because it is the structure that distinguishes persons from pre-human ancestors and from other primates living today. The prefrontal cortex is the judgment seat and thinking cap, where one develops flexible thinking and mental control. It is the personal time machine that integrates the past with the present and anticipates the future. It balances experience with perception to determine appropriate action. The prefrontal cortex is where wisdom resides[4]. Not only is the prefrontal cortex the last area of the brain to evolve in human beings, but it is also the last to develop in individuals. Interestingly, it is one of the first areas of the brain to lose its function due to generalized stress or injury to the central nervous system. Is the prefrontal cortex the headquarters of suicidality? The frontal cortex serves as an important area of the brain involved in suicidality, both through suicidal thoughts and suicidal acts.

Suicidal thinking activates the frontal cortex. Brain changes can be imaged during the task of thinking, not limited to, but including, *suicidal* thinking. A scan of a patient actively thinking shows increased activity in the prefrontal cortex. This could be a PET scan of an actively suicidal patient.

It is known that suicidal thoughts are a common and important antecedent to suicidal acts[5]. In most cases, recurrent suicidal thoughts and ideation is *not* accompanied by a suicide attempt. However, almost all suicidal patients had thought of suicide previously, as evident by communicating the direct or indirect intentions or by retrospectively interviewing patients who attempted suicide. The presence of a detailed suicidal plan is an especially ominous occurrence. As patients age, they generally become less impulsive, so suicidal thoughts and well thought out suicidal intentions and plans may be more difficult to detect. Suicides that involve intense planning and thinking can be more lethal than unplanned ones. The greater planning of suicidal acts implies a psychological deterioration over time. A logical, preventive strategy emphasizing improved screening and detection of this mental deterioration is necessary for clinicians to detect and prevent suicidality.

The suicidal act, itself involves a different area of the frontal lobe. The primary motor strip of the frontal lobe is activated during an act. The motor task causes increased activation of the motor strip and supplementary motor cortex to carry out the act as illustrated in a PET scan. This area in the brain is involved doing a task, a motor task when physically acting out suicide, such as such as pulling the trigger of a gun (firearm suicide) suffocation/hanging, poisoning, falling, cutting/piercing, drowning, setting fire. Any motor behavior or act, not limited to but including the suicidal act, involves activation of the motor strip of the frontal lobe to execute the task.

If that action is the act of suicide, then it can have differing degrees of lethality, even though the task itself can be simple to execute. A motor task, as simple as movement of the right foot in the context of pushing the foot of an automobile gas pedal, can be a suicidal act to crash a car in a suicide attempt. Such a case of a motor vehicle- assisted suicide is described: a the person had tied rope between a stationary object and the neck; then pushing the gas pedal with his foot and driving the vehicle away, that resulted in forces great enough to cause fracture of the cervical spine and virtual decapitation[6].

Impulsivity can affect the degree to which one acts out, and the type of acting out of suicidal behavior. For example, low lethal suicide attempts have been associated with more impulsivity in younger patients; whereas high lethal suicide attempts are associated in older less, impulsive patients. Highly lethal types of suicidal acts may be extremely violent. For example, using a firearm at close range, jumping from a height into a moving train or traffic, hanging, drowning, and stabbing can be considered violent and lethal. Examples of less violent, but just as lethal acts include: swallowing as in intentional overdose, wrist slashing, poisoning, and suffocation[7]. The single, lethal act may be planned or unplanned. Unplanned suicidal acts account for a greater proportion of completed suicides than is generally recognized. For example, researchers who studied patients hospitalized for medically serious suicide attempts demonstrated that 24% of that patient sample thought about the suicidal act for less than five minutes beforehand. In another study, 17% of a series of completed suicides involved less than twenty minutes of planning. Finally, another study concluded that 40% of adolescent suicides showed no evidence of planning. Thus, screening and detection of suicidality, with primary care physicians to detect and treat depression, may not be the most efficient strategy in unplanned suicide risk reduction.

Using neuroimaging techniques, such as a PET scan of the brain in action, will help clinicians begin to understand the biological factors associated with suicide. Although images are difficult to obtain in an actively suicidal patient, PET scans help clarify areas of the brain involved in suicidal thinking and the actual suicidal act. Positron emission tomography may eventually offer a means to measure neurobiological correlates of different types of suicidal behavior, thereby allowing the identification of individuals at more acute risk of suicide completion. PET scan studies in suicidal patients may offer a distinct advantage. One way is allowing for more precise identification and study of the activity of brain regions that differ in those who have survived a suicide attempt of high lethality compared to those who have survived a low-lethality attempt[8].

## Neurobiochemical Aspects of Suicide

There were peripheral biological markers of suicidality before the more recent advancements in imaging the central nervous system in psychiatry were known. They remain important in the biological underpinnings of suicidality. Biological markers associated with increased risk of suicide include the following:

1) An abnormal electroencephalogram. The EEG records electrical impulses on the surface of the brain. The EEG's of suicidal people suggest minor and nonspecific brain dysfunctions, not epilepsy or other obvious pathologic states.

2) Rapid habituation of the skin conductance reaction to unexpected stimuli. The skin's conductance of small electrical currents is affected by the rate of sweating. Habituation of the body's alarm system to stop reacting

occurs when the person is repeatedly exposed to strong stimulation. In suicidal people, the skin conductance reaction diminishes especially fast.

3) Low serum cholesterol. A relatively high concentration of lipids is a unique biochemical feature of brain itself. Nearly fifty percent of the dry weight of the human brain is lipid, compared with 5–20 percent in other organs of the body. Furthermore, brain cholesterol occurs almost exclusively in the free form, in contrast to other tissues of the body. There is only a minute amount that undergoes biochemical esterification.

The abnormal, lipid bi-layer of the nerve cell membrane can result in abnormal alterations in membrane fluidity, viscosity, and function of neuro-receptors and neurotransmission, leading to neuropathological states. Reduced plasma cholesterol could suppress the cholesterol/phospholipid ratio of the nerve cell membranes. Brain lipid metabolism, biochemical reactions that methylate lipids, affects the nerve cell, lipid, bi-layer membrane. In addition to pure cholesterol, brain lipids include glycerides and sphingolipids of very complex composition. When methylated, brain lipids are translocated across the cell membrane, and that process reduces the viscosity of the nerve cell membrane. That activity facilitates the lateral mobility of receptors, which in turn triggers a variety of intracellular events. The intracellular events include generation of cyclic-adenosine monophosphate (cAMP), release of other neurotransmitters, calcium fluxes, and activation of precursor lipids used to signal cascades occurring within the cell.

One study demonstrated no association of low cholesterol and suicidality with respect to cholesterol transport proteins such as apolipoprotein E[9]. However, low serum cholesterol and leptin levels have been studied in relation to suicide. A low serum cholesterol state, or hypocholesterolemia, is associated with a higher risk of suicide and aggressiveness, impulsivity, and violence in patients with a variety of psychiatric disorders[10]. Low serum cholesterol may be associated with increased suicide attempt risk[11].

4) Increased production of the stress hormone, cortisol. Neuroendocrine chemicals, including cortisol, are studied in psychiatric research for disorders such as depression and anxiety, as well as symptoms of aggression and impulsivity are studied in relation to suicide. The frontal lobe of the brain has direct connections with glands in the body. With respect to the adrenal gland, the frontal-limbic-hypothalamic-pituitary-adrenal axis is the pathway whereby the frontal lobe of the brain can influence adrenal gland secretion. Cortisol is synthesized in the adrenal glands. Cortisol production increases in stressful situations, especially in situations that are beyond the individual's control[12]. In addition, increased cortisol from stress can have devastating effects on the brain, such as dendritic pruning.

Postmortem studies have found evidence in suicide victims of chronic limbic-hypothalamic-pituitary-adrenal axis activation resulting in adrenal gland hyperplasia, down-regulation of corticotropin releasing hormone (CRH) receptors, and increases in pro-opiomelanocortin mRNA. Pro-opiomelanocortin is the precursor for ACTH in the pituitary. It is not known whether these changes in suicide are due to depression, to the stress surrounding suicidality itself, or to a neurobiological abnormality common to all suicides irrespective of diagnosis.

Stressor induced, increased cortisol secretion may be measured by urinary cortisol levels, a peripheral marker to assess central neurotransmission functioning. Urinary cortisol levels are significantly higher in patients with violent suicidal behavior compared to those without violent suicidal behavior. However, there are no differences between patient groups regarding severity of anxiety or depressive symptomatology. This observation suggests that violent suicidal behavior is associated with increased cortisol secretion[13]. Because of this fact, some clinicians consider the dexamethasone suppression test (DST) more associated with suicidal behavior in depressed patients compared to the standard demographic and historical risk factors currently used as clinical markers[14].

5) Low peripheral serotonin. Serotonin is the neurotransmitter conveying signals between nerve cells in the brain regulating many functions such as aggressive behavior, mood, memory, and sleep. Serotonin has a major role in defining the suicidal threshold. Serotonin is synthesized, packaged, and released by one nerve. It then binds to serotonin receptors on the next nerve cell, and thereby causing changes. The changes may be excitatory or inhibitory in nature. Serotonin facilitates communication between nerves at the nerve terminals. Although several central nervous system neurotransmitters including dopamine, norepinepherine, glutamanine, GABA (gamma-aminobutyric acid), and acetylcholine, are also considered to be involved in suicide, most of the suicide research has been done specifically with the neurotransmitter serotonin.

Of all the neurotransmitters, serotonin remains historically and currently the most intimately involved with neuropsychopharmacology. Originally found in serum causing powerful contraction of smooth muscle organs, serotonin was discovered in the mid-nineteenth century. A hundred years later scientists at the Cleveland Clinic succeeded in isolating this substance as a possible cause of high blood pressure. High concentrations were found in chromaffin cells of the intestinal mucosa. The material isolated from the bloodstream was given the name serotonin while that from the intestinal tract was called enteramine. Subsequently, both materials were purified, crystallized, and shown to be 5-hydroxy-tryptamine (5-HT), which could then be prepared synthetically, still possessing all the biological features as the natural substance. The indole nature of this molecule resembles the psychedelic drug LSD. When 5-HT was first found within the central nervous system, the theory arose that various forms of mental illness could be related to biochemical abnormalities in its synthesis. This idea was extended when reserpine was observed to deplete brain 5-HT, and profound behavioral depression was observed.

Serotonin is found in many cells that are not neurons, such as platelets, mast cells, and enterochromaffin cells. Only one to two percent of the serotonin in the whole body is found in the brain. Because 5-HT cannot cross the blood-brain barrier, it is clear that brain cells must synthesize serotonin. For brain cells, the first important step is the uptake of the amino acid tryptophan, which is the primary substrate for the synthesis. Plasma tryptophan arises primarily from the diet, and elimination of dietary tryptophan can profoundly lower the levels of brain serotonin. Plasma tryptophan has a daily rhythmic variation in its concentration, and this concentration variation could influence the rate and synthesis of brain serotonin.

There are known metabolic pathways describing the synthesis and metabolism of serotonin. There is a relatively brief sequence of synthetic and degradative steps involved in serotonin turnover. Major enzymes include tryptophan hydroxylase. Serotonin is further metabolized to melatonin in the pineal gland. Serotonin can be catabolized to 5 hydroxy-indole-acetic acid (5-HIAA) by deamination with the enzyme monoamine oxidase (MAO). Although most early neurochemical pharmacology assumed that brain 5-HT was a neurotransmitter, more than a decade elapsed before it could be established with certainty that 5-HT in the brain is actually contained in nerve cells and involved in specific nerve circuits. Dynamic re-uptake and turnover of serotonin occurs in a fashion similar to that described for other neurotransmitters.

The serotonin deficiency hypothesis of depression was originally proposed in 1965. Although it is a somewhat simplistic idea of attempting to relate a behavioral effect to a changing level of a single neurotransmitter, the connection between serotonin and suicide has been repeatedly reproduced in more than a dozen studies. The changes in serotonin function and suicide are not just confined to depressive illness, but also occur in many other psychiatric disorders and states. In fact, biological and molecular genetic studies have suggested that dysfunction of the serotonergic system is associated with susceptibility to suicidal behavior, regardless of psychiatric diagnosis[15].

Serotonin deficiency is characteristic of those suicidal patients who make dangerous and planned suicide attempts. Cerebrospinal fluid levels of the serotonin metabolites may indirectly and peripherally measure and reflect central serotonin activity of the brain. This method has been used to study suicide victims since the 1970's. The serotonin metabolite, 5-hydroxy-indoleacetic acid (5-HIAA), is measured in the cerebrospinal fluid rather than serotonin itself, which is less accessible. The serotonin metabolite, 5-hydroxyindoleacetic acid (5-HIAA), can be measured in the cerebrospinal fluid via a lumbar puncture. Serotonin activity measured this way is presumed to reflect central serotonergic brain activity, but this measurement does not localize where in the brain that serotonin activity originates and leaves a certain percent of 5-HIAA circulating freely in the cerebrospinal fluid before collection. Abnormally low serotonin function is associated with impulsive and aggressive behaviors. Conversely, patients with high 5-HIAA tend to be more fearful. Studies report a relationship between certain violent crimes, like manslaughter and arson, and low 5-HIAA levels in the cerebrospinal fluid of these individuals.

Whole blood tryptophan is another indirect and peripheral way to measure central serotonin function. Tryptophan is a biochemical precursor of serotonin. Recent clinical studies have measured peripheral serotonin in high-risk suicidal patients. One group included pre-pubertal psychiatric in-patients and compared measurements with normal children. Pre-pubertal children with a suicide attempt or suicidal ideation had whole blood tryptophan levels measured. Additionally, platelet serotonin related measurements, including platelet serotonin content and serotonin-amplified platelet aggregation, were also measured. These results demonstrate that the whole blood tryptophan content is lower among in-patient children with suicidal ideation and a recent suicide attempt, as compared with those among normal controls or in-patients without suicidality. In addition, in-patient children with a mood disorder had higher platelet serotonin content than those without a mood disorder. These results suggest that whole blood tryptophan and platelet serotonin content should be further studied for validity as a risk factor for suicidal behavior in youth.

Key scientists who introduced the neurobiological aspects of suicidality are listed. This knowledge is essential to gaining understanding of some of the neurophysiological changes in suicidal patient. It also forms a basis for an understanding of the biochemical basis of antisuicidal neuropsychopharmacology.

JJ Mann's work in the neurobiology of suicide led to the direct understanding regarding the relationship between central and peripheral serotonin indexes in depressed and suicidal psychiatric inpatients. This material provides a fundamental understanding of the biology of suicide.

M. Asberg studied the serotonin metabolite 5-HIAA in the cerebral spinal fluid as a potential biochemical suicide marker; he also worked in cerebrospinal fluid monoamines metabolites in melancholia. This research leads to an early understanding of the association between serotonin dysfunction and suicidality. Measuring cerebrospinal fluid amines and higher-lethality suicide attempts in depressed patients is one aspect of such studies. In a case series in Karolinska Hospital, low CSF 5-HIAA identified men who committed suicide early proved to be more valid then the Beck Suicide Intent Scale or the Beck Hopelessness Scale.

M.A. Oqendo has used positron emission tomography (PET scans) of regional brain metabolic responses to develop a serotonergic challenge and lethality of suicide attempts in major depression. Recent genetic research suggests an association between suicidal behavior and serotonin transporter promoter polymorphisms.

However, the most striking, recent finding in the brains of suicide victims, described by C. Tamminga, documents the specific neuro-biological changes in the suicide patients' brain, revealing a massive abnormal number of serotonin type 2A receptors in the prefrontal cortex[16].

A group of experiments, neuroendocrine challenges, help measure biological changes in suicidal patients. The neuroendocrine challenge concept was recently demonstrated in depressed patients who have an impaired prefrontal cortical response to serotonin release, compared with psychiatric control subjects. This measurement was done using a prolactin response to fenfluramine hydrochloride, a serotonin agonist, with subsequent measurements of cerebrospinal fluid levels of the serotonin metabolite. High-lethality suicide attempts in depressed patients are associated with even lower cerebrospinal fluid 5-hydroxy-indole acetic acid levels as well as a more blunted prolactin response to fenfluramine, a serotonin agonist, as measured during a neuroendocrine challenge. This prefrontal lobe hypofunction and impaired serotonergic responsivity are clinically associated with the proportional lethality of the suicide attempt, and they may mediate the effects of suicide intent and impulsivity on lethality.

## Brain Tissue and Cellular Changes in Suicidality

The neuron represents the functional unit of the brain. The human brain is composed of several billion neurons. Each neuron consists of a cell body with multiple fibers, or dendrites, which receive information from other neurons. Each neuron also has the axon extending from the cell body. The axon transmits information from the cell body to other neurons. Electrical impulses arising in the cell body travel throughout the axon to the synapse. Electrical impulses cannot jump the gap from one neuron to the next. Communication between them is dependent on the release of neurotransmitters; this is called junctional transmission.

At the cellular level, the biochemistry and the physiology of neurons include neurotransmitters, which act at junctions rather than on the events that occur with axonal conduction or within the cell body. Except for local anesthetics, which interact with axonal membranes, most neuropharmacologic and psychopharmacologic medications seem to be involved primarily with synaptic events.

Nerve cells have at least two special properties that distinguish them from all other cells in the body. They can conduct bioelectric signals for long distances without any loss of signal strength. In addition, they possess specific intercellular connections with other nerve cells and with innervated tissues such as muscles and glands.

Under the microscope, the nerve cells are heterogeneous with respect to both size and shape. Despite wide variations in cell shape, size, and volume, most nerve cells possess large amounts of unattached organelles, such as ribosomes for synthesis of intracellular materials such as enzymes and structural macromolecules. In addition, the cell body is filled with varying quantities of rough and smooth endoplasmic reticulum indicative of cells that package synthetic material for transcellular secretion. Thus, the neuron has dynamic secretory cell properties with broad synthetic capabilities. Eric Kandel, MD recently won the Nobel Prize for demonstrating synaptic plasticity in the central nervous system. That is, the brain is not hard wired, but it is constantly undergoing changes such as the development of new neuronal connections. In fact, one theory of learning itself is based on the biochemical modification of the strength of existing neural connections. That the basic paradigms of learning could all arise from changes in synaptic strength is a developed concept.

Since junctional transmission takes longer than could be accounted for based on electrical activity in the preterminal axon or on the electrotonic conductive properties of the postsynaptic membrane, other factors are involved. When an ideal excitatory pathway is stimulated, the presynaptic element liberates an excitatory transmitter that activates an ionic conductance of the postsynaptic membrane. If the resultant depolarization is sufficient to reach threshold, the cell can discharge. Synaptic sites are not directly electrically excitable and central synaptic transmission is chemical. The length of its course of action is determined by the release of the neurotransmitter and its termination by local enzymes, diffusion, and reuptake by the nerve ending.

At the molecular level, an explanation of the action of a psychotropic medication is often possible. At the synaptic ending neurotransmitter such as serotonin is released and diffuses across the synaptic cleft, thereby transmitting information to the dendrite of the next neuron. Psychotropic agents exert their primary effect at synapses. These medications can act post-synaptically by either blocking or regulating receptor activity; they can also alter the synthesis, storage, release, reuptake, or metabolism of the transmitter. The psychotropic medications, including those given for suicidal patients with mental disorders, work at this level of the brain. For example, tricyclic antidepressants such as desipramine, inhibit the reuptake of norepinepherine in a central noradrenergic neuron. The selective serotonin reuptake inhibitors, such as fluoxetine, sertraline, and paroxetine inhibit the reuptake of serotonin in a central serotonergic neuron.

The central serotonergic pathways in the brain include projections from the brainstem to the prefrontal cortex, basal ganglia, hypothalamus and other areas. Agents that enhance serotonergic transmission in the brain are capable of decreasing suicidal behavior. Serotonergic function is low in patients who attempted and/or completed suicide, particularly in those who used violent methods. Several studies have suggested that the major driving factor leading to suicide is aggressive and impulsive behavior, especially in teenagers. Abnormalities in serotonin function have been implicated in these impulsive/aggressive behaviors. Most of the pathophysiology of suicide may be associated with abnormal serotonin function. Patients with low levels of serotonin are six to ten times more likely to commit suicide[17]. These low serotonin levels are stable over time, so a patient can present at any time for evaluation. The serotonin is detectable and independent of timing. It does not matter if the suicide attempt happened eight months or eight hours prior. However, simply having low levels of serotonin is insufficient as a marker of suicide. It has more to do with the predisposition to suicide than to generating suicidal behavior. In evaluating the function of the serotonin system, identification of patients who are vulnerable may result in planning more specific pharmacological intervention[18].

## Intraneuronal Cellular Changes in Suicidality

The true electogenic synapse in the central nervous system remains to be described. However, it seems likely that some neurotransmitters can activate the synthesis of chemicals such as cyclic nucleotides, which in turn can activate intraneuronal protein kinases, phosphorylate specific membrane proteins, and cause reactions to occur. For example, the phosphorylation of a membrane protein could be expected to alter its ionic permeability. Biochemical changes in the prefrontal cortex of suicide victims include abnormalities in enzymatic reactions on the cell surface and within the neurons.

Specific intraneuronal neurobiological changes in the prefrontal cortical neurons of the brain of suicide victims include the alternation of the phosphoinositide signaling biochemical cascade. Low phosphoinositide-specific phospholipase C activity and low expression of phospholipase CB1 protein is present in the prefrontal cortex of teenage suicide subjects.

The enzyme phosphoinositide-specific phospholipase C (PI-PLC) is a component of the phosphoinositide signal transduction system. Compared with normal subjects, the teenage suicide subjects without a history of mental disorders had significantly lower PI-PLC activity and immunolabeling of the specific PLC beta one enzyme in both nerve membrane and cytosol fractions of Broadmann's areas 8 and 9 combined (the prefrontal cortex)[19].

The cAMP-dependent enzyme protein kinase A phosphorylates intracellular neuronal proteins upon activation. This enzyme plays a major role in mediating various physiological functions in the brain. The role of this enzyme in suicidal behavior was examined using the catalytic and regulatory activities of protein kinase A in the postmortem membrane and cytosol fractions of the prefrontal cortex from the brain of suicide victims. Results showed that cAMP binding to the regulatory subunits of protein kinase A, as well as the phosphotransfer catalytic activity of protein kinase A, are lower in the prefrontal cortex of suicide victims[20].

## Central Serotonin Neuroreceptor Changes in Suicidality

The concept that most psychotropic medication, hormones, and neurotransmitters produce their biological effect by interacting with receptor substances in cells was introduced by Langley in 1905. It was based on his observations of the potency and specificity with which some drugs (agonists) mimicked a biological response while others (antagonists) prevented it. Receptors have been identified for most all of the proven neurotransmitters as well as for other substances such as neuropeptides and hormones.

The ability of vast numbers of nerve fibers to transmit information between the billions of neurons within the brain involves a large number of neurotransmitter substances and their specialized sites of action or receptors. The receptors for neurotransmitters such as serotonin are localized on the surface of the cell. With few exceptions, the mechanism of action of most neuroactive drugs refers to their effect on specific receptors.

One approach to studying receptors in the human brain is by measuring ligand binding to a homogenate or slice preparation. This technique is feasible with the development of ligands of highly specific radioactivity and a high affinity for the receptor. The direct method used is to incubate the labeled agonist or antagonist with the receptor preparation and then separate and measure the receptor-ligand complex.

LSD is known to bind to serotonin receptors. Earlier studies have examined specific serotonin receptors, 5-HT2A receptors, by means of radioligand binding techniques with different radioligands. The radioligand used is [125I]-LSD. The levels of 5-HT2A receptors were determined through examination of [125I]-LSD binding to these serotonin receptors. This [125I]-LSD binding to the serotonin receptors in the brain of teenage suicide victims was compared to normal controls. Results demonstrate higher levels and numbers of 5-HT2A receptor binding sites in patients who committed suicide. It was found that the serotonin type 2-A receptor binding sites are much more numerous in the prefrontal cortex of the brain of teenage suicide. This astonishing finding is almost a blueprint for suicidality evident in the frontal lobe of suicidal individuals.

The particular area of the frontal lobe can be even further defined using postmortem serotonin receptor binding mapping studies. These studies demonstrate that brain serotonergic abnormalities associated with suicide are localized specifically to the ventral portion of the prefrontal cortex[21].

Cellular localization of the 5-HT2A receptors can also be determined by means of gold immunolabeling. Using 20um sections of the prefrontal cortex (Broadmann's area 9 of the human brain) obtained from teenage suicide victims, the sections are prepared for immunogold labeling for the 5-HT2A receptors. Gold immunolabeling can be done using antibodies conjugated to gold particles and the 5-HT2A receptor. The immunogold particles are then discerned and counted. When there is dense immunolabeling, immunogold particles overlap. The measurement of the mean value of positive neurons of 5-HT2A receptor is calculated by the number of gold particles/100um2 field area.

Visualized under the microscope at low magnification in a photomicrograph are various cortical layers of different areas of the brain; the right hemispheric prefrontal cortex, hippocampus, and amygdyla. At low microscopic magnification, the results show the expression of the 5-HT2A receptors to be most dense in pyramidal neurons in layers III, V, and VI and, in their apical dendrites.

At higher magnification, the cellular changes in serotonin receptors of the neurons in layer V are strikingly different in the suicidal brain. Greater magnification of layer V in particular and most exclusively shows pyramidal neurons with a higher expression density of serotonin receptors in the teenage suicide victims than in the normal subjects. This 5-HT2A receptor protein expression is higher only in the pyramidal cells of cortical layer V restricted to this specific area, cortical layer V. This receptor protein expression is found to be greatest in the in cortical layer V in the pyramidal cells of the somata.

Studies have reported decreases in serotonin (5-HT2A) binding in the prefrontal cortex after chronic antidepressant administration, whereas the opposite change, 5-HT2A up-regulation, is found in the prefrontal cortex of suicide victims.

The 5-HT2A receptor protein levels can be measured with specific antibodies to the 5-HT2A receptor. One method of measuring protein expression uses of the Western blotting technique with a specific serotonin 5-HT2A receptor antibody. It is a method that also demonstrates greater protein expression, localized on pyramidal cells in cortical layer V of suicide victims.

In the postmortem brains of teenage suicide victims, the greater expression of serotonin receptors in the pyramidal cells (the somata of cortical layer V) in the prefrontal cortex of the frontal lobe is a unique finding. Those pyramidal neurons occupy a unique position in the human brain frontal lobe, as they modulate and integrate neuronal functions mediated by serotonergic, glutamatergic, GABA-ergic, and dopaminergic systems. The soma (nerve cell bodies) and dendrites of pyramidal neurons of layer V receive synaptic contact from dopamine terminals and GABA-containing neurons. These higher levels of serotonin type-2A receptors in the pyramidal cells may cause an imbalance between the 5-HT2A and the GABA-ergic system; this plays an important role in suicidal behavior, independent of psychiatric diagnosis. This layer of the prefrontal cerebral cortex is an area that modulates and integrates neuronal functions mediated by serotonergic and dopamine systems. The higher levels of serotonin receptors in pyramidal cells may cause an imbalance between the serotonin receptors and dopaminergic systems; this may play an important role in suicidal behavior, too. The serotonin type 2A receptor pattern in the prefrontal cortex is specific and unique in suicidal patients. These postmortem brain sample studies suggest that abnormalities of 5 HT receptors subtypes are associated with suicide independent of the psychiatric diagnosis.

## Genetics Aspects of Suicidality

There is a known increase risk of suicide in some families[22]. The American Amish population experienced twenty-six suicides in the past century; 75% of these occurred in only four families, whereas many other families experienced depression but not suicide[23]. In violent families with an index case of a suicide attempt, suicidal behavior is significantly more prevalent than in other families with depressions[24].

Suicidal behavior, including completed suicide, seems to cluster in families. First-degree relatives of individuals who have committed suicide have more than twice the risk of the general population. One study calculated heritability for completed suicide at about 43%. However, the absence of complete concordance for suicide in identical twins leaves room for environmental contributions. In a rare study of adoptees aimed at differentiating inherited and environmental causes, suicide was much more common in the first-degree biological relatives than in the relatives of the adoptive families. Nevertheless, the mode of inheritance of suicidal behavior is almost certain to be complex, involving many genes. Research results suggest that behavioral, biological, and genetic mechanisms most likely underlie suicidal behavior. A trait related suicidal threshold has been proposed. In vulnerable (low threshold) patients, this threshold is exceeded easily resulting in the inability to suppress or contain suicidal thoughts, which then leads to the suicidal act.

For identical co-twins of suicides, the relative risk increases to about 11. Thus there is evidence of genetic factors for suicide, and concordant suicidal tendency is found more frequently in monozygotic than dizygotic twins. Other personality and temperament variables, such as impulsivity, aggression, hopelessness, and depression, have a genetic influence on suicidal behavior.

Although an early twin study found no evidence of increased concordance for suicide in monozygotic twins, several other twin studies on suicide have found a significantly greater risk of double suicides among identical, rather than fraternal, twin pairs.

Concordance for suicide in twins may indicate imitative behavior in the surviving twin, although it is also plausible that suicide in a twin may discourage suicide in the surviving twin.

Whether or not the genes predisposing to suicide are identical with those predisposing to a mood disorder is unknown. Since about one half of those committing suicide have a diagnosis of major depression, it seems probable that the overlap is incomplete. Several lines of evidence indicate that genetic abnormalities in the functioning of the central serotonergic system are involved in the pathogenesis of depressive illness and suicidal behavior. Aggressive and impulsive traits, alcoholism, and substance abuse all carry an elevated risk of suicide and are also associated with serotonergic abnormalities.

Not one, but many genes are most likely involved in the complex mode of inheritance of suicidal behavior. Candidate genes include those genes implicated in serotonergic transmission. Genetic factors do partly explain the risks for major depression and for suicide. However, which genes are precisely involved is unknown. Genetic factors affect serotonergic activity, as indicated by the heredity of cerebrospinal fluid levels of 5-hydroxyindolacetic acid in non-human primates.

The most widely reported serotonergic abnormality in major depression and suicide involves the serotonin transporter (5-HTT). Both functional imaging and postmortem brain studies indicate less 5-HTT binding in the brain of depressed patients, along with the findings of fewer platelet 5-HTT sites and reduced platelet serotonin uptake.

However, platelet 5-HTT binding may be unrelated to levels of brain 5-HTT binding; therefore, direct studies of the brain are necessary to determine the state of 5-HTT binding in major depression and suicide. Since structural abnormalities in major depression involve diverse psychopathologic features involving more brain areas than just the ventral prefrontal cortex, the lower 5-HTT binding throughout the dorsal-ventral extent of the prefrontal cortex, in the occipital cortex, and in the midbrain is also observed in the brain of patients with mood disorders. Thus, the reduction of 5-HTT binding associated with major depression involves not only several cortical regions, but also subcortical regions including the brainstem.

The changes specific to suicide involve the changes in ventral pre-frontal cortical function, which underlies the major diathesis for impulsive aggression and suicide.

More specific than the serotonin binding pattern observed in major depression, 5-HTT binding to the prefrontal cortex of suicides is lower compared with non-suicide controls only in the orbital or ventral prefrontal cortex 18% lower in Broadman areas 45 and 47. Within a group with a history of major depression, suicides had lower 5-HTT binding than non-suicides. Suicide is associated with lower 5-HTT binding in Brodmann area 47 of the ventral prefrontal cortex. The alterations in 5-HTT binding specifically related to suicide risk, as opposed to major depression in general, are concentrated in the ventral prefrontal cortex. Binding of 5-HTT to the prefrontal cortex of patients with a history of major depression is significantly lower compared with those without a history of major depression in widespread brain regions: in the gyrus and sulcus of most Broadmann areas. In contrast to major depression, 5-HTT binding to the PFC of suicides was lower only in the orbital or ventral PFC. Major depression and suicide are associated with fewer serotonin transporter (5-HTT) sites. A localized reduction in the serotonin transporter binding in the ventral portion of the prefrontal cortex of suicides may reflect reduced serotonin input to that brain region, underlying the predisposition to act on suicidal thoughts. This change may represent a trait rather than a state marker in suicide. Therefore, serotonergic input into this brain region might underlie an impairment of behavioral inhibition or restraint, as well as an increased propensity for suicidal acts in patients who feel depressed or hopeless. This notion is supported by acquired ventral prefrontal cortical injuries that are notably characterized by disinhibition and by an increase in impulsive behaviors including aggression and suicide attempts.

Since the same gene encodes both brain and platelet serotonin receptors, peripheral serotonin receptors on blood platelets may indirectly reflect central brain serotonin receptor activity. Studies have shown that the number of brain and platelet serotonin transporter binding sites is reduced in patients with depression and in suicide victims. There are a greater number of 5-HT2A receptors in the platelets of suicidal patients with different mental disorders. The higher level of platelet 5-HT2A receptors observed in suicidal patients is independent of diagnosis. Thus, platelet 5-HT2A receptors might serve as a biological marker of suicidal behavior.

Gene transcription and translation resulting in these increased numbers of serotonin (5-HT2A type) receptors are associated with higher levels of receptor, higher levels of protein, and increased mRNA expression in the prefrontal cortex. A higher level of 5-HT2A receptors may be a specific neurobiological abnormality associated with suicide in a patient independent of psychiatric diagnosis. The higher 5-HT2A receptor levels in the prefrontal cortex may represent a greater genetic vulnerability for suicide. Perhaps so-called "suicide gene therapy" may someday modulate this pathology.

Genes that code for proteins, such as tryptophan hydroxylase, the 5-HT transporter, and the 5-HT2A receptor, are involved in regulating serotonergic neurotransmission and considered major candidate genes for association studies of suicide and suicidal behavior. Genetic variations in the serotonin-system-related genes might be associated with suicidal ideation and completed suicide. For example, one study showed that the 102 C allele in 5-HT2A receptor gene was significantly associated with suicidal ideation in depressed patients. Patients with a 102C/C genotype had a significantly higher mean HAM-D item #3 score (indication of suicidal ideation) than T/C or T/7 genotype patients. These results suggest that the 102T/C polymorphism in 5-HT2A receptor gene is primarily associated with suicidal ideation in patients with major depression and not just with depression itself. In addition, the 5-HT transporter gene S/L polymorphism is significantly associated with completed suicide. Here the frequency of the L/L genotype in depressed suicide victims is almost double that found in control groups. The association between polymorphism in serotonergic genes and suicidality supports the hypothesis that genetic factors can modulate suicide risk by influencing serotonergic activity.

Serotonin is synthesized in the neuron from precursors such as tryptophan. The rate-limiting step in its synthesis is governed by the enzyme, tryptophan hydroxylase. This enzyme converts tryptophan to serotonin within the neuron. The enzyme is genetically regulated. The tryptophan hydroxylase gene can be studied. One study showed that the polymorphisms in intron 7 of the tryptophan hydroxylase gene were not associated with the pathogenesis of mood disorders or suicidal behaviors. No direct correlation with suicide and polymorphisms of this enzyme had been demonstrated. However, in another study, a less common tryptophan hydroxylase U allele occurred with greater frequency in patients who attempted suicide. This confirmed an association between tryptophan hydroxylase genotype and lifetime history of suicide attempts.

RNA encodes the human serotonin receptor. Alterations in RNA editing can change the amino acid sequence in the intracellular loop of the serotonin receptor. These alterations in RNA editing in the prefrontal cortex of control individuals and subjects diagnosed with schizophrenia or major depressive disorder reveal no significant differences in RNA editing among them. However, among patients who had committed suicide, regardless of diagnosis, a significant elevation of editing at the A site occurs, resulting in the generation of a serotonin receptor population differentially responsive to serotonergic drugs. These alternations in RNA editing of the serotonin receptor are different in patients who committed suicide, regardless of the psychiatric diagnosis. The elevation of editing at the A site is predicted to change the amino acid sequence in the second intracellular loop of the serotonin 2 receptor. These alterations in RNA editing may not only contribute to, but also complicate therapy in certain psychiatric disorders. For example, treatment with the SSRI, fluoxetine, may reverse the abnormalities in the pre-mRNA editing or coding sequence of the serotonin receptor.

The DNA related changes described involve the transcription and/or translation of the 5-HT2A receptors in patients who complete suicide. These changes in gene transcription (mRNA levels) of 5-HT2A receptors at the translation level occur since protein expression levels of the receptors in the prefrontal cortex are higher in the suicide victims. The mRNA content for the 5-HT2A receptors is measured by the use of a quantitative reverse transcription polymerase chain reaction. The mean 5-HT2A receptor mRNA, measured in attomoles of total RNA, in the prefrontal cortex is higher in suicide victims. Levels of mRNA by means of quantitative reverse transcription polymerase chain reaction demonstrate greater mRNA levels in these brain samples. Using this method, the 5-HT2A receptor mRNA levels can be quantified. They are significantly greater in the prefrontal cortex, again indicating that the higher 5-HT2A receptor mRNA in suicide victims is specific to certain brain areas. This is the first study to demonstrate higher levels of gene expression of serotonin type 2A receptors and of the encoded serotonin 2 receptor protein in the prefrontal cortex of suicide victims. This trait may be associated with a polymorphism in candidate genes.

In one study, two polymorphic variants of the 5-HT2A receptor gene (102T/C polymorphism and His452Tyr functional polymorphism) and a functional polymorphism in the regulatory region of the 5-HT transporter gene have been determined in genomic DNA obtained from postmortem brain samples of twenty-four depressed suicide victims. The density (Bmax) of 5-HT uptake sites (labeled with 3H-paroxetine) and of 5-HT2A receptors (labeled with 3H-ketanserin) was determined in the prefrontal cortex samples. Results showed a higher frequency of the 5HT transporter gene long (L) allele in depressed suicides. The density of 3HT paroxetine binding sites is higher in subjects expressing the short (S) allele of 5HT transporter gene. The conclusion provides the first evidence suggesting that a functional polymorphism in the regulatory region of serotonin transporter gene may be associated with suicide in depressed subjects.

# CHAPTER 1 END NOTES

1) Let's Play PET, 1992, Regents of the University of California. Available at: http://www.crump.ucla.edu/software/lpp/clinpetneuro/function.html. Accessed February 8, 2003.

2) "How PET works from "The PET Scan: A New Window Into the Brain", Sabbatini in *Brain & Mind Magazine*, March 1997. Available at: http://www.epub.org.brcm/n01/pet/petworks.htm. Accessed February 7, 2003

3) National Institute of Mental Health, Positron Emission Tomography (PET). Available at: http://www.nimh.nih.gov/hotsci/petscan.htm. Accessed February 7, 2003.

4) The Human Brain. Protection. The Prefrontal Cortex-Headquarters of Humanity. Available at http://sln.fi.edu/brain/injury/prefrontal.html. Accessed February 1, 2003.

5) Kwo WH, Gallo JJ, Tien AY: Incidence of suicide ideation and attempts in adults: the 13 year follow-up of a community sample in Baltimore, Maryland. *Psychol Med* 2001; 31:1181-91

6) Byard RW, Gilbert JD: "Cervical fracture, decapitation, and vehicle-assisted suicide", *J Forensic Sci* 2002. 47: 392-4

7) de Moore GM, Robertson, AR. Suicide Attempts by Firearms and by Leaping from Heights: A comparative study of survivors. *Am J Psychiatry*. 1999; 156: 1425-1431

8) Serotonin Receptor Imaging in Suicide Attempters: Do the Neurobiology of Depression and Suicidal Behavior Diverge? Brent, D, Western Psychiatric Institute and Clinic, Pittsburgh, PA. Available at: http://www.wpic.pitt.edu/reseach/City/Grants/GrantPETstudy.htm. Accessed November 9, 2002.

9) Garcia-Baca E, Sastre-Diaz C, Resa-Garcia E, Ceverino A, Ramirez A, et al. Lack of association between plasma apolipoprotein E and suicide attempts. *J Clin Psychiatry* 2004; 65:580-81

10) Modai I, Valevski A, Dror S, et al. Serum cholesterol levels and suicidal tendencies in psychiatric inpatients. *J Clin Psychiatry* 1994;55:252-254

11) Lester D. Serum cholesterol levels and suicide: a meta-analysis. *Suicide Life Threat Behav* 2002; 32:333-346

12) van Heeringen K, Audenaert K, van de Wiele L, et al. Cortisol in violent suicidal behavior: association with personality and monoaminergic activity. *J Affect Disord* 2000. 60: 181-9

13) Stress, Serotonin Receptors, and the Neurobiology of Depression. University of Michigan, Ann Arbor. Available at: http://www-personal.umich.edu/jflopez/Depression.html. Accessed February 1, 2003.

14) Coryell W, Schlesser, M. The Dexamethasone Suppression Test and Suicide. *Am J Psychiatry*. 2001. 158: 748-753.

15) Mann JJ. The neurobiology of suicide. *Nat Med*. 1998; 4:25-30.

16) Pandey GN, Dwivedi Y, Rizavi HS, Ren X, Pandy SC, Pesold CP, Roberts RC, Conley RR. Tamminga CA. Higher expression of serotonin 5-HT2A receptors in the postmortem brains of teenage suicide victims. *Am J Psychiatry* 2002; 159:419-429.

17) Mann J, McBride A, Brown R, et al. Relationship between central and peripheral serotonin indexes in depressed and suicidal psychiatric inpatients. *Arch Gen Psychiatry*. 1992; 49:442-446.

18) An Interview by American Foundation for Suicide Prevention with Dr. Marie Asberg. Available at:

http://www.lorenbennett.org/safsbiological.htm. Accessed November 11, 2002.

19) Mann JJ, Yung-yu Huang, MS, Underwood MD, Kassir SA, Oppenheim S, et al. Serotonin transporter gene promoter polymorphism (5-HTTLPR) and prefrontal cortical binding in major depression and suicide. *Arch Gen Psychiatry.* 2000; 57:729-738.

20) Gross-Isseroff R, Biegon A, Voet H, et al. The suicide brain: a review of postmortem receptor/transporter binding studies. *Neurosci Biobehav Rev* 1998 22; 653-61

21) Courtet P, Baud P, Abbar M, et al. Association between violent suicidal behavior and the low activity allele of the serotonin transporter gene. *Mol Psychiatry.* 2001; 6:338-341.

22) Roy A, Nielsen D, Rylander G, et al. Genetics of suicide in depression. *J Clin Psychiatry.* 1999; 60 (suppl 2):12-17.

23) Egeland J, Sussex J. Suicide and family loading for affective disorders. *JAMA* 1985; 7 (Part II):191-195.

24) Wender PH, Kety SS, Rosenthal D, et al. Psychiatric disorders in the biological and adoptive families of adopted individuals with affective disorders. *Arch Gen Psychiatry.* 1986; 43:923-929.

# Chapter 2

## Psychiatric Disorders and Suicide

IN A RECENT local newspaper, the *Reno Gazette-Journal,* an article titled "Some Come to Gamble, Some Come to Die" caught my attention. It describes the fact that at least more than once a month, a Las Vegas visitor commits suicide.

Between 1991 to 2002, 4,994 people committed suicide in the state of Nevada. Of those, about 11 percent or 547, were from out of state. Most suicides take place in Southern Nevada's populous Clark County, home to the Strip. More than 90 people, both tourists and locals, have committed suicide inside a casino or on hotel properties in Clark County since 1998. Twenty have jumped from casinos and parking garages, including three from mega resorts.

This report illustrates the fact that every year, desperate men and women make the pilgrimage to the gambling capital to kill themselves. More than once a month, a visitor commits suicide according to Clark County coroner records dating to October, 1998. By comparison, Atlantic City, New Jersey had about one third as many non residents take their lives during that period. In the same six years, no one committed suicide at Disney World. They pick Las Vegas and kill themselves. Why is not exactly known. Some report it may be due to the city's culture of anonymity to despair, in some cases, over gambling losses. But, each case is different. As one suicide note stated, "here there are no answers."

I read the article where I lived and always thought it could be true. As a practicing psychiatrist in Nevada, both in Las Vegas in Clark County for five years and Reno in Washoe County for five additional years, I have had over ten years of substantial, direct clinical experience treating suicidal patients in such an environment. Sometimes such a person would seek brief mental health care prior to the suicide. This drives home the personal clinical experience I have had in cases of suicidal patients, and it is a major motivation in the need to address the problem of suicidality in general.

In 1998, a national conference in Reno, Nevada resulted in the U.S. Surgeon General's Call to Action for suicide prevention and the creation of a comprehensive national strategy for suicide prevention in the United States. In the first five years following the Reno conference, many states created their state plan for suicide prevention, based on individual state priorities. A state plan serves as a blueprint for suicide prevention efforts. Implementing a comprehensive plan that uses a public health prevention model is considered most effective in preventing suicides, as no organization or agency working in isolation can adequately achieve this goal. Individual state plans for suicide prevention are being developed, implemented, and then compared. Each plan can be compared to the U.S. National Strategy for Suicide Prevention to observe the extent of alignment between goals and objectives of individual states with those in the National Strategy. Models used in the development of each state's plan can be considered in order to determine the presence of a public health approach to suicide prevention, including any public-private partnerships and other collaborative efforts.

Internationally, about one million people commit suicide each year in the world, 120,000 in Europe and more than 30,000 in the United States[1]. Suicide is a leading psychiatric and medical challenge that can be fairly characterized as a rise in the rate and an international public health emergency.

In the United States in 1998, there was an average of 84 suicides per day, or 3–4 per hour. For the first time ever, the U. S. Surgeon General has declared suicide a serous public health threat and has called for a national strategy for suicide prevention in the hopes that such a program will achieve a significant, measurable, and sustained reduction in suicidal behaviors[2]. Suicide is the eighth leading cause of death in the United States, greater than homicides. The number of suicides per 100,000 persons, nationally, is about 11–12[3]. Suicide rates are generally higher than the national average in the western states and lower in the eastern and mid-western states. Nine of the top ten suicide states in the country are in West.

The State of Nevada consistently among the top states in the nation in per capita suicide rates[4]. In 1995, Nevada's suicide rate was 26 per 100,000 or more than double the national rate. Suicide is the sixth leading cause of death among all residents of Nevada.

Within the State of Nevada, in Washoe County, where I practice psychiatry, the suicide rate is double the national average. The rate is 19.6/100,000. Suicide is the third leading cause of death among Washoe county residents under the age of 25. It is the second leading cause of death in teens, now more than motor vehicle accident deaths. The rate of suicide among men in Washoe County is about four times that of women. Over ninety percent of suicides in the county were white. A total of 749 suicides among Washoe county residents between 1990-2000 were recorded. Five hundred and nine victims were between the age of 25 and 64. Ninety-seven were between the age of 1 and 24. One hundred and forty suicide victims were over age 65, and three were of an unknown age[5].

Explanations of suicidal behavior have largely shifted from moral philosophy to sociological, psychological, biological, medical, and ultimately psychiatric factors to a psychopathological act. An association of suicide with mental illness has been recognized for many centuries; suicide itself was taken as evidence of mental disturbance. Research shows that perhaps 90% of suicides arise in relation to a primary psychiatric or substance related disorder, or both. The suicidal patient should seek psychiatric evaluation since virtually all mental disorders have an increased risk of suicide. The distribution of psychiatric illness in suicide victims differs across the life course. One or more major psychiatric conditions were diagnosable in 90% of suicide victims[6].

Psychiatric illness is most often an ongoing risk factor for suicide. Suicide is highly correlated to the presence of psychiatric disorders, especially depression and substance abuse. It is often in a response to negative life events, which cause a marked psychological distress. Two or more psychiatric disorders may interact synergistically to greatly increase the risk of suicide compared to a level that either diagnosis alone might carry. For example, alcohol dependence and co-morbid major depression is a particularly high-risk combination, with spells of alcohol intoxication providing periods in which the disinhibited patient is at higher risk for impulsive suicidal acts.

Suicide is a distinctly human behavior and it presupposes an awareness of the possibility of self-inflicted death. Animals do not kill themselves and small children do so extremely rarely. "It is thoughts and acts performed by an unhappy or desperate or angry human being, who perceives this as the only remaining solution to his problems. However, human beings differ in their tolerance for the adversities that give rise to such desperate feelings, and also in their capacity to block impulses, to sit down and think, and to construct to solutions to their problems"[7].

Suicidality is not a disease, but it includes suicidal thoughts, ideas, and plans; suicidal feelings; suicidal impulses, attempts, and completions; and suicidal behavior. Suicide can best be described as a psycho-neuropathological entity. Suicide is almost always intentional. Suicidal persons report a range of needs, especially for counseling, medication, and information. More than half of those with suicidal ideation and those who had attempted suicide and reported any needs felt that their needs had not been fully met. Suicidal persons are more likely to perceive that they have needs[8].

Medical doctors have one of the best opportunities to tackle the problem of suicidality. As a psychiatrist, I attended medical school and earned a doctorate of medicine (M.D.). Physicians who want to specialize in psychiatry undergo at least three more years of specialty training than just as a cardiologist, neurologist, or pulmonologist would. Psychiatry is a medical specialty recognized by the American Board of Medical Specialties. A board-certified psychiatrist is certified as a Diplomate of the American Board of Psychiatry and Neurology. Psychiatrists are best able to evaluate a suicidal patient in a variety of venues, such as in a general hospital in consultation, in a psychiatric emergency room, in a psychiatric hospital or clinic, and in the general population.

Nowadays, few psychiatrists are even trained in psychoanalysis or psychotherapy. Psychotherapy is done more by psychologists or social workers. Many psychiatrists now emphasize pharmacotherapy. Knowledge of general medicine is most helpful for a prescribing psychiatrist.

Many patients who attempt or complete suicides do not receive needed treatment. In one study, a random sample of patients admitted to a county hospital following a suicide attempt were evaluated for their history of suicide attempts and treatment in the previous six months. The median number of suicide attempts was two, with 75% of the sample having made at least one. In the previous six months, half the suicide attempters (53%) received outpatient behavioral health treatment; 46% went to an Emergency room; 19% had been on an inpatient psychiatric unit; 68% had seen a nurse or doctor; and 11% had called a crisis clinic. More than two thirds (70%) of the sample had been seen during the six months before their attempt explicitly for psychiatric reasons. When including medical reasons, 84% of suicide attempters were seen by a health care provider prior to their attempt. Therefore, it would seem that clinical interventions and suicide prevention efforts so far raises the question, "What is not working?"

The challenge in working with a suicidal person is that the psychiatrist has to be familiar with a wide range of treatments. Regardless of the disorder being treated, the psychiatrist has to be wary of when suicide can occur in a particular patient[9].

Suicidal thoughts and behaviors may present across the entire spectrum of diagnostic categories. Large varieties of therapeutic interventions are included under the broad umbrella of the psychiatric management of suicidal patients. Adequate treatment of psychiatric disorders and improved detection and treatment of psychiatric illness are essential strategies in suicide risk reduction. Diagnosing and treating patients with suicidality requires a high degree of vigilance for subtle clues of suicidal behavior. Because suicide risk has no pathognomonic signs, clinical judgment is required[10].

More than 90% of persons who die from suicide satisfy the criteria for one or more psychiatric disorders for which there is usually some effective treatment. Furthermore, awareness of specific high-risk diagnoses and modifiable risk factors helps identify treatment targets and clarifies treatment planning in both the short and long term[11].

Suicidal patients can have a variety of different psychiatric diagnoses. Psychiatric diagnoses common with completed suicide include the following: substance related disorders, mood disorders, psychotic disorders, eating disorders, and personality disorders. In most cases involving potential suicide, pharmacotherapy will probably be required. When discussing interventions such as psychopharmacologic treatment of suicidality, suicidality should be considered in the nosological context of primary psychiatric disorders, substance related disorders, and general medical conditions. Initial diagnosis and treatment focuses on the primary mood, anxiety, psychotic, or substance related disorder symptoms.

The following is a useful list of disorders or conditions that increase the risk of suicide relative to the general population, arranged in order of highest risk.

| Condition | SMR (standardized mortality ratio) Relative risk |
|---|---|
| ratio > 1 indicates increased risk compared to general population | |
| Previous suicide attempt | 38.4 |
| Eating Disorders | 23.1 |
| Bipolar disorder | 21–15 |
| Major depression | 23–20.4 |
| Sedative abuse | 20.3 |
| Mixed drug abuse | 19.2 |
| Opoid abuse | 14 |
| Dysthymia | 12.1 |
| Obsessive-compulsive disorder | 11.5 |

| Panic disorder | 10.0 |
| Schizophrenia | 8.45 |
| Personality disorders | 7.08 |
| AIDS | 6.58 |
| Alcohol abuse | 5.86 |
| Epilepsy | 5.11 |
| Pediatric psychiatric | 4.73 |
| Cannabis abuse | 3.85 |
| Spinal cord injury | 3.83 |
| Neuroses | 3.72 |
| Brain Injury | 3.50 |
| Huntington's chorea | 2.90 |
| Cancer | 1.80 |
| Mental retardation | 0.88 |

From Harris EC, Barraclough B. Suicide as an outcome for mental disorders: a meta-analysis. *Br J Psychiatry.* 1997; 170:205-208.

## Substance Related Disorders and Suicidality

Though addiction itself can be viewed as a slow form of suicide[12], signs that suggest an immediate threat to life include the addict's assertion that he intends to kill himself, serious co-morbid mental illness such as mood disorder or psychosis[13], prior suicide attempts, and hopelessness. The suicidal addict often has the means to end his life when he feels most suicidal. Some addicts feign suicidal thoughts or use them as a cry for help. Any mention of suicide in a patient with substance related disorder marks a severely disturbed patient who needs a complete psychiatric evaluation. The addict who even hints at suicide should undergo a thorough medical and psychiatric evaluation and then engage in whatever treatment is indicated. Consulting with a colleague can offer a fresh look, allowing two clinicians to balance the need for treatment against concerns such as bed availability and possible malingering[14].

Substance related disorders play a significant role in suicide. In a recent review of patients in the State of Nevada, as many as 80% had associated substance related disorders[15]. Substance use disorders are the most frequent diagnoses in suicide patients, followed by mood disorders and primary psychotic illness.

Establishing a causal relationship between substance related disorders and occurrence of major behavioral disturbances, such as suicidal behavior is suggested. There are different ways substance related disorders can contribute to suicidality. Substance related disorders include the following: substance dependence, substance abuse, intoxication, and withdrawal. Depending on the substance, a variety of psychiatric symptoms can ensue including dementia, psychosis, mood and anxiety disorders, sexual, sleep, and other disorders.

Substance use alone, even in the absence of substance abuse or dependence, is a significant risk factor for unplanned suicide attempts among patients with suicidal ideation[16]. The dose of the substance used is significant too, since many substances have dose dependent responses. It is the most important parameter in drug induced behavioral disinhibition with alcohol, benzodiazepine, and cocaine.

Alcohol:
The best-known precipitant of behavioral disinhibition is alcohol, which can induce aggressive behavior. An alcohol-dependent person is thirty-two times more likely to commit suicide than the non-addicted individual is[17].

Alcohol intoxication preceding suicide occurs in specific age, ethnic, and gender based patterns. One study showed more than 40% of white teenage suicide victims had alcohol intoxication preceding suicide, whereas comparable African Americans teens did not. Overall, alcohol use was much more common among white victims of suicide of all age groups[18].

Compared with alcoholics who had never attempted suicide, significantly more of the alcoholics who had attempted suicide reported that a first or second-degree relative had committed suicide. Thus, a family history of suicide may indicate that an alcoholic has a higher risk of attempting suicide. First-degree relatives of alcohol dependent patients with suicide attempts show a significantly higher rate of suicide attempts[19].

Alcohol dependent individuals with a history of suicide attempts are found to have more severe course of alcohol dependence, a higher prevalence of both independent and substance induced psychiatric disorders, and other substance dependence[20].

Screening and subsequent treatment of substance related disorders and major mental illness are crucial in preventing suicide attempts and completions. Alcohol dependency and co-morbid major depression is a particularly high-risk combination; further, spells of alcohol intoxication provide periods in which the disinhibited patient is at higher risk for impulsive suicidal acts[21].

Alcohol can induce delirium with intoxication or delirium during withdrawal as well as a persisting dementia. Alcohol during intoxication or withdrawal can induce psychotic, mood, anxiety, sexual, and sleep disorders.

Alcohol, Tobacco, and Caffeine:
A study of the joint heavy use of alcohol, cigarettes, and coffee and the risk of suicide demonstrated that although joint heavy use of all three substances is rare, an interesting relationship appeared. The adjusted relative risk of suicide increases linearly with increasing level of joint heavy use. Among subjects with heavy use of one substance, the risk was 1.55; with joint heavy use of two substances it was 2.22; and with joint heavy use of all three substances, risk was 3.99. Thus clustering of the heavy use of alcohol, cigarettes and coffee could serve as a new marker for increased risk of suicide in the general population. suicidality[22].

Benzodiazepines:
Benzodiazepines are known to disinhibit. Often prescribed for anxiety and insomnia, benzodiazepines can cause emergency syndromes directly related to their potency. Short acting benzodiazepines include lorazepam; long acting ones are clonazepam and diazepam. Alprazolam is now available in both immediate release and extended release preparations. Immediate release alprazolam is potent and causes a severe withdrawal syndrome when high doses are stopped abruptly[23].

Anterograde amnesia is often present in those who attempted suicide by benzodiazepine overdose. Immediate and delayed recall is significantly lower the first two days after patients attempted suicide by benzodiazepine overdose. Less than half of the patients recognized the psychiatrists and knew that they were the ones they had spoken to the day before[24].

Used in combination with alcohol, benzodiazepines can lead to respiratory depression and death. Poisoning in a young girl in coma and respiratory depression with positive family history of suicide attempts by father, mother, and sister was reported. Benzodiazepine was available in large amounts in the form of physician samples, as her elder sister was a drug representative[25].

Suicide attempts in high dose regular benzodiazepine users are most strongly associated with co-morbid borderline personality disorder[26].

Benzodiazepines are more often detected in suicide victims in postmortem toxicology tests than antidepressants, antipsychotics, or mood stabilizers. Because benzodiazepine addiction often begins with prescribed medication, caution is advised especially in suicidal patients. Controlling the amount of the substance prescribed is critical. The amount or number of pills can be written for one week or less. This approach is sometimes needed in high-risk patients.

Cocaine:
The addicted person who jumps off a roof, believing he can fly, may think perfectly clearly when not using crack-cocaine. Thus, cocaine intoxication represents a substance-induced state that can trigger suicidal behavior even in the absence of another diagnosable psychiatric disorder.

Male cocaine dependent suicidal patients, who have attempted suicide at least once, report a significant history of childhood emotional abuse, physical abuse, sexual abuse, and emotional and physical neglect compared with male cocaine dependent patients who have never attempted suicide[27]. Whereas, female cocaine dependent suicidal patients have more co-morbid polysubstance dependence, general medical conditions, and mental illness including a family history of suicidal behavior, childhood trauma and depression, introversion, and neurotic and hostile tendencies[28].

Cocaine dose is related to violent behavior including suicide, as demonstrated by its pharmacological actions on the central nervous system. The chronic use of cocaine induces a limbic dyscontrol syndrome, based on the altered activity of limbic structures.

Stimulants, most commonly cocaine and smoked methamphetamine, can cause myocardial infarction, cardiac arrhythmia, cerebral hemorrhage, hyperpyrexia, and status epilepticus[29]. Because no antidote exists for stimulant intoxication, supportive care is important as well as monitoring for other sequelae of stimulant use, such as agitation and hypertension[30]. Prescription stimulant abuse and dependence can also be a source of suicidal tendencies. Replacing amphetamines with pemoline or atomoxetine may be more appropriate for some patients.

### Nicotine:

A positive dose-related association between smoking and suicide among white men is reported. The relative risk of suicide is high for former smokers, higher for light and moderate smokers, and highest among heavier smokers. Although inference about causality is not justified, one study showed the smoking to suicide connection is not entirely due to the greater tendency among smokers to be unmarried, to be sedentary, to drink heavily, or to develop cancers[31].

The relative risk of both violent (hanging, firearms) and non-violent suicide (drug overdose) is higher among light to moderate smokers, and highest among heavy smokers, compared with non-smokers. Smoking is associated with an increased risk of suicide[32].

### Cannabis:

Cannabis abusers look particularly for euphoria and relaxing effects. Impairment of judgment is common. Aggression as an adverse cannabis reaction is very rare, and it occurs in most cases in association with other drugs and in predisposed individuals[33]. Cannabis laced with phencyclidine (PCP), amphetamines, or other drugs smoked can have very devastating consequences. Since it is relatively commonly used, it is often detected in blood samples with other substances such as alcohol, nicotine, and caffeine; therefore it is erroneously linked to suicide.

### Inhalant:

The prevalence of lifetime inhalant use in students attending alternative high schools, dropout prevention, and recovery schools in Texas is almost 30%[34]. Inhalant users report less family support and cohesiveness and lower self-esteem, and they also report significantly more lifetime thoughts of suicide, suicide attempts, neighborhood gang activity, peer and parental substance abuse, intentions to engage in illegal behavior, substance related criminality, and other substance abuse compared with non-inhalant users. Students reporting lifetime inhalant use were less likely to be financially supported by their parents and/or guardians, more likely to use alcohol/tobacco, marijuana, and cocaine, and more likely to carry weapons and consider suicide[35].

### Ecstasy:

Ecstasy, 3, 4-methylene-dioxymethamphetamine, is not only a serotonin neurotoxin in primates; it also causes profound loss of dopaminergic axons. Its recreational use may be a risk for Parkinson's disease and sustained long-lasting destruction of brain dopamine neurons. It may lead to long-term alterations of neuronal function in the human central nervous system and cause psychiatric disorders[36].

Life threatening consequences generally occur when adequate water is unavailable to a group of intoxicated dancing teenagers. The more common emergency presentations include sudden hypertension, tachycardia, vomiting, depersonalization, panic attacks, and psychosis. It causes dehydration and hyperthermia, which can lead to rhabdomyolysis, kidney failure, and death[37]. However, there is insufficient information about long-term use of ecstasy to estimate its role in the occurrence of suicidal behavior.

Sexecstasy is a combination of ecstasy and viagra or other medicines for erectile dysfunction. This combination is often used by teens at a party for example. Its contribution to suicidal behavior in teens has not been systematically studied.

Heroin:
Suicide is a major clinical issue among heroin users. Heroin users are fourteen times more likely than peers to die from suicide[38]. A study of drug related deaths in Los Angeles, California showed heroin and cocaine each caused the highest number of deaths when even when compared with alcohol. Most heroin deaths, 73% were considered accidental or unexpected, but as much as 19% were considered suicidal[39].

Drugs as a method of suicide play a larger role in suicide among heroin users than in the general population. While heroin overdose is common among methadone maintenance patients, the most common methods employed for suicide attempts are overdose of a non-opioid drug and other methods such as slitting of wrists. A deliberate heroin overdose as a means of attempted suicide was reported by only 10% of patients. Heroin overdoses appear overwhelmingly to be accidental. Over 90% of those who had overdosed reported that their most recent overdose was accidental. Attempted suicide presents a major clinical problem at drug treatment programs, but one distinct from heroin overdose. While both overdose and suicide present increasing clinical problems, they are separate problems and require different responses[40].

Anabolic Androgenic Steroids:
Suicides associated with anabolic androgenic steroids are associated with current use and recent discontinuation. In one patient, suicidal ideation became suicide after the patient started to use them. During current use, patients may exhibit hypomanic symptoms immediately preceding the suicide. Patients may commit other acts of violence while using anabolic androgenic steroids. The acts of violence exacerbated the patient's problems in personal relationships or at work, which in turn seems to have precipitated the suicides. Homicides, suicides, and poisoning determined accidental or indeterminate in anabolic androgenic steroid use is related to impulsive, disinhibited behavior characterized by violent rages, mood swings, and/or uncontrolled drug intake. Thus there is an increased risk of violent death from impulsive, aggressive behavior[41]. As part of lethal polypharmacy, they have been associated with accidental poisoning. Cardiac changes are also observed and cardiovascular complications can contribute to possible lethal affects. In addition, depressive symptoms associated with anabolic androgenic steroid withdrawal have been described when suicide was committed after recent discontinuation[42].

Antidepressants:
Suicidal tendency as an adverse reaction to antidepressants is rare, especially with atypical antidepressants. The risk of acting out exists, and the responsibility of antidepressant agents in the genesis of suicidal tendencies has been reported[43]. Antidepressant induced suicidality, such as the emergence of intense suicidal preoccupation during fluoxetine treatment, has been reported[44]. However, suggestions that some antidepressants may actually increase suicide risk owing to their direct lethality on overdose or to specific adverse behavioral effects such as agitation, restlessness, or insomnia are substantiated[45]. Even small doses of the older tricyclic antidepressants, in contrast to large doses of SSRIs, can be lethal in a suicidal overdose. Depressed patients only use antidepressants 5% of the time in suicidal acts.

Combinations of Drugs:
Combinations of drugs or herbs taken simultaneously may be associated with suicidal behavior. For example, alcohol is frequently combined with other substances such as cocaine, heroin, or benzodiazepines. The combinations of substances result in multiple drug on drug interactions. Very little is known about the effects of these drug interactions on violence and suicide in humans. The number of substances used can be more important than the types of substances used in assessing suicidal behavior.

Postmortem toxicology tests in suicide victims detect rates of different classes of psychoactive substances. The pattern has not changed much in the past decade, and it emphasizes the notion that combinations are common.

Detection of alcohol, cocaine, or cannabis in about 40% of suicides and of benzodiazepines and opiates in 20% of the sample supports the clinical practice of discouraging consumption of these substances in depressed patients. Toxicological findings are helpful in detecting the presence of psychoactive substances in suicides. Alcohol is detected in about 30% of suicides. Prescription psychoactive substances with a high abuse potential such as benzodiazepines and opiates are present in one fifth of the suicides. Continued reporting of routine, comprehensive, toxicological findings in suicides is useful to monitor patterns of use of psychoactive substances for suicide risk reduction in clinical practice and public health policy[46].

### Diagnostic Dilemmas of Suicide and Substance Related Disorders

The parallel or dual diagnosis model of substance related disorders and primary psychiatric disorders might be insufficient when evaluating and treating suicidality.

One clinical approach used to evaluate suicidality associated with substance abuse includes psychiatric and medical assessments. The question if the suicidality is substance- induced or if there is underlying primary mental illness and/or general medical condition contributing can be difficult, but it is important to determine.

The psychiatric assessment of a suicidal patient with substance related disorders is critical. Although psychiatric disorders and substance related disorders commonly occur together, only in the last few years have the complex problems of patients with coexisting psychiatric and substance related disorders, the dually diagnosed, been addressed[47]. Psychiatric disorders are under-diagnosed in patients suffering from substance related disorders[48]. In one study of suicidal cocaine addicts, more than half were given a concurrent psychiatric diagnosis and required hospitalization on an acute-care psychiatric unit[49]. Up to 65% of alcoholics entering rehabilitation suffer from a major psychiatric disorder another study showed[50]. Obsessive compulsive disorder is three times more prevalent than expected in patients admitted to an alcohol rehabilitation program, and extensive assessment and treatment of obsessive compulsive disorder improved overall clinical outcome[51].

To explore the issue of under-diagnosing psychiatric disorders in patients with substance related disorders, we published findings on 109 consecutive patients admitted for substance related disorders having a complete psychiatric assessment and medical history and physical examinations. Over 50% of these patients with substance related disorders had undiagnosed, untreated, or under-treated primary psychiatric symptoms that contributed to their addiction. An additional 25% of these patients with substance related disorders had undiagnosed, untreated, or under-treated general medical conditions that contributed to their addiction. Patients with substance related disorders had more general medical problems than patients did with just mental disorders. We concluded, that as many as 75% of patients suffering from substance related disorders have either a primary psychiatric or general medical conditions that significantly contributed to their substance related disorder.

The concept of treating the primary mental illness, such as mood disorder, anxiety disorder, or sleep disorder, in the hope of suicide risk reduction has been an effective clinical approach.

Does the opportunity exist to treat the primary psychiatric disorder that will cause the deliberate self-medication with drugs or alcohol to cease? This is an especially effective question to address when a simple relationship of the primary mental illness and the substance related disorder exists. Examples of a simple relationship of primary mental illness in a self medicating patient are manic patients using alcohol to decrease mania or depressed patients using intravenous amphetamines. If treating the primary psychiatric disorder causes the substance abuse to cease, this may result in less morbidity and mortality, less general medical conditions, a better clinical outcome, and a higher quality of life.

Suicidal patients with *both* substance related disorders and primary psychiatric disorders (dual diagnosis) often have significant general medical conditions (a triple diagnosis) increasing morbidity and mortality[52]. There is an increased morbidity and mortality from general medical conditions in patients suffering from both substance related disorders and primary psychiatric illness, compared to suffering from either substance related disorders or primary psychiatric illness alone.

That physical illness is common among suicidal mentally ill patients seen in an emergency setting is no surprise. However, it is worth noting that physical pathology is not evenly distributed in this group of patients. Suicidal patients additionally suffer the medical effects of substance related disorder generated from the substance itself or route of administration of the substance. The high prevalence of cardiac and respiratory problems among the patients with dual diagnoses is mainly hypertension and arrhythmias and chronic obstructive pulmonary disease and bronchitis. Among patients with substance related disorders only, chronic back pain accounts for a majority of the orthopedic complaints. Liver disease and complications of peptic ulcer disease were the most common of the gastrointestinal diagnoses, found in over 3/4 of those patients. HIV infection or AIDS accounts for more than half of the infectious disease diagnoses among the substance abusers[53].

The following clinical vignettes of suicidal patients highlight the interruption of the cycle centering on substance related disorder, primary mental illness, and general medical conditions.

*Vignette 1:*
*A 56-year-old, white, male, bipolar patient, manic and undiagnosed has been self- medicating with alcohol for many years, and he is now suffering from cirrhosis, GI bleeding, recurrent falling, legal complications, and divorce. He presents himself to the out-patient psychiatric clinic with suicidal ideations. This patient finally is diagnosed with bipolar disorder and treated with lithium monotherapy. He stops drinking. His medical problems improve. His quality of life improves. He wishes he saw a psychiatrist many years ago.*

*Vignette 2:*
*An 18-year-old, white female is self-medicating to treat an underlying depression with intravenous amphetamines. She drinks alcohol with the amphetamines. No previous treatment for depression is noted. She is having heart palpitations, insomnia, paranoia, poor impulse control, and recurrent skin and soft tissue infections; she has recently been diagnosed with hepatitis B and C. The patient presents herself to the outpatient psychiatric clinic with depressive disorder. She starts bupropion and stops using amphetamines. Patient's quality of life improves, and she remains abstinent.*

*Vignette 3:*
*A 48-year-old, black female with schizophrenia is drinking alcohol to "stop the voices." Patient is developing complications of alcohol abuse including delirium, autonomic instability, and seizures. She finally gets back on the antipsychotic medication to stop the voices telling her to kill herself. The patient's general medical condition improves. She is no longer drinking alcohol and has a better quality of life.*

*Vignette 4:*
*The 40-year-old, white, male opiate addict had an original underlying severe, chronic, lower back pain or sciatica. Inadequate pain control has lead to superimposed heroin and narcotic analgesic abuse over the past two years. There is no treatment plan for this patient with chronic lower back pain, which leads to self-medication with heroin to decrease the pain. The intravenous drug use, the normal route of administration of street drugs, caused hepatitis, HIV, and cellulitis, and its potential for suicidal overdose is marked with increasing suicide attempts. He is hospitalized and detoxified from the narcotic analgesics. He had undiagnosed posttraumatic stress disorder and/or borderline personality disorder. He received pharmacotherapy for both and is attending a monthly parallel program, remaining abstinent, and caring for his children again.*

These clinical vignettes illustrate that interruption of the vicious cycle of untreated primary mental illness, substance related disorders, and resulting life threatening general medical conditions, decreases morbidity and mortality, from natural and unnatural causes.

In summary, the Center for Disease Control and Prevention report almost all people who kill themselves have a diagnosable mental or substance related disorder, or both. Therefore, early recognition and treatment of primary psychiatric disorders and substance related disorders offers a promising means of reducing suicide and suicidal behavior.

Unfortunately, suicidal patients with substance related disorders tend to fall between the clinical cracks. Both psychiatrists and general practitioners are reluctant to treat such patients despite their very high risk of suicide. General practitioners are reluctant to treat general medical problems in patients with substance related disorders. Psychiatrists are reluctant to treat substance abusers. The result, suicide, is a frequent outcome.

Moreover the widespread biochemical effects that the substances can have in areas of the brain such as the frontal cortex are extensive. Just as cocaine abusers have decreased ability to remove dopamine from most central nervous system dopamine synapses, ecstasy abusers have a decreased ability to remove serotonin from the nerve terminals in large areas of the brain. It is no wonder that co-morbid substance related disorders make treating suicidal behavior, associated with mental illness or general medical conditions, with psychotropic medication more difficult.

Current psychopharmacologic treatments for substance related disorders are still limited. There are antabuse, acamprosate calcium methadone, naltrexone, LAAM, and nicotine replacements.

Antabuse or disulfiram is an aid in the management of selected chronic alcohol patients who want to remain in a state of enforced sobriety so that treatment may be applied to best advantage. Disulfiram is not a cure for alcoholism. When used alone, without proper motivation and supportive therapy, it is unlikely that it will have any substantive effect on the drinking pattern of the chronic alcoholic. It is contraindicated in patients who are receiving or have recently received alcohol or alcohol containing preparations such as cough syrups. It produces sensitivity to alcohol, which results in a highly unpleasant reaction when the patient under treatment ingests even small amounts of alcohol. Accumulation of acetaldehyde in the blood produces a complex of highly unpleasant symptoms referred to as the disulfiram alcohol reaction. The average maintenance dose is 250 mg daily[54].

Naltrexone is used in the maintenance of alcohol and opiate cessation, an opiate-free state, in individuals formerly physically dependent on opiates who have successfully undergone detoxification. Naltrexone may diminish or eliminate opiate seeking behavior by blocking the euphoric reinforcement produced by self-administration of opiates and by preventing the conditioned abstinence syndrome that occurs following opiate withdrawal, including heightened sensitivity to stimuli, abnormal autonomic responses, dysphoric mood, and intense opiate craving. By blocking opiate induced euphoria and potentially preventing the redevelopment of opiate dependence, naltrexone therapy in conjunction with a medically supervised behavior modification program may contribute to the prevention of relapse in the post addiction period. Noncompliance with naltrexone therapy, unlike methadone or levomethadyl acetate (LAAM) maintenance therapy, is not associated with unpleasant symptoms of withdrawal[55].

One anecdotal case described a heroin addict, participating in a placebo controlled randomized trial, who was prescribed naltrexone as an aid to heroin relapse prevention. The patient tried to commit suicide by taking a heroin overdose after learning that he was HIV-positive. He was taking naltrexone at the time, and, as a result, he survived what would probably have been a fatal overdose[56].

When psychiatric symptoms develop from the substance related disorders, substance induced intoxication or withdrawal, such as delirium, psychosis, mood, anxiety, sleep or sexual disturbances, psychotropic medications are often needed.

Prescription drug abuse, such as narcotic analgesic or benzodiazepine abuse, can result in an accidental or deliberate fatal outcome. Since that possibility is highest in the suicidal patient, alternatives to the more lethal prescription medications should be considered when treating suicidal patients.

Alternatives to opiates for pain in suicidal patients with substance related disorders might include anticonvulsants such as gabapentin. Gabapentin has been shown to be efficacious in numerous small clinical studies and case reports in a wide variety of pain syndromes. It has been clearly demonstrated to be effective for the treatment of neuropathic pain in diabetic neuropathy and post- herpetic neuralgia. This evidence, combined with its favorable side effect profile and lack of drug interactions, makes it an attractive agent for the suicidal substance abuser with pain syndromes[57].

Alternatives to benzodiazepines for anxiety in suicidal patients with psychiatric disorders include antihistamines, selective serotonin reuptake inhibitors, trazodone, buspirone, and even low dose mood stabilizers or atypical antipsychotic medication. Hydroxyzine has been effective for anxiety and it is not addicting. Paroxetine is indicated for panic disorder. At low dose, trazodone, an antidepressant, has been effective for insomnia, anxiety, and depression. Non-addictive antianxiety agents, such as buspirone, may be effective for generalized anxiety symptoms. These alternatives to benzodiazepines should be considered for the suicidal, anxious, substance abusing patient. Some recent studies have reported low dose quetiapine, a major tranquilizer is effective for certain refractory benzodiazepine related disorders.

Controlling the amount of these types of drugs prescribed is also important when treating suicidal patients. Rather than writing a prescription for one hundred and eighty alprazolam tablets and instructing the patient to take one or two every four to six hours as needed for anxiety, a smaller number of pills such as thirty with specific instructions about how to take the medication is vital. Often a week or less of the substance is prescribed in high-risk suicidal patients. A vigorous attempt should be made by the prescribing clinician is not to give the suicidal patient the means to do it.

## Dementia and Suicide

The relationship between suicide and dementia has yet to be investigated systematically. The prevalence of both dementia and suicide increase with age. In contrast to patients with other psychiatric disorders, patients with dementia were not found to die from suicide more often than expected. The diagnosis of dementia does not contribute to the elevated suicide risk in old age. Dementia is rarely diagnosed in elderly suicidal victims. Suicide attempts in patients suffering from dementia are rare[58]. One report showed two patients with Alzheimer's disease who committed suicide by self inflicted gunshot to the head and by jumping from a nineteenth story window. These patients shared several clinical features with others, including being at the early stages of Alzheimer's disease, having a high level of education, having preserved insight, having access to firearms, and being aware of not responding to pharmacological treatment. Furthermore, dementia itself is a risk factor for late life depression and suicide.

Depression, as an important common risk factor of suicide and dementia, is found in patients with Alzheimer's disease as well as in patients with multi-infarct or vascular dementia. Major depression is found more often in vascular dementia than in dementia of the Alzheimer type. Suicidal thoughts and intentions, wishes to die, and feelings that life is not worth living are reported in patients with dementia, especially if these patients also suffer from depression. This association between cognitive deficits, insight in early stages of dementia, and suicidality needs further investigation.

Other cognitive disorders include mild cognitive impairment and age-related cognitive decline. Mild cognitive impairment is a descriptive term referring to persons, who may be functioning quite well in their daily lives and do not meet clinical criteria for dementia, yet may complain of memory problems and show mild impairment in cognitive tests on memory. Understanding mild cognitive impairment is useful for identifying persons who are at high risk for developing Alzheimer's disease in the future. Vascular dementia may also contribute to the development of Alzheimer's disease[59].

The earlier neuropathology in Alzheimer's disease is primarily in the parietal and temporal lobes as revealed by a PET scan. Neuroimaging with PET can show a pattern of regional glucose metabolism that improves early diagnostic accuracy. A PET scan is being considered as a routine part of the diagnosis of dementia[60].

Many different medications are used for behavioral problems associated with dementia including anticonvulsants, antipsychotics, anxiolytics, beta-blockers, selegiline, serotonergic agents, trazodone, tryptophan, estrogen, and opiates. The cholinergic enhancers, however, are a good first choice. Because of the beneficial effect on behavior, these cholinergic enhancers may lead to a decrease in concomitant treatments with antidepressants, antipsychotics, and anxiolytics.

Psychiatrists have under utilized the cholinergic enhancers, or cholinesterase inhibitors. They are indicated for Alzheimer's disease, but they are also being studied in vascular dementia, mixed vascular and Alzheimer's dementia, and even mild cognitive impairment. The cholinesterase inhibitors delay intra-synaptic acetylcholine degradation, improving memory and attention. These medications include tacrine, donepezil, rivastigmine, and galantamine. These agents can be considered as first line agents for dementia. They provide symptomatic treatment rather than modifying disease agents[61].

## Psychotic Disorders and Suicide

Patients with psychotic disorders, including schizophrenia, account for 10 to 15 percent of suicides. Suicide may occur at any point during the course of schizophrenia. There is a relatively high lifetime rate of completed suicide, 10%, and suicide attempts, 30%–50%, in patients with schizophrenia. Rates of suicidal behavior are high across a broad spectrum of patients with psychotic disorders. There are over 3500 suicides per year in schizophrenic patients. Twelve percent of all suicides occur in schizophrenic patients[62]. The suicide rate for schizophrenics is actually increasing, most likely due to decrease in the average length of stay of the hospitalization and inadequate treatment and discharge planning[63].

Intense suicidal thinking and depression is most often associated with increased risk of suicide. However, even in the absence of depression, impulsivity and substance abuse increases the risk. The number of previous suicidal attempts and number of hospitalizations to prevent suicide in schizophrenics are major historical risk factors. Comorbid substance abuse, alcohol and smoking; mood disorders; depression; and severity of parkinsonism; and side effects of antipsychotic medication are more often associated with suicide in schizophrenic patients, rather than age, gender, level of functioning[64].

Both active illness and depressive symptoms are prevalent immediately before suicide in a patient with schizophrenia[65]. First, episode psychotic patients should be asked about suicidal ideation and substance misuse[66]. Factors associated with suicide attempts among patients with schizophrenia include earlier age of onset of illness, earlier age at first hospitalization, and greater number of lifetime depressive episodes[67].

A marked variation in depressive symptoms, alcoholism, and suicide methods are found among sexes and age groups in suicidal schizophrenic patients. For example, alcoholism is most common among middle-aged men, whereas middle-aged women had a high rate of depressive symptoms. Younger male subjects most often use violent suicide methods. Recurrent intense suicidal thoughts and suicidal plans communicated to someone during the previous three months coupled with depression observed during an interview are clinical features associated with suicide in schizophrenic patients.

The recognition of suicidality in schizophrenic patients is important in guiding the treatment. Is the suicidality due to depression or psychosis? Or could it possibly be drug-induced? These are important clinical questions to consider.

The time of prodromal symptoms of psychotic disorder, that is the early phases of the illness, is also the period of highest risk. Risk factors include psychological distress, low self-image, chronic stress, and hopelessness.

Depressive symptoms leading to hopelessness and suicide in a schizophrenic patient may be a part of a major depressive disorder or schizoaffective disorder. Depression in schizophrenic patients can occur in the prodromal phase or post psychotic phase, or it can be an inter-current episode. Treating depression aggressively may relieve such symptoms, but it can also exacerbate a psychosis[68].

Command auditory hallucinations directing the patient to kill him or herself is another cause of suicidality in psychotic patients. Patients with schizophrenia, based on extent of physical injury, make more medically dangerous suicide attempts[69].

Drug-induced akinetic depression, dysphoria, akathisia, pseudoparkinsonism, restless, and agitation secondary to the traditional antipsychotics has been associated with depression and suicide in schizophrenic patients[70].

The different schizophrenic subtypes and impact of positive and negative symptoms on suicide risk should be evaluated. The paranoid schizophrenia subtype was associated with an elevated risk of suicide. Prominent suspiciousness, in the absence of negative symptoms, defines a relatively high-risk group. Two positive symptoms in particular, suspiciousness and delusions, were more severe among successful suicide. Patients with delusions, hallucinations, and severe agitation with suicidality often benefit from atypical antipsychotic medication. The presence of delusions does not distinguish persons with or without a history of suicide attempt[71]. The deficit subtype of schizophrenia associated with a reduced risk of suicide. Prominent negative symptoms such as affective flattening, alogia, or avolition countered the emergence of suicidality in patients with schizophrenia spectrum[72].

Both active psychotic illness and depressive symptoms are highly prevalent immediately before suicide. Other present state risk factors in suicidal psychotic patients include anxiety symptoms, irritability, and agitation.

That suicidality in schizophrenia appears to be a symptom domain separate from other symptoms such as psychosis is suggested, especially since successful treatment of positive symptoms does not eliminate risk of attempted or completed suicide. Although one study found no correlation between the degree of psychosis or negative symptoms and the degree of suicidality, some correlation was found between mood symptoms and suicidality.

The major risk factor for suicide events in schizophrenic patients include previous suicide attempts, previous hospitalizations to prevent suicide, current or past substance abuse, depression, and parkinsonism.

The PET scan of schizophrenic patient's brain shows decreased frontal lobe activity, which perhaps makes schizophrenic patients more at risk of suicide. Another finding documents a reduction in gray matter brain volume early in schizophrenia, and loss seems to be progressive[73].

The suicide rate in schizophrenia is approximately 0.2–0.3%, a rate that has remained constant despite the introduction of antipsychotic therapy. In particular, the incidence of suicide in schizophrenia has not changed with traditional antipsychotic use. Some evidence suggests that atypical antipsychotics may be somewhat more effective than typical or conventional antipsychotics in fighting suicide. One study found a lower rate of suicide attempts among patients taking atypical antipsychotics versus those taking typical agents.

It may be initially important to gain an appreciation of the older, typical, or traditional antipsychotic medication by listening to the patients who needed to take such medication. Many of these patients were hesitant or afraid of these major tranquilizers, the class of psychotropic medication used to treat those disabling psychotic symptoms. Patients refer to the older, traditional antipsychotics as "causing permanent brain damage." The "thorazine-shuffle" is a term used by patients experiencing disabling side effects from these older traditional antipsychotics. Patients also complain of being or feeling like a zombie, unable to function.

In many ways, the patient is accurate, since the traditional antipsychotics do have more disabling neurological side effects such as parkinsonism and tardive dyskinesia.

Anticholinergic medications are most commonly prescribed to counter acute dystonia or parkinsonism induced by these typical antispychotic medications. The anticholinergics are less effective for treatment of akathisia and even worsen tardive dyskinesia. Prophylactic use of these medications to reduce the incidence of extrapyramidal side effects (EPS) is usually determined on a case by case basis.

Patients with co-morbid substance abuse and mood disorders are prone to developing even more side effects from these traditional antipsychotic medications, which can lead to even more non-compliance, relapse, and suicide. Finally, inadequate treatment that occurs in all phases of the illness results in negative attitudes about these medications.

In the past decade, several new and safe, first-line atypical antipsychotics such as Risperdal (risperidone), Zyprexa (olanzapine), Seroquel (quetiapine), Geodon (ziprasidone), Abilify (aripiprazole) have been made available with much less of those disturbing side effects. They selectively target specific dopamine, serotonin, and other neurotransmitters thought to be responsible for the generation of disturbing psychotic thoughts and suicidal behavior.

The main advantage of first line atypical antipsychotic medication such as risperidone instead of the traditional, first line agents such as haloperidol is the fewer propensities to cause neurological side effects. With these new medications, there is a whole order of magnitude less chance of troubling neurological side effects including parkinsonism, dystonia, akathisia and tardive dyskinesia. For example, elderly patients with dementia, a group most at risk for developing tardive dyskinesia, who were prescribed haloperidol had ten times more frequent incidence of tardive dyskinesa; 26% were on haloperidol, compared to 2.6% of patients on risperidone[74].

Because of the lower intensity and frequency of those neurological side effects, these second generation, first-line atypical antipsychotic medications are safer than the traditional antipsychotics. The favorable side effect profile allows clinicians to use these medications more often and for more conditions.

In a recent study published in the *New England Journal of Medicine*, risperidone was shown to prevent relapse of schizophrenia more effectively than haloperidol. This the first study demonstrating that the atypical antipsychotic, risperidone is not only more safe, but also more effective than haloperidol[75].

The following clinical vignettes illustrate basic observations made when switching patients from the older typical antipsychotic medications with more disabling side effects such as chlorpromazine, trifluoperazine, and haloperidol, to the new first line atypical antipsychotics, such as risperidone and olanzapine.

*Vignette 1:*
*C.D. is a 39-year-old, white male diagnosed with psychotic disorder. He had a history of suicide attempt by hanging years ago. He was maintained on 600 mg chlorpromazine per day. He had psychomotor retardation and the "thorazine-shuffle". His quality of life was poor. The medication was changed over four weeks to risperidone at 4 mg per day. He did not exhibit any side effects; his psychotic symptoms improved; and he felt like he was no longer tranquilized.*

*Vignette 2:*
*N.D. is a 50-year-old, white male diagnosed with major depressive disorder with psychosis. Psychotic symptoms included paranoid delusions that he was being harmed. He was taking 2 mg trifluoperazine per day and 4 mg benztropine per day, but he complained of intolerable side effects. The medication was switched to olanzapine at 5 mg per day over the course of two weeks. His EPS resolved with a marked improvement in his quality of life over the next eight months. He stated, "Stelazine caused jaw tightness and twisting, and moodiness, and I was afraid to tell someone. Since I've been on this olanzapine, I'm doing great!"*

*Vignette 3:*
*F.F. is a 52-year-old, white male diagnosed with schizoaffective disorder, depressed type. He was maintained on 5–10mg fluphenazine per day, 2 mg benztropine per day, and 150 mg sertraline per day. This medication was changed to risperidone at 6 mg per day over the course of three weeks. He exhibited less EPS and significantly fewer negative symptoms. His quality of live improved over the following eight months, and he reported getting a haircut, playing the guitar more often, and socializing. He stated, "I am constantly in a good frame of mind. That's growth! The other medications dragged me down and made me crazy."*

*Vignette 4:*
*R.A. is a 24-year-old, Hispanic male diagnosed with schizoaffective disorder bipolar type. He was doing marginally well on a regimen of 10 mg haloperidol per day and 2 mg benztropine per day. He exhibited marked\psychomotor retardation. The medication was switched to risperidone at 4 mg per day over the course of two weeks. The patient showed marked improvement in relief of psychomotor retardation, as well as less intense delusions and hallucinations, less affective flattening, and no side effects. His quality of life improved over the next two months, as he was more active.*

*Vignette 5:*
*D.W. is a 44-year-old, white male diagnosed with schizoaffective disorder depressed type. He was maintained on trifluoperazine at 4 mg per day and desipramine at 75 mg per day. He developed side effects including severe akathisia and tremors. The medication was changed to olanzapine at 5 mg per day over the course of two weeks. His extrapyramidal symptoms disappeared, and his quality of life improved over the next two months without other side effects.*

Thus, patients are better able to tolerate these new generation major tranquilizers. Biological studies suggest the new antipsychotic medications may have a neuroprotective effect. Therefore, treatment goals should include the following: improving cognitive function, diminishing psychosis, decreasing substance abuse, decreasing depression and hopelessness, and decreasing isolation from family and others, as well as restoring work and social function and improving general health.

A central goal in the treatment should ultimately be remission. Remission is a significant reduction of the core symptoms of schizophrenia such as delusions and hallucinations, excitement/hostility, and cognitive and mood symptoms.

Treatment with these better tolerated atypical antipsychotics, now made available in a wide variety of preparations, is a remarkable option for suicidal patients. In some patients, I share the recent reports that with each schizophrenic relapse, further gray matter damage occurs; compliance with effective medication is just one way the patient can benefit. No longer should antipsychotics be considered neurotoxic, (chlorpromazine believed to cause brain damage). It is important to educate patients and families about the advancements in psychotropic medication.

## Mood Disorders and Suicide

Mood disorders place individuals at a greatly increased risk of suicide, and the National Institute of Mental Health has declared that the first line of defense against suicide is to recognize and treat mood disorders[76]. Major mood disorders are associated with about half of all suicides.

The bipolar disorder spectrum includes bipolar type I, bipolar type II, cyclothymia, and bipolar disorder not otherwise specified. In contrast to major depressive disorder, bipolar disorder is made up of several distinct states: depression, hypomania, mania, and mixed states. Since bipolar patients can move between states and experience multiple states in their lifetimes, it is not surprising that patients with bipolar disorder kill themselves more frequently than those with major depression[77].

Individuals with bipolar disorder comprise a patient population at high risk for suicide related morbidity and mortality. Twenty-five to fifty percent of patients with bipolar disorder attempt suicide at least once during their lifetime and ten to fifteen percent die from suicide. Almost one half of patients with bipolar disorder make at least one suicide attempt[78]. Most suicides are carried out within the first few years after onset of the illness. While half of suicides in bipolar illness occur within six years of onset, the other half can occur at any time; there is no completely safe period. A high risk of suicidal behavior is observed very early in the course of bipolar illnesses, especially among young people who become very demoralized after their first episode in the first few years coupled with the considerable delay in starting therapy. There is a serious concern that diagnosis and intervention should take place much earlier[79].

Past and current depressive states are commonly associated with suicide among persons with mood disorders, often in association with severe anxiety or agitation. Prior suicide attempts and current or prior depression is foreseeable of suicide in severe bipolar patients. Bipolar patients spend more weeks during the year being depressed, much more than being manic. For example, one study showed bipolar type I patients spend thirty-one weeks depressed, but only ten weeks manic. Bipolar II patients spend 50% of time depressed and only 2% of the time manic. This emphasizes the significance of the depressive phase of bipolar disorder and increased suicide risk, especially since depressive episodes dominate in bipolar II disorder. Although the risk of suicide attempt in bipolar patients taking lithium is more than eight times lower than among those not taking the medication, even with lithium, the rate of suicide in bipolar patients on lithium is greater than in general population[80].

Co-morbid alcoholism is associated with a higher rate of attempted suicide among family members with bipolar disorder[81]. The increased risk of suicide across all states of bipolar disorder could result from drug and alcohol abuse, a common and corrosive co-morbid condition.

Among all disorders associated with suicide risk, bipolar disorder has the highest mortality, even greater than major depression or mixed drug abuse. The lifetime suicide risk for bipolar disorder is 15.5%, and for major depression, it is 14.6%. No other DSMIV psychiatric diagnosis has such a high suicide lifetime risk (percentage), incidence (percent year), or relative risk.

Suicide attempts in patients with bipolar disorders have more lethal implications than in patients with major depression or than that of the general population. This concept helps explain why the ratio of attempted suicide to fatal suicides in bipolar patients is less than in the general population; that is, more bipolar patients who attempt suicide complete suicide. In contrast to general depression where risk for fatalities is usually higher among males, the mortality rate for women with bipolar disorder is higher than men with the same disorder.

Mania and hypomania are rarely associated with suicidal behavior. Mania confers the lowest risk for completed suicide compared to depression and mixed states. Suicidality is more common in mixed than in manic bipolar disorder[82].

Mixed, excited-dysphoric-agitated mood states present a much higher risk of suicide than pure mania. Mixed bipolar disorder is characterized by symptoms of depression with coexisting symptoms of mania. Therefore, an agitated depressed patient, a dysphoric manic patient, and a patient with depression and a flight of ideas represent mixed bipolar characteristics. Mixed bipolar states are symptoms that meet minimum criteria for major depressive disorder plus three or more of the following: 1) unrelenting dysphoria, irritability, and lability 2) dramatic expressions of suffering, 3) psychomotor agitation against a background of retardation, 4) intense sexual excitement, 5) extreme fatigue with racing thoughts, 6) free-floating anxiety as well as panic attacks, and 7) suicidal obsessions.

This description of mixed bipolar is not very clinically useful. Another description of this state centers on the clinical presentation.

When evaluating the suicidal patient with mixed bipolar disorder it is important to observe the mood, thinking, and behavior. These parameters serve as a useful guideline in evaluating patient's risk level for suicide in a mixed bipolar state. Such patients can have depressed mood but racing thoughts and psychomotor agitation which suggests depressive-anxious mania. Patients in a mixed state can have depressed mood, poverty of thought, and psychomotor agitation which suggests an excited or agitated depression. Patients in a mixed state can have depressed mood, racing thoughts, and psychomotor retardation, which suggests depression with flight of ideas. These are examples of mixed states. Patients with mixed bipolar disorder are at very high risk of suicide.

When treating mixed bipolar disorder, low dose atypical antipsychotic medication and/or mood stabilizers can be prescribed with or without an antidepressant. Antidepressants alone can activate the patient more. Benzodiazepines may disinhibit, and they pose a substantial risk of dependence and misuse in these types of patients. Mood stabilizers require pre-laboratory screening and often take several days for symptomatic relief. Combination pharmacotherapy is discussed in the next chapter.

The majority of suicides among patients with bipolar disorder occur in association with the depressed phase[83]. Severity of concurrent depressive symptoms in mania, rather than a mixed or manic state, is associated with suicidality in bipolar patients. Dysphoric mania is the bipolar subtype associated with the highest risk of completed suicide. Dysphoric mania is most often diagnosed and treated as agitated depression. Another reason for the higher risk of suicide among those in mixed states may be that manic symptoms during a depressed episode, especially irritability and tension, are particularly difficult to tolerate; they cause patients to feel trapped. Suicide is one way to rid oneself of this intolerable state[84].

A complete suicide assessment including asking a bipolar patient whether they think about or have ever attempted suicide is advisable because of the high lifetime risk of suicide and suicide attempts. Suicidal ideation in this group appears to be one of the best short-term indicators of future attempts.

A PET scan of a bipolar patient's brain shows increased activity of monoamines in sub-cortical areas, even when the patient may not be in a manic phase. There is a clear difference in the density of monoamine releasing cells, releasing brain chemicals dopamine, serotonin, and norepinephrine, in the brains of bipolar patients even when they are not having active manic symptoms[85]. This neuroimaging allows us to understand the basic changes in the brain of bipolar patients and the relationship to the course of illness and suicidal symptomatology.

New neurobiological findings in bipolar patients reveal an actual loss of gray matter, atrophy of the cells, and loss of cortical volume, both in neurons and glia. There is a morphologic signature in bipolar disorder of decreased neuronal and glial density in association with glial hypertrophy. These reductions in neuronal and glial density occur in the prefrontal cortex in bipolar patients[86].

The dorsolateral prefrontal cortex was analyzed using postmortem brains from bipolar patients that reveal distinct alterations in cellular architecture. It was noted that this area of the prefrontal cortex has reduced neuronal density in layer III and pyramidal cell density in layers III and V. In addition, a reduction in glial density was found in sub-layer III coupled with enlargement and changes in shape of glial nuclei spanning multiple layers. Of note is that this pattern is distinct from elevations in neuronal density in schizophrenia, rather instead resembling the reductions in cell density found in major depressive disorder[87].

Even within the nerve cell itself, there is a deficiency of second messenger precursor chemicals, specifically reduced frontal cortex inositol levels, in the postmortem brain of suicide victims with bipolar disorder[88].

After a patient with bipolar disorder is determined to be at high risk for suicide, measures can be initiated including pharmacotherapy. Naturalistic studies suggest that lithium is associated with lower rates of suicide attempts and completions, independent of its mood stabilizing effect. Suicidal behaviors can return once patients stop taking the medication. Lithium's antisuicidal properties are superior to those of anticonvulsants, although most of the studies have not been matched for past suicidal behavior and may therefore not be comparable in terms of risk.

There are generally two classes of mood stabilizers 1) lithium and 2) anticonvulsants such as divalproex sodium (valproate, valproic acid), carbamazepine and oxcarbamzepine, lamotrigine, gabapentin and tiagabine, topiramate, zonisamide, and levtiracetam.

Lithium, divalproex, and lamotrigine are the mood stabilizers approved by the FDA for use in patients with bipolar disorders. The atypical antipsychotic, olanzapine, is the first antipsychotic (major tranquilizer) that is also approved as a mood stabilizer[89].

Lithium has been clearly demonstrated to be superior to anticonvulsants in non-rapid cycling and to be equal to divalproex in rapid cycling types of bipolar disorders. Only lithium has been able to show its effectiveness in preventing or attenuating future episodes of the phases of the illness. In bipolar illness, this would mean preventing recurrences of mania, hypomania and depression[90]. It is antisuicidal for bipolar patients, unlike the anticonvulsants.

Divalproex effect for mania is supported by considerable evidence for both acute mania and maintenance treatment. Antimanic response is generally associated with a valproate serum level under 45 to 50 mg/L. Most patients treated with valproic acid respond within one to four days after achieving an adequate serum level[91]. Divalproex loading for rapid stabilization of acute mania is described as effective as haloperidol or olanzapine[92]. In a Canadian survey of outpatient geriatric care, the number of new valproate users surpassed the number of lithium users and went up from 183 in 1993 to over 1,000 in 2001.

Divalproex activates enzymatic pathways used to synthesize endogenous growth factors for neurogenesis[93]. It activates the ERK MAP kinase pathway used to enhance neuronal connectivity.

Divalproex is effective for mania but not depression, and not suicidal depression. It can help with instability and impulsivity. It has side effects including weight gain; hair loss (reversible with the over-the-counter Centrum Silver vitamin, which contains equipotent mixture of zinc and selenium), ovarian dysfunction, sex-steroid binding changes, menstrual irregularities, low platelets, and elevated liver enzymes. Cases of hyperammoniaemia, which requires lactulose, can also occur.

Carbamazepine and oxcarbamazepine are popular alternatives to lithium and valproic acid, but they are not FDA approved for the treatment of acute mania. Both lithium and divalproex, however, are more effective than carbamazepine in patients with rapid cycling bipolar disorder. In one report, the combination of lithium and carbamazepine was more effective in preventing a manic episode than with lithium or carbamazepine alone. There is a poorer long-term outcome on carbamazepine compared to lithium.

The side effects of carbamazepine, including rash behaviors, neurtropenia, iron deficiency anemia, in addition to the extensive drug-drug interactions, limits it use.

Carbamazepine enzymatically induces its own metabolism and the catabolism of many medications as well. For example, it can break down birth control pills and render a woman pregnant while taking birth control pills. It is not a good choice for patients taking other psychiatric or medical medications.

I start carbamazepine 100 mg three times daily. Monitoring for tolerability and for initial side effects such as rash, fever, or ataxia, I then gradually introduce the 200 mg tablets twice daily, finally titrating up to 1000 mg per day in some cases. Monitoring the CBC, CMP, and carbamazepine levels are required.

Gabapentin has not shown to be effective for acute mania in several clinical trials. An initial positive effect diminishes over time. Early enthusiasm for its use as a primary treatment for bipolar disorder seems to have been premature[94]. Some studies show that placebo is actually more effective than gabapentin in bipolar patients with mania as a monotherapy.

Lamotrigine is more effective than gabapentin and placebo in treating bipolar disorder. Other studies with lamotrigine had no statistically significant differences with placebo in patients with bipolar disorder. The side effect of Steven Johnson Syndrome, a life threatening skin rash, decreases by slower dosage titration, but slower titration may reduce lamotrigine's usefulness in acute mania[95]. It is FDA approved for bipolar disorder. Lamotrigine is more effective in preventing depression, however, rather than mania.

Topiramate, tiagabine, leviracetam, ethosuximide, and zonisamide have not extensively been studied for suicide risk reduction, but they are potential maintenance treatments for bipolar disorder currently.

In general, the anticonvulsants are not as effective for depression, the phase with the most risk of suicide, of bipolar illness, as is lithium. The two proven effective mood stabilizers for mania, lithium and divalproex, have special effects on the brain morphology in patients suffering from bipolar disorder.

Lithium has been shown to increase neurogenesis in dentate gyrus of adult mice. Lithium increases glial density and increases gray matter volumes in bipolar patients. Lithium may both prevent the damage caused by psychiatric illness and repair it by stimulating new cell growth[96].

Both lithium and divalproex increase Bcl-2, a major neuroprotective protein in the frontal cortex, and both signal protein synthesis for endogenous growth. These neurotrophic effects enhance neuronal connectivity, unlike medications such as desipramime, haloperidol or carbamazepine, which do not. Lithium and divalproex activate the ERK MAP kinase signaling for endogenous nerve growth not only Bcl-2, but also pERK 42, PERK 44, pRSK, pCREB, and pBAD[97].

Lithium is the only mood stabilizer that is anti-suicidal[98]. Prophylactic lithium treatment reduces the risk of suicide in patients with bipolar disorder. A 22-study literature review in over forty years of experience with the use of lithium treatment in bipolar patients revealed that, in patients taking lithium, suicidal acts reduced by 85%[99]. Bipolar patients had a 6.4 fold higher risk for suicide before taking lithium than during lithium treatment. When discontinuing lithium treatment, a patient's risk increased 7.5 fold[100].

There have been some studies comparing lithium and other anticonvulsants in patients of suicide risk with bipolar disorder. Suicide and suicide attempts among bipolar patients randomly assigned to either lithium or carbamazepine demonstrated lithium to be more effective. In addition, there is a 2–3 fold relative risk of suicide events in bipolar patients taking lithium rather than divalproex. Lithium is essentially more effective in bipolar suicidal patients than divalproex[101].

In severely ill, bipolar patients, double mood stabilizer pharmacotherapy can be effective with lithium and divalproex. Patients may be more compliant with a combination of lithium and divalproex than either medication alone because these medications have synergistic actions and different side effect profiles. Also, when given in combination the doses and therefore the side effects of these medications may be reduced[102].

Atypical antipsychotics as monotherapy or adjunct therapy for acute manic or mixed episodes associated with bipolar type I disorder are now FDA approved.

Olanzapine is approved for both acute and maintenance therapy in bipolar disorder.

Risperidone is approved for acute therapy either alone or in combination with lithium or valproate. Quetiapine is also approved for acute bipolar mania as monotherapy or in combination with those mood stabilizers. Ziprasidone and aripiprazole are also approved for the treatment bipolar disorder.

The depressive disorder spectrum includes major depression, dysthymia, minor depression, and depression disorder not otherwise specified. They comprise a group of patients at very high risk of suicide, especially since suicidal thoughts is actually a core symptom of a major depressive episode[103].

Depression as the major cause of suicide is a prevalent but an under-detected, under-diagnosed, and under-treated illness; this is particularly true for depressed suicide victims[104]. This clinical phenomenon highlights the National Institute of Mental Health Collaborative Depression Study that depression treatment can be characterized by an unmet need. A major depressive episode is perhaps the most common psychiatric syndrome that predisposes to suicide. Depressive disorders and substance related disorders are perhaps the most common psychiatric disorders that suicidal patients suffer.

In the two years after discharge from the psychiatric hospital for major depression, patients have increased the risk of a suicide attempt seven fold. For each suicide attempt in a subject's history, the risk for an attempt in the follow up period increases by 30%.

Major depressive disorder can be single, episodic, recurrent, or chronic. The severity of the major depressive episode can be mild, moderate, and severe without psychotic features, severe with psychotic features, or severe with mood congruent or mood incongruent psychotic features. The major depressive episode can be in partial remission, full remission, or unspecified. It can have catatonic, melancholic, or atypical features, or a postpartum onset.

A major depressive episode forms the foundation for a major depressive disorder. A major depressive disorder is a major depressive episode that is not better accounted for by schizophrenia, schizoaffective, or another psychotic disorder. In addition, it is not due to a substance related disorder or general medical condition. That there has never been a manic, hypomanic, or mixed episode is also a requirement.

A major depressive episode is a cluster of symptoms that has been present during at least a two-week period nearly every day, and it represents a change from previous functioning. At least one of the symptoms is either depressed mood most of the day, as indicated by either subjective report or observation made by others, or markedly diminished interest or pleasure in all, or almost all, activities. Other symptoms include the following: significant weight loss when not dieting, weight gain, decrease or increase in appetite, insomnia or hypersomnia, psychomotor agitation or retardation, fatigue or loss of energy, feelings of worthlessness or excessive and inappropriate guilt, diminished ability to think or concentrate or indecisiveness, and finally recurrent thoughts of death, recurrent suicidal ideation without a specific plan, a suicide attempt, or a specific plan for committing suicide.

These symptoms must cause clinically significant distress or impairment in social, occupational, or other important areas of functioning. Finally, symptoms can not meet diagnostic criteria for a mixed episode, not be due to the direct physiological effects of a substance or general medical condition, and not be better accounted for by bereavement.

Bipolar depression is often difficult to recognize, especially early in the course of illness. Bipolar depression is depression in a patient with bipolar disorder. Thus, initially treating this type of depressed patient can induce mania. Pure activating antidepressants, such as SSRIs or SNRI's, may activate such a patient. This clinical caveat is important since most bipolar depressed patients are more likely to present for treatment in a depressed rather than manic phase. When the history is gathered, the patient may not recall manic or hypomanic periods or recognize hypomania as pathologic. Bipolar depression may be more likely than unipolar depression to present with severe fatigue, hypersomnia, marked irritability, severe anxiety, or racing thoughts. It is important to recognize the illness and to inform the patient that they are cycling—the problem is not just the depression. Mood-stabilizing medications are the mainstay of treatment[105].

Treating bipolar depression acutely and over the long term can be challenging. Compared with bipolar mania, much less is known about the most effective strategies for treating bipolar depression. Several treatment guidelines based on expert consensus have addressed bipolar depression, but many unanswered questions remain. For bipolar depression, mood stabilizer therapy is the cornerstone of bipolar relapse prevention therapy. Results from some studies suggest that combination therapy may be more effective than monotherapy. A mood stabilizer or combination mood stabilizer/atypical antipsychotic are needed prior to beginning an antidepressant. Symbyax (Lilly) is a combination of olanzapine and fluoxetine that is now FDA approved for the treatment of bipolar depression. Recently, this medication is the first ever approved for bipolar depression.

Treating bipolar depression can be clinically challenging, since prescribing an antidepressant can induce mania. One of the pharmacological treatment goals of bipolar depression is to reduce depression and suicidal thoughts as an acute treatment strategy. Relapse prevention and maintenance goals also include reducing the risk of suicide attempts. Acute treatment of bipolar depression calls for a mood stabilizer alone or in combination with an antidepressant. It is important to avoid using unimodal antidepressant therapy in patients with bipolar I depression because of the risk of switching to mania.

Minor depression is frequently overlooked or related to general medical conditions. Recurrent brief depressive disorder and major depressive disorder share the same diagnostic picture of depression, and both are associated with increased suicide attempt rates.

Combined depression is characterized by longitudinal diagnostic shifts from recurrent brief depressive disorder to major depressive disorder or vice versa. It is a mood disorder that has a substantially high risk of suicide attempts. Patients with combined depression show significantly higher suicidal behavior in comparison with recurrent brief depressive disorder and major depressive disorder patients. The coexistence of a greater propensity for suicidal ideation and impulsivity in recurrent brief depressive disorder might also explain why such patients are more prone to attempt suicide, even if they do not meet the duration criteria for major depressive disorder[106].

A major depressive episode can occur despite having other psychiatric disorders such as a substance related disorders, dementia, psychotic, anxiety, and personality disorder, general medical conditions, or with severe psychosocial stressors.

Co-morbid depression and substance abuse greatly increases the risk for suicide. Major depression that occurred before the patient became substance dependent is associated with increased severity of suicidal intent. Major depression that occurs during abstinence is most associated with an increased number of suicide attempts. Depression based on the timing of the occurrence of depression in relation to substance dependence is important in evaluating suicidal risk among these patients[107].

Co-morbid depression and panic disorder may to increase the risk for lifetime suicide attempt. The presence of greater anxiety in the non-attempters warrants further investigation[108].

Depression in those forms can be treated equally well by all antidepressants provided that the patient stays on the medication. The response rate to a completed therapeutic trial of a medication from any of the antidepressant classes is roughly the same: 60 to 65%[109].

Three depressive subtypes, psychotic depression, depression with atypical features, and winter depression, require further explanation in relation to suicidality.

If a depressed patient becomes psychotic, the psychotic feature itself does not necessarily increase risk of suicide. In one study, psychotic and non-psychotic depressed patients did not differ with respect to attempted suicide. However, suicide in psychotic major depression is more violent and associated with more dangerous suicide methods compared to non-psychotic depressed suicides[110]. Psychotic depression does not respond well to antidepressants alone. In general, the antidepressant needs to be helped along by an adjunctive antipsychotic agent for the treatment of psychotic depression. Some consider psychotic depression to be a separate subtype of depression[111].

Depression with atypical features such as profound sensitivity to rejection, overeating, leaden fatigue, sleeping too much, and mood reactivity (meaning that the patient feels better when something good happens) seems to respond to MAO inhibitors or SSRIs. Tricyclic antidepressants are not effective for atypical depression.

Winter depression, also known as seasonal affective disorder, responds to all antidepressant medications as well as most other forms of depression. The specifier "with seasonal pattern" is used by psychiatrists to apply to the pattern of major depressive episodes in bipolar type I disorder, bipolar type II disorder, or recurrent major depressive disorder. The essential feature is the onset and remission of major depressive episodes at characteristic times of the year. In most cases, the episodes begin in fall or winter and remit in spring. Less commonly, there may be recurrent summer depressive episodes. Young women are at highest risk for winter depressive episodes. For those patients who are partially compliant with medication, winter depression is the one depressive subtype where phototherapy can also be effective. In fact, bright visible spectrum light alone in treatment may be associated with switches into manic or hypomanic episodes.

The variation in light-dark cycles superimposed upon human mood is influential effects suicide rates. The light -dark cycles in nature in conjunction with a person's mood can help understand suicide. Suicides peak in the summer and spring months. Although depression in the winter season is common, there is a spring peak for suicide. The occurrence of suicide has been more common during the spring since at least the Middle Ages[113]. The month of May is associated with maximum suicide risk in many countries of the Northern Hemisphere[114].

There is an annual rhythm for violent suicides in both sexes. Among males a four cycles per year pattern is seen alongside the more relevant one cycle per year distribution. Among females, a six cycle per year pattern is seen alongside the one cycle per year distribution. The annual rhythm found in that study of violent attempted suicide in relation to climate and seasonal change confirms the importance of taking chronobiological variables into account when evaluating of patients at risk of suicide[115].

It has not been determined whether seasonal differences in suicide rates can be attributed to sunlight, temperature, or prevalence of acute psychiatric illness. The prevalence of suicide increases with higher latitudes. A positive linear relation between the variation in suicide rate and geographic latitude across twenty countries demonstrates that latitude is directly related to variation in suicide rates.

A temperature relationship with attempted suicide has also been noted. Higher temperatures positively correlated with attempted suicides, whereas cooler temperatures seem to exert a protective effect.

The relationship between the intensity of cosmic rays, the level of solar and geomagnetic activity, and the monthly numbers of deaths from fatal suicides in Israel and Lithuania was studied. Cosmic rays intensity, as measured by proton flux of energy levels between 60 and 90 MeV, correlated strongly with monthly numbers of deaths from suicide[116].

These environmental factors coupled with depressive symptoms can place a person at higher risk for suicide, and these factors require close attention in patients who are suicidal with mood disorders.

During a depressive episode, the subjective perception of stressful life events may be more germane to suicidal expression than the objective quantity of such events. A more optimistic perceptual set, despite equivalent objective severity of depression, may modify hopelessness and may protect against suicidal behavior during periods of risk, such as during a major depressive episode. Assessment of reasons for living should be included in the evaluation of suicidal patients.

Understanding some of the structural and functional abnormalities of the brain in patients suffering from mood disorders gives insight into the changes in the brain in suicidal patients with mood disorders.

Gray matter is reduced in mood disorders, such as bipolar and major depression, particularly in the prefrontal cortex. Whether missing neurons and glia, supporting nerve structures, were never present or the diseases led to structural changes such as cell atrophy over time is unclear.

Patients with major depressive disorder and a history of a suicide attempt demonstrate significantly more subcortical gray matter hyperintensities in the basal ganglia compared to depressed patients without such a history. These MRI findings in depressed patients with suicidality suggest that patients with abnormal MRI findings may be at higher risk for mood disorders and suicide attempts because of disruption of critical neuroanatomic pathways[117].

Neuroimaging with PET shows the most remarkable changes in the brain before and after treatment of depression. There is great increased activity in the brain and particularly within the prefrontal cortex after successful treatment[118].

Patients with major depression have an impaired prefrontal cortical response to serotonin release. Physiological activity is decreased during major depressive episodes in the dorsal prefrontal cortical areas. These areas of deactivation during the depressed state may reflect neuropsychological interactions between cognitive and emotional processing, and they may relate to the subtle cognitive impairments associated with major depressive episodes. These abnormalities reverse with symptom remission[119].

In a notable report, combining biologic and physiologic changes in the brain of suicide attempters with major depression, it was found that lower serotonergic activity correlated with high-lethality suicide attempts in depressed patients. Postmortem studies of serotonin receptors in suicides localize changes to the prefrontal cortex. Depressed patients with a history of a high-lethality suicide attempts were compared to those with low-lethality suicide attempts with respect to level of depression, suicidal ideation, intent, impulsivity and aggression. PET scans measuring regional cerebral uptake of fludeoxyglucose and a fenfluramine challenge were done. Localized prefrontal cortex hypofunction and impaired serotonergic responsivity were found to be proportional to the lethality of the suicide attempt and may mediate the effects of suicide intent and impulsivity on lethality. Results showed depressed high-lethality suicide attempters had lower activity in the prefrontal cortex compared with low lethality depressed suicidal attempters. The difference was more pronounced after fenfluramine administration. This low activity in the prefrontal cortex is associated with higher lifetime impulsivity, higher suicidal intent and planning, and higher-lethality suicide attempts[120].

A neuropsychological study showed patients whose prior suicide attempts of high lethality performed significantly worse than all groups on tests of executive functioning. They were the only group to perform significantly worse than non patients on tests of general intellectual functioning, attention and memory, which suggests neuropsychological deficits in depressed patients with prior high-lethality suicide attempts have impairment of executive functioning beyond that typically found in major depression. This more extensive neuropsychological impairment in the context of depression may be a risk factor for severe suicide attempt[121].

The pathophysiology of suicidal behavior in major depressive disorder also emphasizes the hypothalamic-pituitary-adrenal (HPA) axis and its interplay with the serotonin system. Although no typical demographic and historical risk factors distinguishes depressed patients who commit suicide from those who do not, the biochemical test, the dexamethasone suppression test, is a practical measure of HPA-axis hyperactivity that provides a tool considerably more powerful than the clinical ones currently in depressed patients[122].

It seems that few suicide attempters with major depression receive adequate treatment for depression before the suicide attempt and that, despite their well-known high risk for suicide, the treatment situation is not necessarily any better after the attempt. For example, during the month just before a suicide attempt, only 16% of patients had received antidepressants in adequate doses. Within one month of the suicide attempt, only 17% of these depressed patients were receiving antidepressants in adequate doses in a recent study in Finland[123]. In another study in Hungary, where the suicide rate is highest in Europe, drug treatment prior to suicide with anxiolytics or hypnotics (33%) was more common than treatment with antidepressants (18%) or lithium (2%)[124].

Antidepressant treatment of depressed patients is strikingly inadequate, even in suicide attempters known to be at higher risk for suicidal acts. This deficiency undermines the ability to measure the antisuicidal effects of antidepressants in naturalistic studies[125].

Clinicians need not be fearful in treating suicidal patients with major depressive disorder with an adequate dose and duration of antidepressant pharmacotherapy for fear of activating the patient and contributing to the suicidality[126]. Early reports that certain antidepressants such as fluoxetine could actually induce intense suicidal ideation or increase suicidal behavior by energizing depressed patients to act along preexisting suicidal thoughts, or by inducing akathisia with associated self-destructive impulses is a clinical concern[127].

Only an average of 5% of suicidal patients on average use their prescribed antidepressant to commit suicide. Under-prescription of antidepressants and failure of antidepressant therapy appear to be of greater practical importance than the toxicity of individual compounds. A suicide preventing effect has not been demonstrated conclusively for antidepressants. Yet, successful treatment of depression can relieve suicidality.

Depression, the major cause of suicide, is prevalent but an under-detected, under-diagnosed, and under-treated illness, and this is particularly true for depressed suicide victims. However, several studies consistently show that successful treatment of depression not only relieves depressive symptoms, but also decreases suicidal risk. In contrast to lithium, antidepressants have not been shown to be anti-suicidal or to prevent suicide. The data on the impact of antidepressants on suicide risk is unconvincing. However, effectively diagnosing and treating depressive disorders can certainly be beneficial. If the rate of treated depressions in the population increases gradually, at a given point it will appear in the decline of the suicide rates. Although absolute evidence is lacking at present, recent reports from some European countries strongly suggest that increasing utilization of antidepressants is one of the most important contributing factors in the decrease in suicide rates.

## Anxiety Disorders and Suicide

Acute or present-state severe and extreme anxiety or agitation is highly correlated with suicide. In a study of hospitalized psychiatric in-patients and suicide, that is patients who committed suicide (mostly by hanging, suffocation, or jumping) while in a psychiatric hospital (on a pass from the unit, or absconded from the unit) or immediately after discharge (within seven days), the patients with severe and extreme anxiety and agitation highly correlated with suicide completion. During the seven days prior to suicide completion of in-patient psychiatric hospital suicides, nearly 80% had evidence of severe anxiety and/or severe or extreme agitation.

Severe present-state psychic anxiety or agitation is highly associated with increased suicide risk. Changes in the severity of the symptoms, where patients would seem improved usually for only a short duration is an important clinical observation. Of note is that 80% of those patients also denied suicidal thoughts and intent at their last communication before their suicide. That finding, consistent with other reports, shows that suicidal ideation was not an acute correlate, and even the nonsuicidal patients had a higher percent of expressed suicidal ideation. Denying suicidal ideations alone, therefore, is not a reliable basis for a suicide risk assessment. In addition, clinicians could not rely on a patient's ability to agree to a "no-suicide" contract as being a deterrent to suicide. Although a high prevalence and severity of anxiety and agitation in these patients existed, the relevant medication usage was quite low. The aggressive treatment of severe anxiety/agitation may well be capable of reducing acute suicide risk, even before the depression is in full remission[128].

Severe psychic anxiety (as determined by the intensity of the experienced anxiety as well as its duration throughout the patient's day), panic attacks, and global insomnia are symptoms that appear to be present in depressed patients shortly prior to suicide or serious attempts. Thus, rapid treatment may reduce the risk of suicide even before the positive effects of antidepressant medications occur. It is suggested that psychic anxiety, panic attacks, and global insomnia differentiate suicides from non-suicides among severely depressed patients from a week to a year, whereas expressed suicidal ideation, prior suicidal ideation, and hopelessness do not separate them acutely, only at two to ten year follow-up.

One may consider treatment of anxiety, panic, and insomnia symptoms to reduce the likelihood of suicide. Clonzaepam, not as a sedative hypnotic but as a long acting anxiolytic-anticonvulsant, is an adjunct to antidepressant treatment. Its short-term use may lessen the risk of suicide. Certain benzodiazepines require extreme caution when prescribing them. Alprazolam has been reported to induce dyscontrol in borderline personality disorder patients. Anxious patients in all diagnostic categories should be closely guided by means of intensified psychotherapeutic interventions if undergoing a benzodiazepine reduction in the setting of suicidal ideation.

Other agents such as atypical antipsychotic medications that block serotonin (5-HT2A) receptors and anticonvulsants like divalproex, are especially useful in some patients with severe agitation and anxiety, including patients with bipolar mixed states. If there are such modifiable severe anxiety symptoms that are associated with suicide, then aggressive treatment of these symptoms may reduce suicide. Pharmacological treatment may need to be added to the antidepressant, given the known delay of action of antidepressants and the possible failure in producing therapeutic benefit.

Anxiety disorders, even when controlled for co-morbid depression and substance abuse, are implicated in fifteen to twenty percent of suicides. The major anxiety disorders include panic disorder with or without agoraphobia, specific phobias, social phobia, obsessive-compulsive disorder, posttraumatic stress disorder, acute stress disorder, and generalized anxiety disorder.

Although previous reports of suicide risk in patients with anxiety disorders have been inconsistent, suicide risk in patients with anxiety disorders is higher than previously thought[129]. Patients with anxiety disorders warrant explicit evaluation for suicide risk. Patients with suicide attempts were more likely than patients who completed suicide to have a current diagnosis of anxiety disorder[130].

Obsessive compulsive disorder has obsessions as part of the symptoms. If these obsessions involve suicidal thoughts, there can be an increased risk of suicide in these patients. Obsessions increased the risk of suicidal thoughts, and suicidal thoughts, depression, and obsessions increase suicidal attempts[131].

Posttraumatic stress disorder develops after being exposed to a traumatic event in which the person experiences, witnesses, or is confronted with actual or threatened death or serious injury or a threat to the physical integrity of the person or others. The person's response in adults involves intense fear, helplessness, or horror, but in children, it may involve disorganized or agitated behavior. The traumatic event is persistently re-experienced. There is avoidance of stimuli associated with it and increased arousal. The disturbance lasts more than one month and causes clinically significant distress or impairment in social, occupational, or other areas of functioning. It can be acute if duration of symptoms is less than three months or chronic. It can have a delayed onset if the onset of symptoms is at least six months after the stressor.

Since one out of two adult Americans will experience a traumatic event at some time in their life, there is a contradiction to the commonly held belief that being exposed to a traumatic event is rare and outside of the range of usual human experience. Approximately twenty-five percent of those exposed to a trauma will develop PTSD, leading to a lifetime prevalence of eight percent in the American population. It used to be thought that PTSD is a disorder primarily of male combat veterans, but it is twice as prevalent in women as it is in men, and the duration is substantially longer in women. Only fifteen percent of all PTSD cases are related to combat. The more common stressors are related to sexual violence and accidents.

PTSD appears to be associated with an increased risk of suicide. Patients with PTSD have the highest risk of lifetime suicide attempts when compared with patients having other anxiety disorders. Patients with PTSD have a high risk of suicide even when compared to patients with mood disorders. Posttraumatic stress disorder patients have an increased risk of suicide and suicidal behavior[132], especially with high levels of impulsivity and little social support[133]. The sub-clinical or sub threshold posttraumatic stress disorder also significantly raises the risk for suicidal ideation, even after controlling the major depressive disorder. Higher numbers of sub-threshold PTSD symptoms are associated with greater impairment, co-morbidity, and suicidal ideation[134].

Suicidal behavior in patients with current or past panic disorder was not associated with suicidal behavior in the absence of other risk factors. However, co-morbid mood disorders, substance related disorders, eating disorders, personality disorders, and female sex with panic disorder are risk factors to consider[135].

Advances in brain imaging techniques involving PET have increased our knowledge of which brain structures regulate human anxiety: the amygdala, the hippocampus, the orbital frontal cortex, and other regions of the prefrontal cortex. For example, patients with panic disorder have a decreased number of benzodiazepine receptors in the brain[136]. In addition, patients with posttraumatic stress disorder have GABA dysfunction in the medial prefrontal cortex[137].

In chronic posttraumatic stress disorder, many studies have shown a reduction in the volume of the hippocampus as well as dysfunction of the medial prefrontal cortex. It is not known if the smaller brain volumes of the hippocampus result from stress or if it is an inborn trait that is a risk factor for PTSD. The SSRIs can promote neurogenesis. For example after starting treatment with an SSRI, patients showed 35% improvement in memory and an associated 5% increase in hippocampal volume within one year after starting treatment. That fluoxetine can promote hippocampal neurogenesis suggests increased neurogenesis might be one of the ways SSRIs decrease psychiatric symptoms[138].

Studies definitively show that stress is bad for neurons—particularly neurogenesis or the development of new neurons in the brain. With the onset of stress or anxiety, neurogenesis is decreased in the adult brain. Stress decreases the dendrite branching of neurons in the hippocampus.

The amygdala is involved in fear reactions that occur like a reflex and without thought. Emotional inputs to the amygdala frequently use the excitatory neurotransmitter glutamine, which is regulated by both GABA and serotonin neurons. This biochemical understanding of anxiety helps guide treatment recommendations in the hope of reducing suicidality.

Modern guidelines for psychopharmacologic treatment of anxiety disorders have evolved from recommending GABAergic (gamma-aminobutryic acid) benzodiazepines to recommending serotonergic agents for first line use. This trend, along with adverse publicity about the dependence potential of benzodiazepines, might lead one to suspect that use has declined. Nevertheless, benzodiazepines are still more widely prescribed than antidepressants for the treatment of anxiety disorders. Although serotonergic antidepressants have largely replaced benzodiazepines as the recommended first-line treatments for anxiety disorders in treatment guidelines, benzodiazepines are in fact still used more frequently. For example, alprazolam is more often prescribed than paroxetine for generalized anxiety disorder. Risk conscious pharmacotherapy for the suicidal patient include dispensing only amounts of medications consistent with clinical needs and risks, refilling prescriptions only with adequate clinical monitoring, avoiding under-treatment, avoiding unnecessary abrupt discontinuation of medications, and choosing the least toxic, effective drug available.

New GABA agents have the potential of less sedation and dependence liability, and they may be useful in the future, as third generation minor tranquilizers, for treatment of anxiety[139].

Now, an innovative stage-based pharmacotherapy for posttraumatic stress disorder, involving different treatments during the course of the disorder, has evolved[140]. Immediate treatment during the first hours centers on reducing terror. Dampening down the terror and fear with adrenergic blocking agents such as beta-blockers (propranolol) is quite an effective approach. Treatment during the first days to reduce sensitization and help memory consolidation involves the use of the adrenergic blockers and mood stabilizers. Treatment during the first months continues to reduce symptoms incorporating SSRIs and low dose trazodone for sleep disturbance. Treatment after the first year involves reducing symptoms and co-morbidity with adrenergic blockers, SSRIs, and mood stabilizers. Finally, in complex posttraumatic stress disorder, atypical antipsychotic augmentation is reported to be effective. Although a popular belief at benzodiazepines for posttraumatic stress disorder are most effective, they are actually not helpful for certain patients, especially with co-morbid substance abuse and high risk of suicide[141].

## Adjustment Disorders and Suicide

An essential feature of an adjustment disorder is the development of clinically significant emotional or behavioral symptoms in response to an identifiable psychosocial stress. The symptoms develop within three months after the onset of the stressor and must resolve within six months of the termination of the stressor. Typical stressors include the following: break-up of a relationship, marital problems, marked business difficulties, and living in a crime-ridden neighborhood.

Many patients suffering from an adjustment disorder have had a documented suicide attempt in the past; almost all had been suicidal during their admission to the hospital; and one-half had attempted suicide before their hospitalization. Adjustment disorder diagnoses in patients with suicide attempts is associated with high levels of suicidality. The most commonly used method of suicide attempts was overdosing. A majority of the patients had co-morbid Axis II personality disorders and substance related disorders[142].

Thwarting one suicide attempt does not necessarily solve the problem. A recent report showed the risk of suicide among individuals with a history of parasuicide continues for many years after the initial event. Clinicians should pay particular attention to the management of patients immediately after an episode of suicide attempt. Previous, deliberate self-harm remains a potent risk for subsequent suicide, even if it occurs many years prior[143].

## Eating Disorders and Suicide

The death rate for patients with anorexia nervosa is the highest among patients with psychiatric conditions, dying from physiologic causes (arrhythmia, gastric hemorrhaging) and suicide[144]. Suicide attempts are equally, if not more, common in women with eating disorders compared to women with depression[145].

Eating disorders are severe, relatively chronic conditions that are associated with co-morbid psychopathology and adverse medical conditions.

The vast majority of those afflicted with eating disorders are adolescent and young adult women. Distorted body image, obsession with food and weight, drastic reduction in food intake often to the point of starvation, and extreme weight loss characterize anorexia nervosa.

Anorexia nervosa is associated with a substantial risk of death and suicide. The risk of suicide in a patient with eating disorder is twenty-three times that of the general population. Features correlated with fatal outcome are longer duration of illness, binging and purging, co-morbid substance abuse, and co-morbid mood disorders[146].

Bulimia nervosa, more common than anorexia nervosa is characterized by binge eating and compensatory purging by vomiting, use of laxatives, diuretics, diet pills, exercise, or fasting. Binge behavior and loss of control of food intake characterize binge eating disorder with an absence of purging[147].

Suicidal thoughts in women with bulimia nervosa and binge eating disorder is associated with markedly poorer functioning and much higher levels of disability, health problems, insomnia, psychosocial stress, and co-morbid psychiatric disorders[148].

Disturbances of the serotonergic pathways within the brain have been linked to the onset, persistence, and recurrence of eating disorders. Studies have linked bulimia nervosa, suicide and self-injurious behavior to alterations in brain serotonin activity[149]. Suicide attempts are frequent, often serious, and multiple in women with bulimia nervosa. The treatment for eating disorders includes selective serotonin reuptake inhibitors. Interventions targeting depressive and impulsive features associated with bulimia nervosa are essential to reduce the risk of suicide attempt in women with this disorder[150].

## Sleeping Disorders and Suicide

Suicidal patients often report problems with their sleep. Sleep-related complaints such as insomnia, hypersomnia, nightmares, and sleep panic attacks are common in suicidal patients. The subjective quality of sleep, as measured by self-rated questionnaires, also appears to be more disturbed in suicidal depressed patients.

The frequency of nightmares is directly related to the risk of suicide. Among patients having nightmares there is an increased relative risk of suicide. There is a direct and graded association between the frequency of nightmares and death from suicide in a general population[151].

Sleep studies in suicidal patients report various findings including increased rapid eye movement (REM) time and REM activity in suicidal patients with a variety of psychiatric diagnoses including depression, schizoaffective disorder, and schizophrenia. One mechanism responsible for this possible association between suicide and sleep could be the role of serotonin. Serotonin not only is related to attempted and completed violent suicide and aggressive dyscontrol, but it also is involved in onset and maintenance of slow wave sleep and in REM sleep. Cerebro spinal fluid-5HIAA levels have been correlated with slow wave sleep in patients with mental illness. Moreover, 5-HT2A receptor antagonists have improved slow wave sleep.

One study investigated serotonin 2 receptors and human sleep by studying the effect of a selective 5-HT2A antagonist on electroencephalogram power spectra. A one milligram oral dose of SR 463349B, a novel 5-HT2A antagonist, was administered three hours before bedtime. This drug enhanced slow wave sleep and reduced stage 2 without affecting subjective sleep quality. In non REM sleep EEG, slow-wave activity was increased and spindle frequency activity was decreased. Thus in enhancing slow wave activity and attenuating the spindle frequency activity, the 5-HT2A receptor antagonist mimicked the effect of sleep deprivation[152].

One mechanism responsible for this possible association between sleep and suicide could be the role of serotonin. Serotonergic function is low in patients who attempted and/or complete suicide, particularly those who used violent methods. Aggression appears to be an intervening factor between serotonin and suicide. Enhanced serotonergic transmission decreases suicidal behavior. Serotonin is also involved in the onset and maintenance of slow wave sleep and REM sleep. Serotonin metabolites have been correlated with slow wave sleep in patients with depression as well as schizophrenia. Moreover, serotonin receptor (type 2) antagonists have improved slow wave sleep. Further studies are needed to investigate the possible role of sleep disturbance in suicidal behavior[153].

## Sexual Disorders and Suicide

Although sexual orientation is not a mental disorder, it is associated with increased risk of suicidal ideation and suicidal attempts. A high rate of depression and suicidal ideation among gay, lesbian, bisexual, and unsure, homeless, substance abusing youth is reported[154]. Gay, lesbian, and bisexual young people are at increased risk of different psychiatric disorders, including major depression, generalized anxiety disorder, conduct disorder, nicotine dependence, or other substance abuse and/or dependence, multiple co-morbid disorders, and suicidal ideation and suicidal attempts. These findings suggest that sexual orientation is related to mental health problems and suicidality[155].

Suicidal ideation among homosexual or bisexual young people is associated with depression, and it may lead to suicidal behavior especially in the presence of a role model of suicidal behavior and among those with unsatisfying friendships[156].

Many autoerotic fatalities share common characteristics with suicide and homicide. These cases can be mis-interpreted. Several cases of autoerotic accidental asphyxia death are initially reported as suicide[157]. Other bizarre cases of suicide illustrate the relationship of various paraphilias, including sexual masochism and fetishism of a suicide from a self-inflicted intra rectal gunshot wound[158]. This case emphasizes the overlap of the impulsiveness, aggression, and suicide.

Serious psychopathological sexual disorders, such as paraphilia, associated with violence, impulse disorders and suicidality and the role of sex hormones and serotonin is becoming more recognized and developed in law and forensic psychiatry[159].

Psychopharmacologic treatment of paraphilia, such as pedophilia and sadism, and sexually aggressive impulsive behavior with the luteinizing hormone-releasing hormone (LHRH) medication, leuprolide acetate, is a potentially effective treatment in reducing the tendency of sexual aggressive behavior. There is a reported reduction of penile erection, ejaculation, masturbation and sexual deviant impulsiveness and fantasies[160].

## Other Psychiatric Disorders and Suicide

Impulse control disorders such as pyromania, kleptomania, intermittent explosive disorder, trichotillomania, and pathological gambling have been associated with increased suicide attempts[161]. The relationship to impulsivity in impulse control disorders and suicide may be independent of depression.

Pathological gambling is an impulse control disorder that tends to be co-morbid with a wide range of other disorders, and it is reportedly associated with a high rate of suicide. With increasing access to gambling facilities through casinos, the Internet, and other venues, pathological gambling is a rapidly emerging mental health concern. For most gamblers, gambling is a form of entertainment, but for many individuals, the activity leads to far reaching disruption of family and work. The personal and societal financial ramifications are severe, and many pathological gamblers end up in the criminal justice system. Suicidal ideation and suicide attempts are prevalent in individuals seeking treatment for pathological gambling. Compared with non-suicidal pathological gamblers, those with suicidal ideation suffered from more psychiatric symptoms, were less satisfied with their living situations, and experienced more days of conflict in the month before entering gambling treatment. Compared with pathological gamblers with no history of suicidal ideation, those with suicidal ideation spent more money gambling in the month before entering treatment and reported greater cravings for gambling[162]. Serotonin is linked to behavioral initiation and disinhibition, which are important in the onset of gambling cycle and the difficulty in ceasing the behavior. Effective treatment including SSRIs and mood stabilizers are potentially useful pharmacological agents[163].

Psychosomatic illness and evaluation of somatic symptoms is important in the assessment of suicide. High levels of medically unexplained somatic symptoms should prompt the clinician for assessing for depression and anxiety, deliberate self- harm, and suicidal ideation. Somatoform disorders are associated with increased risk of suicide[164]. In one study of suicidal ideation and somatic symptoms of patients with mind/body distress in a Japanese psychosomatic clinic, the total number of those with somatic symptoms correlated with suicidal ideation, even after controlling for depression[165].

Body dysmorphic disorder is associated with suicidal behavior. In one study, patients who presented to the plastic surgeon for aesthetic surgery were screened for both body dysmorphic disorder and subclinical body dysmorphic disorder. The prevalence of subclinical body dysmorphic disorder was 18.4%, and suicidal ideation was found in 12.1% of patients. The prevalence of body dysmorphic disorder was 6.3%, and suicidal ideation was found in 49.7% of those patients[166]. Thus, the more severe, but less common form of body dysmorphic disorder is associated with a higher degree of suicidal ideation.

Dissociative identity disorder, formerly known as multiple personality disorder, is a rare disorder that has an interesting relationship to suicide. Compared to similar patients with mood disorders, patients with multiple personality disorder actually had more frequently attempted suicide after being diagnosed and hospitalized[167].

## Personality Disorders and Suicide

PERSONALITY DISORDERS INCREASE suicide risk about six fold[168]. Suicide risk assessment and management can be particularly challenging in patients with personality disorders. Personality disorders, or Axis II disorders, are often more common than Axis I disorders in suicide victims[169].

When personality disorders are present with another major mental disorder, such as major depression or a substance related disorder, the risk of suicide increases further.

The presence of personality disorders may create suicide risk when occurring with disorders usually not thought to have a serious suicide risk. For example, patients with panic disorder who developed suicidal ideation were more likely to have a personality disorder compared to similar patients without a personality disorder diagnosis[170].

Suicide victims with personality disorders were almost always found to have current depressive syndromes, psychoactive substance use disorders, or both[171]. Co- morbid borderline personality disorder and major depressive episode increases the number and seriousness of suicide attempts[172].

One in ten patients with personality disorders complete suicide, but this outcome is not readily preventable and does not necessarily occur during the course of treatment[173]. Patients with personality disorders may be at higher than usual risk at various times in their lives if they develop depression or other co-morbid psychiatric disorders. In many instances, these disorders improve over the life course and the patient no longer meets symptomatic criteria after a number of decades[174]. For instance, borderline personality disorder may improve if the patient survives the tumultuous early decades and settles into a period of relative quiescence in the fourth or fifth decades of life. Consequently, treatment strategies take on special importance with such patients. Unlike suicide risk management in other disorders where older age is the most significant additional factor for completed suicide, the suicide risk may be highest in the earlier turbulent years of the patient's life since these personality disorders may improve over the life course.

The most common personality disorders that carry the most serious suicide risk, similar to those patients with major mood disorders, are the cluster B personality disorders: antisocial, borderline, narcissistic and histrionic personality disorders[175].

The two personality disorders most frequently associated with completed suicide are borderline personality disorder and antisocial personality disorder. No recently published research addressing suicide risk in other personality disorders exists. In several recent large studies of patients who had completed suicide, these cluster B personality disorders, especially in males, were among the top three most common diagnoses found. Another study showed that personality disorders constituted the second most frequently diagnostic category associated with completed suicide[176].

Antisocial personality disorder patients also have a surprisingly high suicide risk. Antisocial personality disorder was one of the top three psychiatric diagnoses in suicide attempters[177].

The risk of lethal suicide attempt for borderline personality disorder patients is at least as high as it is for major depression[178]. Poor social adjustment in school, at work, or in the family are also risk factors for suicide in borderline personality disordered patients. Impulsivity is a major characteristic associated with a higher number of suicide attempts in borderline personality disorders[179]. Childhood sexual abuse, especially in cases of incest or prolonged sexual abuse, is more highly associated with completed suicide in borderline patients than physical abuse[180]. In one study, childhood sexual abuse is associated with whether a borderline patient would attempt suicide and the number of suicide attempts[181].

Assessing suicide risk in patients with borderline personality disorder is complicated. Many borderline patients with a history of repeated suicide attempts have a suicide risk that is much above that of the general population. The patient's level of chronic risk can be estimated by careful history of the previous suicidal behaviors, especially those with the greatest intent and medical lethality. The clinician can then estimate the severity of the patient's ongoing chronic risk for suicide. A patient may have a moderate to high chronic risk for suicide. Managing the chronic level of suicide risk in patients with borderline personality disorder often involves strategic outpatient management such as dialectical behavior therapy, which is effective in reducing suicidal behavior[182].

Characterologically based suicidality and a parasuicidal tendency in the context of the treatment of the patients' personality disorder is a recommendation to decrease the suicidal risk in severe personality disorders[183]. Dialectal behavioral training is particularly effective for some patients. Dialectical Behavior Therapy (DBT) was evaluated in a community mental health center treating high utilizers of inpatient psychiatric units and emergency rooms. During the first year of treatment, DBT showed reductions in the number and severity of medically treated parasuicides compared to treatment as usual in the prior year. There were significant reductions in psychiatric-related emergency room visits, the number of psychiatric inpatient admissions and days, and the number of crisis-treatment systems engaged.

However, then the clinician may evaluate further for acute-on-chronic change in status focusing on the time before the suicide attempt. A recent major depressive disorder, high levels of hopelessness, several recent negative life events, the perception of a loss of support system, or substance related disorder: these are examples of the acute changes. Patients with BPD are also known to be at risk for suicide around times of hospitalization and discharge or other major psychosocial stressors. Using this acute-on-chronic model can be very effective for communication decisions regarding interventions[184].

A patient with borderline personality disorder may be assessed for being at a chronic, but not at an acute-on-chronic risk for suicide, such that short-term hospitalization would have little or no impact on a chronic risk that has been present for months or years. If the patient is not admitted to the hospital, it is important to do an adequate documentation of suicide risk assessment and to arrange close follow-up, since completed suicide is associated with a reduction in continuing care after the last psychiatric clinical encounter[185]. Hospitalizing the patient who demonstrates an acute-on-chronic suicidal risk would be well indicated. In this circumstance, a short-term admission may allow the risk level to return to the chronic, pre-admission level.

Full appreciation of the suicide risk in patients with borderline personality disorder may be limited by inaccurate stereotypes that such patients only make self-injurious gestures, compounded with the fact that suicidal threats are used for secondary gain.

The suicidal gestures and self-injurious behaviors made by patients with personality disorders are often mistaken to be without true lethal intent. The history of self-injurious behavior also increases the risk for suicide[186]. Patients with self-injurious behavior are at risk for suicide attempts because of their high levels of depression, hoplessness, and impulsivity. They also tend to misperceive and underestimate the lethality of their suicidal behaviors.

Some clinicians may underestimate the potential for serious attempts since patients with personality disorders often present a spectrum of suicidal behavior that ranges from obvious feigned or exaggerated threats to completed suicide.

The contingent or instrumental suicide threat combined with an actual threat can appear that almost every encounter with such patient should result in an acute psychiatric hospitalization. However, clinical judgment is clearly required since little or no research evidence exists that psychiatric hospitalization decreases the long-term suicide risk in personality disorder patients; hospitalization can be regressive or counter therapeutic in some situations. If demands for shelter or hospitalization are not met, contingent suicide threats or threats, in which leverage is applied with some threat of killing oneself, are often encountered. Caution is needed however as patients may present manipulation at one time, and yet, on another occasion, they have serious suicide risk.

Adequate treatment of co-morbid mood disorders and substance related disorders is a cornerstone to treatment. Pharmacotherapy is frequently required for these patients.

Many chronically unstable patients benefit from antidepressant treatment with low dose SSRIs to avoid activation, although ultimately higher doses may be needed. The SSRIs have the specific benefit of having low lethality in overdose. Although lithium and valproic acid have serious lethality in overdose, the mood stabilization effects have the potential for reducing suicide risk in some patients. Maintenance single or double-mood stabilizer combination pharmacotherapy coupled with "prn" medication can be effective in reducing the severity and intensity of symptoms. Medication education about the use of medication as needed or "PRN" major and minor tranquilizers is one approach for severely symptomatic and motivated patients. Some patients with chronic propensity to suicidal behaviors benefit from low dose antipsychotic medication. Consideration as to the amount of medication dispensed is another clinical factor since many patients with borderline personality disorder overdose on prescription medications[187].

## Mental Retardation and Other Developmental Disorders and Suicide

While suicidal ideation and attempts are infrequent among patients with mental retardation, completed suicides and potentially fatal attempts have been reported. Suicide attempts by patients with Down's syndrome experiencing dysphoric mood and hopelessness about unmet needs associated with their disability, as well as major depressive disorder are described. These cases emphasize that mental health practitioners should appreciate the seriousness of suicidal ideation among persons who have mental retardation and treat the underlying psychiatric disorder[188].

## Psychosocial Stressors and the Timing of Suicide

Although psychiatric illness is most often an ongoing risk factor for suicide, the timing of suicidal acts tends to be associated with stressful life events. Psychosocial stressors can precipitate suicide. Psychosocial stressors, referred to as Axis IV in DSM IV, can make a vulnerable patient cross the line and become suicidal. Psychosocial stressors not only affect the diagnosis and treatment, but also the prognosis of mental disorders. Suicide may be precipitated by a stressful event even in the absence of any psychiatric disorder[189].

The association of stressful life events and suicidal behavior is strong[190]. Major categories of psychosocial stressors include social problems, negative life events, environmental difficulties, familial or other interpersonal stressors, and inadequacy of social support or personal resources.

The death or loss of friend, inadequate social support, living alone, difficulty with acculturation, discrimination, and adjustment of a life-cycle transition such as retirement are psychosocial stressors related to the social environment that can lead to isolation. Feeling cut off from people and the loss of a relationship are two major risk factors for suicide[191].

Death of a family member; health problems in the family; disruption of the family by separation, divorce, or estrangement; removal from the home; remarriage of parent; sexual or physical abuse; parental overprotection; neglect of a child; inadequate discipline; discord with siblings; and the birth of a sibling represent losses or sudden life changes that can have destabilizing effects. These problems with the primary support group can lead to consideration of suicide.

Death of a family member from suicide or family history of suicide is a risk factor.

Divorce or widowed patients are at a higher risk of suicide. Married patients with children are at less risk perhaps due to the sense of increased responsibility, as well as a bias associated with relatively healthy and successful adaptation[192].

Educational problems include illiteracy, academic problems, discord with teachers or classmates, and inadequate school environment. Difficulty at school may be a warning sign in youth of potential substance-related disorders and psychiatric illness including depression and suicide.

Occupational problems include the following: unemployment, threat of job loss, stressful work schedule, difficult work conditions, job dissatisfaction, job change, and discord with supervisor or co-workers.

The relationship between suicidal behavior and employment status is inconsistent. Unemployment may contribute to suicidal risk indirectly, through its impact on family tension arising from economic depravation and loss of normal social role and self-esteem leading to indignity, isolation, hopelessness, alcohol abuse, and violence. One study showed during a recession, there is less suicide, and an unexpected increase in suicides of both men and women during a period of economic growth, possibly related to increase alcohol use[193].

Economic problems include extreme poverty, inadequate finances, and insufficient welfare support. Suicide is more frequent at both extremes of the socioeconomic spectrum, and there is increased risk following sharp changes of financial status—up or down.

Housing problems include homelessness, inadequate housing, an unsafe neighborhood, and discord with neighbors or the property owner. Homelessness is associated with increase risk of suicidal ideation and behaviors. In one study, more than 60% of homeless persons reported suicidal ideation and over 30% had attempted suicide[194]. Homeless patients with mental illness account for a significant percent of all patient suicides. The most frequent diagnosis in homeless mentally ill patients who commit suicide is schizophrenia.

Resistance to seek treatment; barriers to access; or insufficient health care services including inadequate health care services, no transportation to health care facilities, unavailable or inadequate health insurance, and unavailability of social service agencies are stressors particularly important in both sexes. Females tend to seek help more often and are more likely to be seen and treated for depression and suicidality, in an out-patient psychiatric clinic or even during a primary care visit. In contrast, males tend to wait too long before getting treated and usually first present to the physician in a psychiatric hospital; or they do not seek help at all and end with a fatal outcome. This type of access to health care services seems to contribute to the higher incidence of male suicide in the general population. Perhaps there is a social stigma that males should not get depressed as much as females, and going to the doctor for depression is somehow un-manly[195].

Urban life has often been blamed for creating isolating environments with high suicide rates. Yet, the ten most populated cities in the United States are below the national average for suicide[196]. Suicide is three times more common in rural area than urban centers in Europe and China[197]. Among factors contributing to suicide risk in rural areas include the lack of access to assistance or treatment and general social isolation[198]. In urban cities, easy access to hand guns or other lethal equivalents may confer lethality to what would otherwise be a transient self-destructive impulse. Easy access to lethal methods is a risk factor for suicide.

Problems related to interaction with the legal system and crime, such as arrest, incarceration, litigation, or being a victim of crime, are legal psychosocial stressors that can contribute to suicide. For example, incarceration itself, as well as hearings and sentencing, increase suicidality in jail inmates[199].

One goal is to reduce in-custody suicide while promoting safe management of an inmate with mental illness. This approach requires some innovative suicide risk management programs such as training for jail personnel, telephone/internet access to mental health professionals, a continuous review of jail management protocols, and coordination of local treatment interventions all in an effort to reduce suicide while a person is incarcerated. A better working knowledge of effective suicide prevention techniques in a jail/detention facility setting is needed. Jails and detention facilities are traditionally high-risk environments for suicide, and often times staff is under-trained and inexperienced. Staff is expected to book, hold, and assess individuals brought to their facilities for crimes ranging from murder to trespassing. Educational materials, such as *On Your Watch, The Challenge of Jail Suicide,* a DVD produced by Dan Weisburg, Hollywood director and producer, provides a glimpse into the lives of seven inmates, the circumstances that caused them to be arrested, and the stressors that made them suicidal.

The Youth Rehabilitation and Treatment Center in Geneva is an all-female, adolescent correctional facility operated by the Nebraska Health and Human Services System. Over fifteen years ago, a suicide prevention program titled the Greenline Suicide Prevention Program was developed to assist staff in identifying the suicidal risk factor in this setting. Any trained staff member was able to place a youth on Greenline, which in turn activates the Greenline supervision program composed of three distinct levels of staff supervision: Watch, Warning, and Alert. In addition, a safety plan was provided for those youth that demonstrate long-term, self-injurious behaviors. This innovative strategy of a youth correctional suicide prevention program is useful.

In Kentucky, media attention about the disproportionately high rate of suicide and in-custody deaths in jails prompted the legislature to mandate mental health training for all jail personnel. This innovative suicide and mental health/substance abuse risk management program was developed and implemented in Kentucky jails. It features a network of crisis services including mandatory training for all jail personnel on mental health issues; 24/7 telephonic access to mental health professionals, who use triage instruments, and coordination of local treatment intervention by the community mental health system. The goal of this program is to promote safe management of inmates with mental illness, to increase diversion, and to reduce in-custody suicide.

Another approach to suicidality in this setting involves educating inmates about warning signs of depression and suicide. Then, assisting inmates in identifying others at risk for suicide is the method employed. Inmates in county jails are more likely to express suicidal ideation to peers rather than corrections officers. Teaching inmates the skills to identify peers who may be contemplating suicide and access the help needed may lead to quicker intervention. Finally, an inmate facing the three-strike law may feign suicidal symptoms as a secondary gain; therefore, clinical skill is required to differentiate these suicidal threats to genuine suicidality associated with depression and the need for treatment.

# Chapter 2 End Notes

1) World Health Organization (WHO). Suicide: International rates. Available at: http://www.who.int/mental_health/Topic_Suicide/suicide1.html. Accessed: November 2, 2002.

2) American Association of Suicidology. Suicide Prevention Effort Launched by U.S. Surgeon General. Available at: http://www.suicidology.org/suicidepreveffort.htm. Accessed September 2, 2002.

3) Center for Disease Control. National Center for Injury Prevention. Suicide in the United States. Available at: http://www.cdc.gov/ncipc/factsheets/suifacts.htm. Accessed September 2, 2002.

4) Patton N. National suicide research center comes to Nevada. *Las Vegas Review- Journal*, Wednesday, September 30, 1998. Available at: http://www.lvrj.com/lvrj_home/1998/Sep-30-Wed-1998/news/8313198.html. Accessed September 2, 2000.

5) Washoe District Health Department. *Chronic Disease & Injury Epi-Letter*. March, 2002. Vol. 3, No. 1:1-4.

6) Conwell Y, Duberstein PR, Cox C, Herrmann JH, Forbes NT, and Caine ED. Relationships of age and axis I diagnoses in victims of completed suicide: a psychological autopsy study. *Am J Psychiatry*. 1996; 153:1001-1008.

7) American Foundation for Suicide Prevention. An Interview with Dr. Marie Asberg. Available at: http://www.lorenbennett.org/safspbiological.htm. Accessed November 11, 2002.

8) Pirkis J, Burgess P, Meadows G, Dunt D. Self-Reported Needs for Care Among Persons who have Suicidal Ideation or who have attempted suicide. *Psychiatr Serv*. 2001; 52:381-383.

9) Shea S. *The Practical Art of Suicide Assessment*. New York, NY: John Wiley and Sons Inc.; 1999.

10) Gutheil T, Applebaum PS, *Clinical Handbook of Psychiatry and the Law*, 3rd ed. Philadelphia, Pa: Lippincott Williams and Wilkens: 2000.

11) Risenhoover CC. *The Suicide Lawyers: Lethal Secrets 1st ed*. Ashland, OH: Kiamchi House: 2004.

12) Menninger K. *Man against himself*. New York: Harcourt, Brace and World, 1938:147.

13) Hirschfeld RM. When to hospitalize the addict at risk for suicide. *Ann NY Acad Sci*. 2001; 932:188-196.

14) Westreich LM. Turning alcohol and drug emergencies into catalysts for change. *Current Psychiatry*. 2002:12:51-57.

15) Rosin D. Suicide. Review of suicides of patients in the State of Nevada system. Material presented: Medical Staff Meeting, NNAMH; January 14, 2002; Sparks, Nevada.

16) Borges G, Walters EE, Kessler RC. Associations of substance use, abuse, and dependence with subsequent suicidal behavior. *Am J Epidemiol*. 2000; 151:781-789.

17) Sexia FA. Criteria for the diagnosis of alcoholism. In: Estes NJ, Heinemann MD (eds). Alcoholism: development, consequences and intervention. St. Louis: CV Mosby, 1982:49-66.

18) Garlow SJ. Age, Gender, and Ethnicity differences in patterns of cocaine and ethanol use preceding suicide. *Am J Psychiatry*. 2002; 159:615-619.

19) Roy A. Relation of Family History of Suicide to Suicide Attempts in Alcoholics. *Am J Psychiatry*. 2000; 157:2050-2051.

20) Preuss UW, Schuckit MA, Smith TL, et al. Comparison of 3190 alcohol-dependent individuals with and without suicide attempts. *Alcohol Clin Exp Res.* 2002; 26:471-7

21) Rosenthal RN, Westreich L Treatment of persons with dual diagnoses of substance use disorder and other psychological problems. In: McCrady BS, Epstein EE (eds). *Addictions: a comprehensive textbook.* New York.: Oxford University Press, 1999: 439-476.

22) Tanskanen A, Tuomilehto J, Viinamaki H, Vartiainen E, Lehtonen J, Puska P. Joint heavy use of alcohol, cigarettes and coffee and the risk of suicide. *Addiction.* 2000; 95:1699-1704.

23) Arana G, Rosenbaum JF. *Handbook of psychiatric drug therapy (4th ed).* New York: Lippincott Williams & Wilkins; 2000:179.

24) Verwey B, Eling P, Wientjes H, Zitman FG. Memory impairment in those who attempted suicide by benzodiazepine overdose. *J Clin Psychiatry.* 2000; 61:456-459.

25) Rathod NR. Alprozolam poisoning. *Indian J Med Sci.* 2001; 55:218-221.

26) Lekka NP, Paschalis C, Beratis S. Suicide attempts in high-dose benzodiazepine users. *Compr Psychiatry.* 2002; 43:438-442.

27) Roy A. Childhood trauma and suicidal behavior in male cocaine dependent patients. *Suicide Life Threat Behav.* 2001; 31:194-196.

28) Roy A. Characteristics of cocaine-dependent patients who attempt suicide. *Am J Psychiatry.* 2001; 158:1215-1219.

29) Weiss, RD, Mirin SM, Bartell RL. *Cocaine (2nd ed).* Washington, DC: American Psychiatric Press, 1994: 31-33.

30) Catravas JD, Waters IW, Walz MA, et al. Antidotes for cocaine poisoning. *N Engl J Med.* 1977; 301:1238.

31) Miller M, Hemenway D. Rimm E. Cigarettes and suicide: a prospective study of 50,000 men. *Am J Public Health.* 2000; 90:768-773.

32) Tanskanen A, Tuomilehot J, Vinamaki H, Vartiainen E, Lehtonen J, et al. Smoking and the risk of suicide. *Acta Psychiatr Scan.* 2000; 101:245-245.

33) Gillet C, Polard E., Mauduit N, Allain H. Acting out and psychoactive substances: alcohol, drugs, illicit substances. *Encephale.* 2001; 27:351-359.

34) Fleschler MA, Tortolero SR, Baumler ER, Vernon SW, Weller NF.. Lifetime inhalant use among alternative high school students in Texas: prevalence and characteristics of users. *Am J Drug Alcohol Abuse.* 2002; 28:477-495.

35) Howard MO, Jenson JM. Inhalant use among antisocial your: prevalence and correlates. *Addict Behav.* 1999; 24:59-74.

36) Ricaurte GA. Severe dopaminergic neurotoxicity in primates after a common recreational dose regimen of MDMA ("ecstasy"). *Science.* 2002; 297:2260-2263.

37) Henry JA, Jeffreys KJ, Dawling S. Toxicity and deaths from 3,4-methylene-dioxymethamphetamine ("ectasy"). *Lancet.* 1992; 340-387.

38) Darke S, Ross J. Suicide among heroin users: rates, risk factors and methods. *Addiction.* 2002;97: 1383-1394.

39) Office of Applied Studies. Emergency department trends from the Drug Abuse Warning Network. Preliminary estimates, January-June 2001, with revised estimates, 1994-2000. Rockville, MD: Department of Health and Human Services, February 2002:40.

40) Darke S, Ross J. The relationship between suicide and heroin overdose among methadone maintenance patients in Sydney, Australia. *Addiction.* 2001; 96:1443-53.

41) Thiblin I, Runeson B, Rajs J. Anabolic androgenic steroids and suicide. *Ann Clin Psychiatry.* 1999; 11:223-31.

42) Thiblin I, Lindquist O, Rajs J. Cause and manner of death among users of anabolic androgenic steroids. *J Forensic Sci.* 2000; 45:16-23.

43) Healy D. Emergence of antidepressant-induced suicidality. *Primary Care Psychiatry.* 2000; 6: 23-28.

44) Teicher MH, Glod C, Cole JO. Emergence of intense suicidal preoccupation during fluoxetine treatment.

*Am J Psychiatry.* 1990; 147:207-210.

45) Baldessarini RJ, Tarazi FI. Drugs and the treatment of psychiatric disorders: antimanic and antidepressant agents. In: Hardman JG, Limbird LE, Molinoff PB, et al. eds. *Goodman and Gilman's The Pharmacological Basis of Therapeutics. 10th ed.* New York, NY: McGraw-Hill Press; 2001.

46) Dhossche DM, Rich CL, Isacsson G. Psychoactive substances in suicides. Comparison of toxicologic findings in two samples. *Am J Forensic Med Pathol.* 2002; 22:239-243.

47) Turnbull JM, Roszell DK. Dual diagnosis. *J Prim Care.* 1993; 1:181-190.

48) Mar NS, Gold MS. Dual diagnoses: psychiatric syndromes in alcoholism and drug addiction. *Am Fam Physician.* 1991; 43:2071-2076.

49) Stanislav SW, Sommi RW, Watson WA. A longitudinal analysis of factors associated with morbidity in cocaine abusers with psychiatric illness. *Pharmacotherapy.* 1992; 12:114-118.

50) el-Guebaly N. Substance abuse and mental disorders: the dual diagnoses concept. *Can J Psychiatry.* 1990; 35:261-267.

51) Eisen JL, Rasmussen SA. Coexisting obsessive compulsive disorder and alcoholism. *J Clin Psychiatry.* 1989; 50:96-98.

52) Viner MW, Sutter B, Burchette C. Single, Double, and Triple Diagnoses. *Primary Psychiatry.* 1998; 6:47-52.

53) Viner MW, Waite J, Thienhaus OJ. Co-morbidity and the need for physical examinations among patients seen in the psychiatric emergency service. *Psychiatr Services.* 1996; 47:947-949.

54) Antabuse. *Physicians' Desk Reference.* Montvale, NJ: Medical Economics; 2003: 2370-2371.

55) Medscape DrugInfo. Naltrexone HCL Oral. Uses & Dosage. Available at: http://www.medscape.com/ Druginf?id/htm. Accessed February 16, 20003.

56) Krupitsky EM, Masalov DV, Didenko TY, et al. Prevention of suicide by naltrexone in a recently detoxified heroin addict. *Eur Addict Res.* 2001; 7:87-88.

57) Rose MA, Kam PC. Gabapentin: pharmacology and its use in pain management. *Anaesthesia.* 2002; 57:451-462.

58) Schneider B, Maurer K. Dementia and suicide. *Fortschr Neurol Psychiatr.* 2001; 69:164-169.

59) Petersen RC. Normal aging, mild cognitive impairment, and early Alzheimer's disease. *The Neurologist.* 1995;1:326-344.

60) Small G. Advances in the diagnosis and treatment of dementia. Paper presented at: Annual meeting of the American Society of Clinical Psychopharmacology meeting; November 2, 2003; San Francisco, CA.

61) Kaufer DI. Cholinesterase-inhibitor therapy for dementia: novel clinical substrates and mechanisms for treatment response. *CNS Spectrums.* 2002; 7:742-750.

62) Meltzer HY. Conley RR, de Leo, D, Green AI, Kane JM, Knesevich MA, et al. Intervention Strategies for Suicidality. *J Clin Psychiatry.* 2003; 2:1-18.

63) Mortensen PB, Juel K. Mortality and causes of death in first admitted schizophrenic patients. *Br J Psychiatry.* 1993; 163:183-189.

64) Meltzer HY, Alphs L, Green AI, et al. Clozapine treatment for suicidality in schizophrenia: International Suicide Prevention Trial (InterSePT). *Arch Gen Psychiatry.* 2003; 60:82-91.

65) Heila H, Isometsa ET, Henriksson MM, Heikkinen ME, Marttunen MJ, Lonnqvist JK. Suicide and schizophrenia: a nationwide psychological autopsy study on age-and sex-specific clinical characteristics of 92 suicide victims with schizophrenia. *Am J Psychiatry.* 1997; 154:1235-1242.

66) Sandor A, Courtenay K. First episode psychosis. *BMJ.* 2002; 324:976.

67) Gupta S, Black DW, Arndt S, et al. Factors Associated with suicide attempts among patients with schizophrenia. *Psychiatr Serv.* 1998; 49:1353-1355.

68) Meltzer HY. Treatment of Suicidality in Schizophrenia. *Ann. N.Y. Acad. Sci.* 2001; 932:44-60.

69) Radomsky ED, Haas GL, Mann JJ, et al. Suicidal Behavior in patients with schizophrenia and other psychotic disorders. *Am J Psychiatry.* 1999; 156:1590-1595.

70) Kasantikul D. Drug-induced akathisia and suicidal tendencies in psychotic patients. *J Med Assoc Thai.* 1998;

81:551-554.

71) Grunebaum MF, Oquendo MA, Harkavy-Friedman JM, et al. Delusions and suicidality. *Am J Psychiatry.* 2001; 158:742-747.

72) Fenton WS, McGlashan TH, Victor BJ. Symptoms, subtype, and suicidality in patients with schizophrenia spectrum disorders. *Am J Psychiatry.* 1997; 154:199-204.

73) Cahn W, et al. Brain volume changes in first-episode schizophrenia. A 1-year follow-up study. *Arch Gen Psychiatry.* 2002; 59:1002-1010.

74) Jeste DV, Okamoto A, Napolitano J. Low Incidence of persistent tardive dyskinesia in elderly patients with dementia treated with risperidone. *Am J Psychiatry.* 2000; 157:1150-1155.

75) Csernansky JG, Mahmoud R, Brenner R. A comparison of risperidone and halperidol for the prevention of relapse in patients with schizophrenia. *N Engl J Med.* 2002; 346:16-22.

76) *NIMH: Suicide Facts.* Bethesda, Md: National Institute of Mental Health; 1999. Available at: http://www.nimh.nih.gov/publicat/suicidefacts.cfm. Accessed November 21, 2002.

77) Nierenberg AA, Gray SM, Grandlin LD. Mood disorders and suicide. *J Clin Psychiatry* 2001; 62 (suppl 25): 27-30.

78) Goodwin FK, Jamison KR. Suicide. In: Goodwin FK, Jamison KR, eds. *Manic Depressive Illness.* New York, NY: Oxford University Press; 1990;227-244

79) Sachs GS, Yan LJ, Swann AC, Allen MH. Integration of suicide prevention into outpatient management of bipolar disorder. *J Clin Psychiatry.* 2001 62 (suppl 25): 3-11.

80) Baldessarini RJ, Tondo L, Hennen J. Treating the suicidal patient with bipolar disorder; reducing suicide risk with lithium. *Ann N Y Acad Sci.* 2001; 932:24-38.

81) Potash JB, Kane HS, Chiu Y, Simpson SG, MacKinnon DF, et al. Attempted suicide and alcoholism in bipolar disorder: clinical and familial relationships. Am J Psychiatry. 2000; 157:2048-2050.

82) Strakowski SM, McElroy SL, Keck PE Jr., West SA.. Suicidality among patients with mixed and manic bipolar disorder. *Am J Psychiatry.* 1996; 153:674-676.

83) Isometsa ET, Henriksson MM, Aro HM, et al. Suicide in bipolar disorder in Finland. *Am J Psychiatry.* 1994; 151:1020-1024.

84) Kessler RC, Borges G, Walters EE. Prevalence of and risk factors for lifetime suicide attempts in the National Co-morbidity Survey. *Arch Gen Psychiatry.* 1999; 56:617-626.

85) Gavin K. University of Michigan Health System. U-M team finds evidence of brain chemistry abnormalities in bipolar disorder. http://www.med.umich.edu/opm/newspage/2000/bipolar.htm. Accessed 11/9/02.

86) Drevets WC, Price LJ, Simpson JR Jr, et al. Subguenual prefrontal cortex abnormalities in mood disorders. *Nature.* 1997; 386:834-827.

87) Rajkowska G, Halaris A, Selemon LD. Reductions in neuronal and glial density characterize the dorsolateral prefrontal cortex in bipolar disorder. *Biol Psychiatry.* 2001; 49: 741-752.

88) Shimon H, Agam G, Belmaker RH, et al. Reduced frontal cortex inositol levels in postmortem brain of suicide victims and patients with bipolar disorder. *Am J Psychiatry.* 1997; 154:1148-1150.

89) Frye MA, GItlin MJ, Altshuler LL. Foundational treatment for bipolar disorder. Treating acute mania. *Current Psychiatry. 2003;* 3(suppl) 10-13.

90) Goodwin FK, Baldessarini RJ, Dunner DL. The use of lithium in treating bipolar disorder. *CNS Spectrums.* 2002; 7:1-12.

91) Sachs GS. Bipolar mood disorder: practical strategies for acute and maintenance phase treatment. *J Clin Psychopharmacol.* 1996; 16 (2 suppl 1):32S-47S.

92) Hirschfeld RM, Allen MH, McElvoy JP, Keck PE, Jr., Russell JM. Safety and tolerability of oral loading divalproex sodium in acutely manic bipolar patients. *J Clin Psychiatry.* 1999; 60(12):815-818.

93) Yuan PX, Huang LD, Jiang YM, et al. The mood stabilizer valproic acid activates mitogen-activated protein kinases and promotes neurite growth. *J Biol Chem.* 2001; 276:674-683.

94) Yatham LN, Kusumakear V, Calabrese JR, Rao R, Scarrow G, Kroeker G. Third-generation anticonvulsants

in bipolar disorder: a review of efficacy and summary of clinical recommendations. *J Clin Psychiatry.* 2002; 63:275-283.

95) Calabrese JR, Bowden CL, Sachs GS, Ascher JA, Monaghan E, Rudd GD. A double-blind, placebo-controlled study of lamotrigine monotherapy in outpatients with bipolar I depression. Lamictal 602 Study Group. *J Clin Psychiatry.* 1999; 60:79-88.

96) Moore GJ, Bebchuk JM, Wilds IB, et al. Pharmacologic increase in human gray matter. *Lancet* 2000; 356:1241-1242.

97) Chen G, Zeng WZ, Yuan PX, et al. The mood stabilizing agents lithium and valproate robustly increase the levels of the neuroprotective protein bcl-2 in the CNS. *J Neurochem.* 1999; 72:879-882.

98) Baldessarini RJ, Tondo L. Antisuicidal effect of lithium treatment in major mood disorders. In: Jacobs D, ed. *The Harvard Medical School Guide to Assessment and Intervention in Suicide.* San Francisco, CA: Jossey-Bass; 1998:355-371.

99) Tondo L, Baldessarini RJ. Reduced suicide risk during lithium maintenance treatment. *J Clin Psychiatry.* 2000; 61 (suppl 9):97-104.

100) Tondo L, Baldessarini RJ, Hennen J, et al. Lithium treatment and risk of suicidal behavior in bipolar disorder patients. *J Clin Psychiatry.* 1998; 59:405-414.

101) Goodwin F. Update on treatment for bipolar disorder. Paper presented at: Annual meeting of the American Society of Clinical Psychopharmacology; November 2-3, 2002. San Francisco, CA.

102) Keck PE, McElroy SL, Strakowski SM, et al. Compliance with maintenance treatment in bipolar disorder. *Psychopharmacol Bull* 1997; 33:87-91.

103) *American Psychiatric Association. Diagnostic and Statistical Manual of Mental Disorders, Fourth Edition.* Washington , DC: American Psychiatric Association; 1994.

104) Rihmer Z. Can better recognition and treatment of depression reduce suicide rates? A brief review. *Eur Psychiatry.* 2001; 16:406-409.

105) Shelton RC. Mood-stabilizing drugs in depression. *J Clin Psychiatry.* 199; 60(suppl 5):37-40.

106) Pezawas L, Stamenkovic M, Jagsch R, Ackerl S, Putz C, Stelzer B, et al A longitudinal view of triggers and thresholds of suicidal behavior in depression. *J Clin Psychiatry.* 2002; 63: 866-873.

107) Aharonovich E, Liu X, Nunes E, Hasin DS. Suicide attempts in substance abusers: effects of major depression in relation to substance use disorders. *Am J Psychiatry.* 2002; 159:1600-1602.

108) Giovanni PA, Oquendo MA, Malone KM, Brodsky B, Ellis SP, Mann JJ. Anxiety in major depression: relationship to suicide attempts. *Am J Psychiatry.* 2002; 157:1614-1618.

109) Gitlin MJ. Clinical Rounds. Three depression subtypes respond selectively. *Clinical Psychiatry News* 2003; 1:43.

110) Lykouras L, Gournellis R, Fortos A, Oulis P, Christodoulou GN. Psychotic (delusional) major depression in the elderly and suicidal behavior. *J Affect Disord.* 2002; 69:225-229.

111) Rothschild AJ. Management of psychotic, treatment-resistant depression. *Psychiatr Clin North Am.* 1996; 19:237252.

112) Davis GE, Lowell WE. Evidence that latitude is directly related to variation in suicide rates. *Can J Psychiatry.* 2002; 47:572-574.

113) Minois G. *History of Suicide, Voluntary Death, in Western Culture.* Baltimore, Md: Johns Hopkins University Press; 1999.

114) Altamura CA, van Gastel A, Pioli R, et al. Seasonal and circadian rhythms in suicide in Cagliari, Italy. *J Affect Disord.* 199;53:77-85.

115) Preti A, Miotto P. Influence of method on seasonal distribution of attempted suicides in Italy. *Neuropsychobiology.* 2000; 41:62-72.

116) Stoupel E, Isrealevich P, Gabbay U, Abramson E, Petrauskiene J, Kalediene B. Cosmic rays activity and monthly number of deaths: a correlative study. *J Basic Clin Physiol Pharmacol.* 2002; 13:23-32.

117) Ahearn EP, Jamison KR, Steffens DC, Cassidy F, Provenzale JM, Lehman A, et al. MRI correlates of suicide attempt history in unipolar depression. *Biol Psychiatry.* 2001; 50: 226-270.

118) National Institute of Mental Health. Depression PET scan. Available at: http://www.nimh.nih.gov/ hotsci/scandep.htm. Accessed 11/9/02.

119) Drevets WC. Functional anatomical abnormalities in limbic and prefrontal cortical structures in major depression. *Prog Brain Res.* 2000; 126:413-431.

120) Oquendo MA, Placidi GP, Malone KM, Campbell C, Keilp J, Brodsky B, et al. Positron emission tomography of regional brain metabolic responses to a serotonergic challenge and lethality of suicide attempts in major depression. *Arch Gen Psychiatry.* 2003; 60:14-22.

121) Keilp JG, Sackeim HA, Brodsky BS. Oquendo MA, Malone KM, Mann JJ. Neuropsychological dysfunction in depressed suicide attempters. *Am J Psychiatry.* 2001; 158:735-741.

122) Coryell W, Schlesser M. The dexamethasone suppression test and suicide. *Am J Psychiatry.* 2001; 158:748-753.

123) Suominen KH, Isometsa ET, Henriksson MM, Ostamo AI, Lonnqvist JK. Inadequate treatment for major depression both before and after attempted suicide. *Am J Psychiatry.* 1998; 155:1778-1780.

124) Rihmer Z. Relationship between recognized depression and suicide in Hungary. *International Journal of Methods in Psychiatric Research.* 1996; 6:15-S20.

125) Oquendo MA, Kamali M, Ellis SP, Grunebaum MF, Malone KM, Brodsky BS, Sackeim HA, Mann JJ. Adequacy of antidepressant treatment after discharge and the occurrence of suicidal acts in major depression: a prospective study. *Am J Psychiatry* 2002; 159:1746-1751.

126) Muller-Oerlinghausen B, Berghofer A. Antidepressants and suicidal risk. *J Clin Psychiatry.* 1999; 60(suppl 2):94-99.

127) Leon AC, Keller MB, Warshaw MG, Mueller TI, Soloman DA, Coryell W, et al. Prospective study of fluoxetine treatment and suicidal behavior in affectively ill subjects. *Am J Psychiatry.* 1999; 156:195-201.

128) Busch KA, Fawcett J, Jacobs DG. Clinical correlates of inpatient suicide. *J Clin Psychiatry.* 2003; 64:14-19.

129) Khan A, Leventhal RM, Khan S, Brown WA. Suicide risk in patients with anxiety disorders: a meta-analysis of the FDA database. *J Affect Disord.* 2002; 68:183-190.

130) Beautrais AL, Suicides and serious suicide attempts: two populations or one? *Psychol Med.* 2001; 31:837-845.

131) Abdel-Khalek A, Lester D. Manic-depressiveness, obsessive-compulsive tendencies, and suicidality in Kuwaiti college students. *Psychol Rep.* 2002; 90( 3 Pt 1);1007-1008.

132) Amir M, Kaplan Z, Efroni R, Kotler M. Suicide risk and coping styles in posttraumatic stress disorder patients. *Psychother Psychosom.* 1999; 68:76-81.

133) Kotler M, Iancu I, Efroni R, Amir M. Anger, impulsivity, social support , and suicide risk in patients with posttraumatic stress disorder. *J Nerv Ment Dis.* 2001; 189:162-167.

134) Marshall RD, Olfson M, Hellman F, Blanco C, Guardino M, Struening EL.. Co-morbidity, impairment, and suicidality in subthreshold PTSD *Am J Psychiatry.* 2001; 158:1467-1473.

135) Warshaw MG, Dolan RT, Keller MB. Suicidal behavior in patients with current or past panic disorder: five years of prospective data from the Harvard/Brown Anxiety Research Program. *Am J Psychiatry.* 2000; 157:1876-1878.

136) Bremner JD, Innis RB, White T, et al. SPECT [I-123] iomazenil measurement of the benzodiazepine receptor in panic disorder. *Biol Psychiatry.* 2000; 47:96-106

137) Bemner JD, Innis RB, Southwick SM, . Decreased benzodiazepine receptor binding in prefrontal cortex in combat-related posttraumatic stress disorder. *Am J Psychiatry.* 2000; 157:1120-1126.

138) Bremner JD. PTSD can deter growth of neurons in brain. *Clinical Psychiatry News.* 2003; 2:33

139) Stahl SM. Brainstorms. Don't ask, don't tell, but benzodiazepines are still the leading treatments for anxiety disorder. *J Clin Psychiatry* 2002; 63:756-757

140) Marmar CR, Neylan TC, Schoenfeld FB. Advances in the Psychopharmacology of Posttraumatic Stress Disorder. *The Economics of Neuroscience.* 2001; 3:64-69.

141) Shalev AY, Bonne E. In: Shalev AY, et al, eds. *International Handbook of Human Response to Trauma.* New York, NY; Klumer/Plenum Publishers, 1999.

142) Kryzhanovskaya L, Canterbury R. Suicidal behavior in patients with adjustment disorders. *Crisis* 2001; 22:125-131.

143) Jenkins GR. Suicide risk continues for years after first attempt. *BMJ;* 2002; 325:1155.

144) Agras WS. The consequences and costs of the eating disorders. *Psychiatr Clin North Am.* 2001; 24: 371-379.

145) Bulik CM, Sullivan PF, Joyce PR. Temperament, character and suicide attempts in anorexia nervosa, bulimia nervosa and major depression. *Acta Psychiatr Scand.* 1999; 100:27-32.

146) Herzog DB, Greenwood DN, Dorer DJ, et al. Mortality in eating disorders: a descriptive study. *Int J Eat Disord.* 2000; 28:20-26.

147) Sobel SV. What's new in the treatment of anorexia nervosa and bulimia? Medscape *Women's Health* 1996; 1:5.

148) Johnson JG, Spitzer RL, Williams JB. Health problems, impairment and illnesses associated with bulimia nervosa and binge eating disorder among primary care and obstetric gynecology patients. *Psychol Med.* 2001; 31:1455-1456.

149) Steiger H, Koerner N, Engelberg MJ, Isreal M, Kin Ng Ying NM, Young SN. Self-destructiveness and serotonin function in bulimia nervosa. *Psychiatry Res.* 2001; 103:15-26.

150) Corcos M, Taieb O, Benoit-Lamy S, Suicide attempts in women with bulimia nervosa: frequency and characteristics. *Acta Psychiatr Scand.* 2002; 106:381-386.

151) Tanskanen A, Tuomilehto J, Viinamaki H, et al. Nightmares as predictors of suicide. *Sleep.* 2001; 24:844-847.

152) Landolt HP, Meier V, Burgess HJ, Finelli LA, Cattelin F, ete al. Serotonin-2 receptors and human sleep: effect of a selective antagonist on EEG power spectra. *Neuropsychopharmacology,* 1999. 21:455-66.

153) Singareddy RK, Balon R. Sleep and suicide in psychiatric patients. *Ann Clin Psychiatry.* 2001; 13:93-101.

154) Noell JW, Ochs LM. Relationship of sexual orientation to substance use, suicidal ideation, suicide attempts, and other factors in a population of homeless adolescents. *J Adolesc Health.* 2001; 29:31-36.

155) Fergusson DM, Horwood LJ, Beautrais AL. Is sexual orientation related to mental health problems and suicidality in young people? *Arch Gen Psychiatry.* 1999; 56:876-880.

156) van Heeringen C, Vincke J. Suicidal acts and ideation in homosexual and bisexual young people: a study of prevalence and risk factors. Soc Psychiatry Psychiatr Epidemiol 2000; 35:494-499.

157) Garza-Leal JA, Landron FJ. Autoerotic asphyxial death initially misinterpreted as suicide and a review of the literature. *J Forensic Sci.* 1991; 36:1753-1759.

158) Prahlow JA,. Suicide by intrarectal gunshot wound. *Am J Forensic Med Pathol.* 1998; 19:356-361.

159) Bradford JM. The role of serotonin in the future of forensic psychiatry. *Bull Am Acad Psychiatry Law.* 1996; 24:57-72.

160) Briken P, Berner W, Noldus J, Nika, Michi U. Treatment of paraphilia and sexually aggressive impulsive behavior with the LHRH-agonist leuprolide acetate. *Nervenarzt.* 2000; 71:380-385.

161) Lejoyeux M, Arbaretaz M, McLoughlin M, Ades J. Impulse control disorders and depression. *J Nerv Ment Dis.* 2002; 190:310-314.

162) Petry NM, Kiluk BD. Suicidal ideation and suicide attempts in treatment-seeking pathological gamblers. *J Nerv Ment Dis.* 2002; 190:462-469.

163) Hollander E, Buchalter AJ, De Caria CM. Pathological gambling. *Psychiatr Clin North Am.* 2000; 23:629-642.

164) Dhossche D, van der Steen F, Ferdinand R. Somatoform disorders in children and adolescents: a comparison with other internalizing disorders. *Ann Clin Psychiatry.* 2002; 14:23-31.

165) Nakao M, Yamanaka G, Kuboki I. Suicidal ideation and somatic symptoms of patients with mind/body distress in a Japanese psychosomatic clinic. *Suicide Life Threat Behav.* 2002; 32:80-90.

166) Altamura C, Paluello MM, Mundo E, Medda S, Mannu P. Clinical and subclinical body dysmorphic disorder. *Eur Arch Psychiatry.* Clin Neurosci. 2001; 251:105-8.

167) Fetkewicz J, Sharma V, Mersky H. A note on suicidal deterioration with recovered memory treatment. *J*

*Affect Disord.* 2000; 58:155-159.

168) Foster T, Gillespie K, McClelland R, et al. Risk factors for suicide independent of DSM-III-R Axis I disorder. *Br J Psychiatry.* 1999; 175:175-179.

169) Henriksson MM, Aro HM, Marttunem MJ, et al. Mental disorders and co-morbidity in suicide. *Am J Psychiatry.* 1993; 150:935-940.

170) Starcevic V, Bogojevic G, Marinkovic J, et al. Axis I and Axis II co-morbidity in panic/agoraphobia patients with and without suicidal ideation. *Psychiatry Res.* 1999; 88:153-161.

171) Isometsa, ET, Henriksson MM, Heikkinen ME, Aro HM, Marttunen MJ, Kuoppasalmi KI, Lonnqvist JK. Suicide among subjects with personality disorders. *Am J Psychiatry.* 1996; 153:667-673.

172) Soloff PH, Lynch KG, Kelly TM. Characteristics of suicide attempts of patients with major depressive episode and borderline personality disorder: a comparative study. *Am J Psychiatry.* 2000; 157:601-608.

173) Paris J. Chronic suicidality among patients with borderline personality disorder. *Psychiatr Serv.* 2002; 53:738-742.

174) Kjellander C, Bongar B, King A. Suicidality in borderline personality disorder. *Crisis.* 1998; 19:125-135.

175) Lambert MT. Suicide risk assessment and management: focus on personality disorders. *Curr Opin Psychiatry.* 2003; 16:71-76.

176) Hiroeh U, Appleby L, Mortensen PB, et al. Death by homicide, suicide, and other unnatural causes in people with mental illness: a population-based study. *Lancet.* 2001; 358:2110-2112.

177) Beautrais AL, Joyce PR, Mulder RT. Prevalence and co-morbidity of mental disorders in persons making serious suicide attempts: a case control study. *Am J Psychiatry.* 1996; 153:1009-1014.

178) Cheng AT, Mann AH, Chan KA. Personality disorder and suicide: a case-control study. *Br J Psychiatry.* 1997; 170:441-446.

179) Brodsky BS, Malone KM, Ellis SP, Delit RA, Mann JJ. Characteristics of borderline personality disorder associated with suicidal behavior. *Am J Psychiatry.* 1997; 154:1715-1719.

180) Dubo ED, Zanarini MC, Lewis RE, Williams AA. Childhood antecedents of self-destructiveness in borderline personality disorder. *Can J Psychiatry* 1997; 42: 63-69

181) Soloff PH, Lynch KG, Kelly TM. Childhood abuse as a risk factor for suicidal behavior in borderline personality disorder. *J Personal Disord* 2002; 16:201-214

182) Koerner K, Linehan MM. Reserach on dialectical behavior therapy for patients with borderline personality disorder. *Psychiatr Clin North Am* 2000; 23:151-167

183) Kernberg OF. The suicidal risk in severe personality disorders: differential diagnosis and treatment. *J Personal Disord* 2001; 15:195-208.

184) Yen S, Shea MT, Pagano M, et al. Axis I and axis II disorders as predictors of prospective suicide attempts: findings from the collaborative longitudinal personality disorders study. *J Abnorm Psychol.* 2003; 112:375-381

185) Lambert MT, Bonner J. Characteristics and six-month outcome of patients who use suicide threats to seek hospital admission. *Psychiatr Serv.* 1996; 47:871-873.

186) Stanley B., Gameroff MJ, Michalsen V, Mann JJ. Are suicide attempters who self-mutilate a unique population? *Am J Psychiatry* 2001; 158:427-432

187) Gunderson JG. *Borderline Personality Disorder.* Washington, DC; American Psychiatric Press, 1984.

188) Hurley AD. Two cases of suicide attempt by patients with Down's syndrome. *Psychiatr Serv.* 1998; 49:1618-1619.

189) Conwell Y, Henderson RE. Neuropsychiatry of suicide. In: Fogel BS, Schiffer RB, Rao SM, eds. *Neuropsychiatry.* Baltimore, MD; Williams & Wilkins; 1996: 485-521.

190) Paykel ES, Prusoff BA, Myers JK. Suicide attempts and recent life events. A controlled comparison. *Arch Gen Psychiatry.* 1975; 32:327-333.

191) Jamison KR. Night Falls Fast. New York, NY: Alfred Knopf; 1999.

192) Jacobs D, ed. *Harvard Medical School guide to assessment and intervention in suicide.* San Francisco, Calif: Jossey-Bass; 1998.

193) Platt S. Parasuicide and unemployment. *Br J Psychiatry.* 1986; 149:401-405.

194) Eynan R, Langley J, Tolomiczenko G, Rhodes AD, Links P, Wasylenki D, et al.. The association between homelessness and suicidal ideation and behaviors; results of a cross-sectional survey. *Suicide Life Threat Behav.* 2002; 32:418-427.

195) Murphy GE. Why women are less likely than men to commit suicide. *Compr Psychiatry* 1998; 39:165-175.

196) American Association of Suicidology. U.S.A. *Suicide: 1998 Official Final Data.* Available at: http://www.suicidology.org/index.html. Accessed November 9, 2002.

197) Phillips MR, Liu H, Zhang Y. Suicide and social change in China. *Culture Med Psychiatry,* 1999; 23:25-50.

198) Tonado L. Prima del tempo. *Capire e prevenire il suicidio.* Rome, Italy: Carocci; 2000

199) He XY, Felthous AR, Holzer CE, Nathan P, Veasey S. . Factors in prison suicide: one year study in Texas. *J Forensic Sci.* 2001; 46:896-901.

# CHAPTER 3

## Psychopharmacologic Treatment of Suicidality

In general, research and clinical experience indicate a combination of psychosocial interventions, psychotherapy, and pharmacotherapy, offers the best strategy for reducing suicidal behaviors. However, psychiatrists need to be aware of the range of treatments available for reducing suicide risk. Clozapine, lithium, novel combination pharmacotherapy, and new indications for medications to pediatric and geriatric special populations are advances in psychopharmacologic treatments of suicidality.

### Antipsychotic Pharmacotherapy

Antipsychotic medication is the mainstay of treatment for psychotic illnesses, but it also widely used in many other psychiatric conditions. For example, recognition and aggressive treatment of symptoms of agitation and anxiety in acutely depressed suicidal patients may provide an opportunity for clinicians to intervene and prevent suicide in the short term, while buying time to successfully treat the patients' depressive illnesses with antidepressants and/or lithium. That is, even in the absence of frank psychotic symptoms, antipsychotic medications may be useful in reducing acute suicidal ideation because of their effectiveness in reducing over-stimulation.

Active positive psychotic symptoms, such as delusions and hallucinations (command-type suicidal auditory hallucinations), are associated with an increased risk of suicide in schizophrenic patients, and aggressive treatment of those symptoms is important in suicide risk reduction.

Antipsychotic medications may also be directly involved in reducing chronic suicidal thoughts, although suicidal thoughts have not been traditionally considered clinically psychotic.

Introduced over fifty years ago, antipsychotic medications benefit millions of people by managing their symptoms. For people who respond well, antipsychotics can mean the difference between leading an engaged, fulfilling community life and being severely disabled.

The first-generation antipsychotics are still widely available and are effective in treating positive symptoms of psychosis, such as hallucinations and delusions. They do not alleviate many other common and important aspects of psychotic illness. In addition, the first generation antipsychotics can produce significant extrapyramidal side effects at clinically effective doses. These side effects, which include dystonic reactions, drug-induced parkinsonism, akathisia, and tardive dyskinesia can make treatment intolerable for some people, leading to subjective distress, diminished function, stigma, and nonadherence.

The effort to find medications that are more effective with fewer and less severe neurological side effects led to the development of the second-generation antipsychotics, termed atypical. These have few or no extrapyramidal side effects at clinically effective doses. Many of these newer medications are also more effective than the older agents in treating the negative, cognitive, and affective symptoms of psychotic illness.

Six new atypical or second-generation antipsychotics have become available over the past years. They include the following: Clozaril (clozapine), Risperdal (risperidone), Zyprexa (olanzapine), Seroquel (quetiapine), Geodon (ziprasidone), and Abilify (aripiprazole). Since they are used in a variety of settings, widely, and off label, they have important public health ramifications. Although there is a major emphasis on the lack of the traditional disabling neurological side effects associated with second-generation antipsychotics, they all can be associated with metabolic syndromes. Metabolic concerns that need close monitoring with these second-generation antipsychotics include weight gain, diabetes mellitus, and hyperlipidemia. There are reports of dramatic weight gain, diabetes and diabetic ketoacidosis, an atherogenic lipid profile, increased LDL cholesterol and triglyceride levels, and decreased HDL cholesterol in patients taking these second-generation atypical antipsychotics.

Because of the close associations between obesity, diabetes, and dyslipidemia, there is heightened interest in the relationship between second-generation antipsychotics and the development of these major risk factors for cardiovascular disease[1].

To gain a better understanding of this relationship, the American Diabetes Association, the American Association of Clinical Endocrinologists, and the North American Association for the Study of Obesity developed a consensus and recommendations. In summary, the panel recommends: 1) consideration of metabolic risks when starting atypical antipsychotics; 2) education of the patient, family and care giver; 3) screening (baseline) and regular monitoring of metabolism, with tests such as fasting plasma glucose and lipid profile, blood pressure, height and weight measurements (so the BMI can be calculated), and waist circumference—also, obtaining a personal and family history of obesity, diabetes, dyslipidemia, hypertension, or cardio-vascular disease; and 4) referral to specialized services when appropriate[2].

It is important not to sacrifice efficacy for less neurological side effects in severely ill, suicidal schizophrenic patients. With serious mentally ill patients, the risk of the antipsychotic being less effective or not effective at all needs to be weighed against the benefit of development of less neurological side effects. It may be more of a risk not to aggressively treat the psychotic symptoms most likely responsible for suicide. Furthermore, it is possible that diabetes, associated with dehydration and electrolyte imbalance, can predispose a patient to neuroleptic malignant syndrome, the most life threatening neurological side effect and medical emergency. In animals, hyperglycemia can diminish dopaminergic transmission and increase postsynaptic dopaminergic super sensitivity. Atypical anipsychotic induced hyperglycemia should be recognized and treated promptly to prevent neuroleptic malignant syndrome[3].

Unlike the first generation antipsychotics, the new atypical antipsychotics may actually have a neuroprotective effect. It is known that atypical antipsychotic medications increase glial density and brain volume in the primate prefrontal cortex.

Treatment with atypical antipsychotic medication causes glial proliferation (as much as 33% in prefrontal cortical layer IV) and hypertrophy of the cerebral cortex. Increased cortical thickness in layer V even occurs in the prefrontal cortex of monkeys. Those findings indicate that glial proliferation and hypertrophy of the cerebral cortex is a common response to atypical antipsychotic medication.

These responses play a regulatory role in adjusting neurotransmitter levels or metabolic processes and producing changes in neurotransmitter levels and receptor sensitivity in the cortex[4]. This is a particularly important effect of the atypical antipsychotics, since gray matter volume is significantly less in schizophrenics, especially in the prefrontal cortex[5].

What are the differences among the currently popular atypical antipsychotics? Atypicals such as risperidone and olanzapine were introduced in a way that created confusion about the differences among them. The widespread use of new atypical antipsychotic medications in the 1990s revolutionized the treatment of schizophrenia. The development of atypical antipsychotics has been the most significant advance in the pharmacological treatment of schizophrenia since the introduction of typical antipsychotics in the 1950s[6]. Clozapine, risperidone, and olanzapine are particular antipsychotics that have become very popular among psychiatrists. Which one is best for the patient is a frequently asked question among psychiatrists, primary care physicians, and advanced practitioners of nursing.

The historical backward order in which the atypicals were introduced contributes to the confusion about differences among them. First, clozapine appeared in 1990, but it was strictly reserved as a last-line agent for treatment refractory schizophrenia. Then, later the first-line atypicals were introduced. Risperidone became available in 1993, olanzapine in 1997, and quetiapine in 1998—all as first-line agents. Now others have been made available as more treatment options for patients.

Another factor that contributes to confusion among the atypicals is their unique receptor binding heterogeneity, usually represented with complex pie charts. Although these chemical distinctions with respect to different types of receptor binding profiles are useful, trying to compare them in clinical use, based on those characteristics, can sometimes be misleading. For example, olanzapine is frequently compared to clozapine in this way, as having a similar receptor profile without similar side effects. This association is not useful since each antipsychotic has very different clinical indications. Olanzapine is a first-line agent and clozapine is a last-line agent. In order for a schizophrenic patient to be considered a candidate for clozapine, the patient usually remains very ill with prominent severe psychotic symptoms after failing numerous trials of first-line agents. This distinction is highlighted in a recent study that demonstrated no difference in efficacy between olanzapine and chlorpromazine in the treatment of psychotic symptoms in patients with treatment resistant schizophrenia. Both drugs lead to only marginal improvement. Furthermore, more than half of the patients who failed to respond to olanzapine therapy subsequently showed clinical improvement following clozapine administration[7].

Unfortunately, most clinical guidelines discuss the atypical antipsychotics as a homogenous group; all are similar in safety and efficacy. However, these atypical antipsychotics do differ in efficacy, and that fact is not fully appreciated by evidence-based research at this time. In addition, the atypical antipsychotics differ in side effects. Therefore, there is really no property in which they are clearly homogenous, and the choice of which atypical first-line antipsychotic medication to use should be tailored toward individual patients[8].

In order to distinguish differences among the currently popular atypical antipsychotics, one can use side effect profiles, clinical outcome measures, and the same classification scheme that is used for traditional antipsychotic medication.

High potent, typical antipsychotics tend to be more effective for positive psychotic symptoms (delusions and hallucinations), more likely to cause neurological extrapyramidal side effects (such as parkinsonism), and less sedating than low potent antipsychotics.

Low potent, typical antipsychotics tend to be less effective for positive psychotic symptoms, less likely to cause neurological extrapyramidal side effects, and more sedating than high potent typical antipsychotics.

Thus, haloperidol is classified as a high potent, typical antipsychotic, and chlorpromazine a low potent typical antipsychotic. This well known classification scheme for typical antipsychotics can be extended to the atypical antipsychotics. It lays the foundation for a new classification scheme of atypical antipsychotics.

Risperidone may be then conceptualized as a high potent first-line atypical antipsychotic relative to olanzapine, just as haloperidol is compared to chlorpromazine. Likewise, olanzapine is a low potent, first-line, atypical antipsychotic relative to risperidone, just as chlorpromazine is compared to haloperidol[9].

Risperidone is particularly effective for delusions, hallucinations, suspiciousness, and unusual thought content. It is superior to olanzapine for the treatment of these positive symptoms[10]. Introduced in 1994, it has been the most frequently prescribed antipsychotic in the United States. Adult outpatients with clinically stable schizophrenia or schizoaffective disorder have a lower risk of relapse if they are treated with risperidone than if they are treated with haloperidol[11]. More than 90 % of schizophrenic patients can be maintained well on a dose of less than 6 mg per day[12]. The dose of risperidone used for schizophrenia, in both acute episodes and relapse prevention is usually between 4 to 6 mg per day[13]. Side effects can be minimized with effective dosing. It is not associated with significant weight gain, sedation, and diabetes, or glucose dysregulation. Risperidone exhibits dopamine (D2) blockade and higher doses. It can elevate serum prolactin.

Monitoring for extrapyramidal side effects is important. It is possible to develop extrapyramidal side effects and sometimes anticholinergic medication, such as low dose benztropine mesylate, is needed. There have been reports of the development of akathisia, acute dystonia, parkinsonism, neuroleptic malignant syndrome, and tardive dyskinesia[14]. It is also is a potent serotonin 5 HT2A receptor antagonist at lower doses. Finally, it is reported that risperidone is associated with less sedation than olanzapine[15].

Olanzapine, on the other hand, is associated with significant sedation, or somnolence, and weight gain. Sedation is dose dependent and approaches nearly a 40% incidence at daily doses of 12.5 to 17.5 mg/day. Weight gain was characterized as the most problematic side effect in long term study of patients treated with olanzapine[16].

In a direct comparison study, there were significant increases in body weight and body mass index in the patients treated with olanzapine, but no such significant increases were found in the patients treated with risperidone[17]. It has been recently reemphasized that weight gain should be taken seriously due to the increased risk of cardiovascular disease, diabetes, certain cancers, and osteoarthritis, especially in countries such as the United States where these general medical conditions are already prevalent. Weight gain can also have an adverse psychological impact contributing to the loss of self-esteem[18], an adverse effect to be avoided in depressed, suicidal, schizophrenic patients. Evidence suggests that antagonism of serotonin 5HT2c, or histamine H1 type H1 receptors, plays a role in antipsychotic induced weight gain. Olanzapine has a very low incidence of extrapyramidal side effects such as parkinsonism[19].

Using those views to differentiate among the atypical antipsychotics can help decide which one to prescribe for the relief of serious suicidality associated with positive psychotic symptoms such as delusions and hallucinations. Risperidone appears to be one of the best of the first-line atypical antipsychotics.

The efficacy, safety, and tolerability of quetiapine, ziprasidone, and aripiprazole for the treatment of psychosis in patients with schizophrenia have been determined in a number of clinical trials. However, more clinical experience is needed with these medications in order to study suicide risk reduction in schizophrenic patients. These new first-line atypical antipsychotics increase the clinician ability to treat a variety of mental disorders associated with increased risk of suicide.

Although command suicidal auditory hallucinations are intense and severe and can lead to suicide in psychotic patients, treatment for those particular symptoms can be quite safe and effective. However, most patients with schizophrenia are only partially compliant with oral antipsychotic medication, whether or not the antipsychotic is a conventional typical or novel atypical type.

Compliance with oral psychotropic medication is a challenge to both the clinician and patient. For the clinician faced with a symptomatic schizophrenic patient, decisions as to whether to adjust the dose, augment with another medication, or switch medication are needed.

Partial compliance in schizophrenia begins early and prevalence increases over time. Delay in refilling medications effects hospitalization in patients with schizophrenia. The odds of hospitalization increase twofold even missing one to ten days of medication. The odds increase to nearly three times greater with a delay of eleven to thirty days, and for a maximum delay of over thirty days, the odds of hospitalization are about 4 times higher than for a person with no medication gaps. Compliance is difficult to measure accurately.

Clinician and patient reports overestimate compliance, whereas pill count and microelectronic monitoring of the number of times a pill bottle cap is opened is more accurate and reveals low levels of compliance with oral anitpsychotic medication. Poor compliance with oral antipsychotic medication in schizophrenic patients changes symptoms, increases rehospitalization rate, increases costs, and is a serious obstacle to optimal outcome.

The high rates of relapse, hospitalization, and suicidal behavior associated with untreated schizophrenia indicate that continuous antipsychotic treatment is the most likely contributor to successful outcome. If patient's compliance improves, they are likely to have fewer relapses and less suicidal behavior. The risk for suicidal behavior may increase when patients are not taking medication. A long acting, injectable atypical antipsychotic may help these patients by providing continuous antipsychotic coverage and therefore reduce symptoms that lead to aggressive or violent behavior.

In response to this problem, the development of the first long-acting, injectable atypical antipsychotic has been approved for use by the FDA. Risperdal Consta was approved by the FDA in October 2003. It has been proven safe and effective in adults with schizophrenia. The combination of the efficacy, favorable tolerability profile of an atypical, or newer-generation, antipsychotic and the benefits of a long acting injectable formulation is an important step forward in the treatment of schizophrenia.

Indications for switching from an oral antipsychotic to a long-acting, injectable atypical antipsychotic include patients who have an involuntary out patient commitment, patients taking an oral conventional antipsychotic who are chronically relapsing, patients with a persistent lack of insight or denial of illness, patients taking an oral atypical antipsychotic who are experiencing relapse for reasons that are unclear, patients with a history of or potential for aggressive or violent behavior, and, in addition, patients who want to avoid the stigma of needing to take psychotropic medication several times per day.

Other potential patients to consider for long-acting, injectable atypical antipsychotic include the following: patients with a history of or potential for suicidal behavior, homeless patients, patients with co-morbid substance abuse problems, patients who lack social supports, elderly patients taking an oral conventional antipsychotic who forgets to take medication, and patients taking an oral or long acting injectable conventional antipsychotic who are stable but experiencing neurological side effects.

The starting dose of Risperdal Consta currently recommended for schizophrenia is 25 mg IM every two weeks. Doses of 37.5 mg and 50 mg are available. The technology does not involve an oil based medium such as sesame oil used in older, typical, long acting depot neuroleptics such as haldol decanoate; rather, it incorporates Medisorb Microsphere Technology. The hydrolysis of polymers, made of glycolide and lactide, initiates the decomposition and suspension of microspheres embedded with risperidone, and the breakdown slowly releases active risperidone.

Atypical antipsychotic polypharmacy for severe suicidal schizophrenic patients may be needed. The use of antipsychotic polypharmacy can predispose the patient to serious side effects. It should be reserved for few patients. It should not only be evidenced based, but also cost efficient and effective. Cost inefficient and ineffective atypical antipsychotic polypharmacy is discouraged.

Some patients require atypical antipsychotic polypharmacy to control serious psychotic symptoms. If so, then a careful combination of a high-potent and low-potent antipsychotic may be most effective, regardless of whether it is a traditional or atypical antipsychotic. But, the combination of haloperidol and risperidone should be avoided since it can induce moderately severe extrapyramidal symptoms when prescribed together. Similarly, the combination of two low-potent antipsychotics, whether typical or atypical, can predispose the patient to too much sedation, weight gain, and metabolic complication. Rather, the clinician should strongly consider combining a high potent (haloperidol or risperidone) with a low potent (chlorpromazine or olanzapine). If such antipsychotic polypharmacy is still ineffective in controlling positive psychotic symptoms, especially associated with suicidality, then clozapine should be considered.

## Clozapine and Suicide Risk Reduction

Clozaril remains the gold standard for treatment of schizophrenia. It had been reserved for refractory cases, but now it has recently been approved specifically for suicidal schizophrenia as a first-line agent in these patients. This is particularly relevant since intense and severe positive psychotic symptoms, such as command auditory suicidal hallucinations can be significantly reduced with clozapine.

Clozaril (clozapine) adds a completely new dimension to the psychiatrist's psychopharmacologic armamentarium for suicidality. Clozaril was first widely recognized for the efficacious therapy of treatment- resistant schizophrenia and severe psychotic disorders. It has been considered the gold standard for treatment-resistant schizophrenia[20].

In addition to proven efficacy, clozapine is found to have a distinctive side effect profile. Its use is associated with only minimal EPS, including the near absence of associated parkinsonism, dystonia, and tardive dyskinesia[21]. Clozaril, despite being the first available atypical, has often been used as a last-line agent. It has been prescribed for treatment-refractory schizophrenia. Although clozapine was the first atypical anti-psychotic approved in the early 1990's, it is traditionally reserved only for chronically ill schizophrenic patients who have been poorly responsive to previous treatments. For those reasons, it is common clinical practice to try olanzapine, risperidone, quetiapine, ziprasidone, or aripiprazole before clozapine[22].

Clozapine is, by any definition, an atypical neuroleptic. Some prominent researchers in the field refer to clozapine as a drug class in itself[23]. It is one of the most complicated drugs in psychopharmacology, known to have notable interactions with at least nine different neurotransmitter receptors. One unique property of clozapine is that it spares the nigrostriatal and tubuloinfindibular CNS dopamine tracts. Because of this selective dopamine blockade, neuroleptic-induced, extrapyramidal side-effects are extremely rare. It specifically targets the mesolimbic and mesocortical dopamine tracts most associated with the positive and negative symptoms of schizophrenia[24].

The ability of clozapine to restore function in even the most refractory of schizophrenic patients, its low propensity to cause tardive dyskinesia, and its efficacy in patients with negative symptoms has changed the management of schizophrenia[25]. It has even drawn media attention in mainstream publications such as *Time* magazine, as well as portrayed in the films as in *Out of Darkness*.

When clozapine is combined with psychoeducational interventions, such as the Social and Independent Living Skills training, there is significant functional improvement in the patient's quality of life, better treatment adherence, and a less likely chance of re-hospitalization compared to patients receiving clozapine alone[26].

Clozaril is now the first drug ever with the indication involving suicidal behavior. Clozaril is the first and only pharmacological agent approved as a first-line agent specifically to reduce the risk of recurrent suicidal behavior in patients with schizophrenia or schizoaffective disorder judged to be at risk of suicidal behavior[27]. Not only is there a better response rate to clozapine among patients with acute schizophrenia (57% compared to 36% with standard antipsychotic medication), but clozapine also has the added benefit of decreasing suicidal behavior in these patients.

The efficacy of Clozaril in reducing the risk of suicidal behavior is demonstrated in the *InterSePT* TM study, the largest prospective study ever conducted to examine the impact of any pharmacologic treatment on suicidal behavior. The *InterSePT* study has demonstrated Clozaril to be effective for the treatment of emergent suicidal behavior in patients with schizophrenia or schizoaffective disorder. This study is the first study ever to prospectively evaluate a medication in reducing the risk of suicidal behavior. Clozaril reduced the risk of suicide attempts and hospitalizations to prevent suicide among individuals suffering from schizophrenia or schizoaffective disorder. Patients also required fewer concomitant psychotropic medications. Furthermore, the effects of clozapaine in reducing the risk of suicidal behavior derive from its intrinsic pharmacology and not from the influence of concomitant psychotropic medications[28].

Wider use of clozaril in this population may help save lives. Traditionally used only for treatment refractory schizophrenia, clozaril will be effective for non-treatment refractory schizophrenia or schizoaffective disorder with high risk of suicidality. *The InterSePT* study is a two-year international, open-label, randomized study. It is a landmark study in prevention of suicidal behavior. *InterSePT* demonstrated findings of major significance. The time to a suicide event or hospitalization to prevent a suicide event is longer for the Clozaril patients compared to the Zyprexa (olanzapine) patients. In addition, there is a significant reduction in relative risk of suicidal behavior, including a less number of suicide attempts and hospitalizations to prevent suicide, compared with the patients taking Zyprexa in this study. The Clozaril patients frequently need less concomitant psychotropic medications such as antipsychotics, antidepressants, sedatives, or anxiolytics and mood stabilizers compared to the Zyprexa patients[29].

The following cases are examples of patient's great benefit from the medication:

*Case 1: The patient is a twenty-four year old white male admitted to the hospital for suicide attempt by cutting his throat with a steak knife. The patient suffers from chronic paranoid schizophrenia. He was recently being treated in the clinic with prescribed sertraline at 100 mg per day and olanzapine at 10 mg per day. He did not significantly improve with olanzapine therapy; in fact, he required the addition of haloperidol and benztropine for several months prior to admission for command suicidal auditory hallucinations. He has a history of recurrent suicide attempts. He reported that this was an impulsive act and appeared to be giggling with an inappropriate affect at the time. He had a negative urine drug screen prior to admission. No recent stressors or depression was identified. Apparently, voices were telling him to cut his throat because it would be cool. His past medical history was unremarkable. A decision to switch antipsychotic medication to clozapine was made with the support of the patient and his family. After pre-clozapine medial history and physical labs were within normal limits, olanzapine and sertraline were tapered off and clozapine was gradually introduced at 25 mg every three days, titrating up to a final initial dose of 300 mg per day.*

*During the one-month hospitalization, the patient developed mild asymptomatic tachycardia that was treated with 10 mg of propranolol twice daily. Citalopram was introduced and titrated up to a final dose of 40 mg per day, for post-psychotic depressive symptoms. The patient tolerated with medication well, except he experienced mild sedation. White blood counts remained within normal limits during his hospitalization.*

*Mental status examination prior to discharge showed the patient to be much improved. He was cooperative. Affect was no longer inappropriate to thought content. Thinking showed only mild paranoia. There were no suicidal ideations, intentions, or plans. There was no depression. Attention and concentration improved. Impulse control markedly improved. He exhibited no anxiety or agitation. He was eating and sleeping well.*

*The patient continues to do well, being seen in the outpatient setting. Active involvement of the family, as well as case management, has contributed to his continued well-being. He started school and is working part time.*

*Case 2: The patient is a twenty-five year old white male admitted via a physician's emergency certificate from a local hospital. He reported having electro convulsive treatment (ECT) at a major university hospital approximately two months prior to admission for suicidal ideations, intentions, and plans. He suffers from schizoaffective disorder, depressed type. He reported that he stopped taking his psychotropic medications that included lamotrigine, divalproex, paroxetine, olanzapine, and lorazepam. "I did not take my meds. I bought sleeping pills and vodka, but I came to the hospital instead."*

*The patient reported no recent alcohol or drug abuse or psychosocial stressors. Over the past five weeks prior to admission, he began having increased depression, insomnia, command-type auditory hallucinations, and suicidal thoughts. The patient was going to take two bottles of aspirin with vodka to kill himself, as the voices he was hearing were telling him to do that.*

*The patient has had fifteen previous in patient admissions to a major university hospital. During the last hospitalization there, it was felt that he had treatment-resistant schizophrenia and suicidality, so ECT was recommended and done. He had twelve previous suicide attempts, mostly by overdose of prescription and over-the-counter medications. He had failed numerous trials of antipsychotic medications including haloperidol, risperidone, and chlorpromazine. Haloperidol caused severe extrapyramidal symptoms. Benzodiazepines made the depression worse. Numerous trials of SSRIs such as fluoxetine, venlafaxine, and sertraline were ineffective. Paroxetine and citalopram were partially effective. Recent MRI and CT scans of the head were normal. The patient had no active medical problems, but had a recent history of respiratory arrest secondary to a suicide overdose, which required mechanical ventilation and renal dialysis. The patient appeared obese with gynecomastia.*

*His mental status exam on admission showed a cooperative patient, alert and oriented. Speech was normal. Thinking revealed severe auditory hallucinations of a command type, telling him to kill himself. Affect was blunted and inappropriate. Patient had mild to moderate memory impairment, and poor attention, concentration, and judgment. He had anxiety and agitation, was sleeping excessively, and was with a decreased appetite.*

*The patient agreed to a clozapine trial, since this was not tried before. After baseline medical history and physical and laboratory work were essentially normal, he was started on clozapine and titrated up to a dose of 125 mg per day, by increasing the dose 25 mg every three days. During the twelve day hospitalization, citalopram was gradually introduced and titrated up to 40 mg per day for depression. A small dose of valproic acid at 250 mg twice daily was included for mood stabilization and impulsivity. This combination of medication proved effective, and he did not suffer any side effects. By day twelve, he was asymptomatic. His mental status examination showed a cooperative and compliant patient with good eye contact and normal speech. Affect was appropriate to thought content. There were no delusions or hallucinations, and most notably, there were no command suicidal auditory hallucinations. Insight and judgment improved. Attention and concentration improved. He was eating and sleeping well. He was discharged from the hospital by day twelve and is currently doing well in the out patient setting.*

The third case report, representing one of the earliest case reports in the medical literature of an atypical form of neuroleptic malignant syndrome (NMS), is highlighted as I published it ten years ago. It describes the development of neurotoxicity with clozapine. This case emphasizes the caution in prescribing this medication. It describes the rapid appearance of delirium and other signs of neurotoxicity during the second week after initiating clozapine therapy[30].

*Case 3: Due to symptomatic exacerbation while on trifluoperazine maintenance, Mr. A, a 40-year-old man suffering from schizophrenia for over twenty years, came to the inpatient unit for a clozapine trial. Refractoriness to typical neuroleptics including haloperidol, fluphenazine, and perphenazine was a supported by a detailed medication history, the persistence of psychotic symptoms, and a progressive personal and social deterioration. At admission, the review of Mr. A's systems was unremarkable. Physical examination was entirely normal except for mild obesity: his weight at 228 lb. Blood pressure was 128/72 mm Hg, pulse at 82 beats per minute, respirations at 18 breaths per minute, and temperature at 98.8 degrees F. Laboratory test results, including chemistry and hematology profiles, were normal. Baseline white blood count was 9400/mm3 with normal differential. Results of urinalysis, chest x-rays, ECG, and EEG were are normal.*

*Clozapine treatment was initiated at 25 mg/day, with daily increments of 25 mg. While showing a reasonable symptomatic improvement after the first twelve days of treatment, Mr. A experienced a few, common, adverse reactions associated with clozapine including sedation, salivation, mild tachycardia (his pulse increased to 108 per minute), dizziness, and postural changes in blood pressure.*

*On Day thirteen, while receiving 200 mg/day of clozapine, Mr. A experienced disorientation, slurred speech, fatigue, weakness, ataxia, and autonomic instability. Symptoms reached a crescendo in three to four hours. Examination revealed blood pressure at 142/82, pulse at 122 beats per minute, respirations at 28 breaths per minute, and temperature at 103.7 degrees F. In addition, Mr. A experienced fecal and urinary incontinence, diaphoresis, and dry mouth. Laboratory assessment showed a white blood count of 19,700/mm3 with a marked left shift.*

*The physician withdrew clozapine and gave the patient supportive measures including intravenous fluids, nonsteroidal anti-inflammatory drugs, a cooling blanket, and close observation on the psychiatric unit. Repeated physical examinations were otherwise normal. Muscle stiffness, rigidity, and tremor were never observed, and serial creatine phosphokinase (CPK) enzyme tests were normal. Multiple blood, urine, throat, sputum, and stool cultures were negative for bacteria, parasites, and fungus. Chest x-rays remained normal. Autoimmune workup including antinuclear antibody (ANA), rheumatoid factor, and serum complement was also unremarkable. Although a viral infection was considered, a consultant thought it very unlikely in view of the patient's temperature pattern (a persistent fever for seven days) and hematology profiles (no leukopenia and a marked left shift for seven days).*

*Three days after the discontinuation of clozapine treatment, Mr. A's disorientation, ataxia, and, shortly thereafter, temperature, blood pressure, pulse, respiratory rate, and hematology profile returned to baseline levels. Three weeks after clozapine withdrawal, Mr. A's psychotic symptoms became prominent. Reinstitution of neuroleptic treatment (trifluoperazine) resulted in a modest clinical improvement, allowing discharge to a residential facility.*

To start the patient on clozapine requires very close clinical monitoring. Clozaril use is associated with a substantial risk of seizure, affecting 1 to 2% of patients at low doses, 3 to 4% at moderate doses, and 5% at high doses. The risk of seizures can be reduced with the prophylactic co-administration of valproic acid especially when a high dose of clozapine is prescribed. One of the reasons for a 12.5 mg test dose is to assess for tolerability. One of my recent schizophrenic and autistic adult patients with a seizure disorder on valproic acid concentrate attempted a clozapine trial, but he had a seizure on this initial 12.5 mg test dose.

In clinical trials, clozaril was associated with a 1 to 2% incidence of agranulocytosis, a potentially fatal blood disorder that, if caught early, can be reversed. Mandatory blood monitoring and drug dispensing as specified are required. Early signs of any potential infection, which can lead to sepsis and death since clozapine lowers the white blood cells involved in fighting infection, can be monitored clinically assessing vital signs for temperature and physical examination for any infections. Some clinicians use lithium to raise the WBC count while on clozapine. I have not found this to be useful since there is a potential for an antipsychotic/lithium drug-drug combination neurotoxicity as has been reported in the medical literature with other antipsychotic medications and lithium. In extreme cases, granuocyte stimulating factor has been used in such cases.

Due to the significant risk of side effects, such as agranulocytosis, seizures, myocarditis, other adverse cardio respiratory events, and rare neurotoxic syndromes associated with its use, clozapine has traditionally been prescribed for patients who have failed to respond adequately to treatment with appropriate courses of standard first line typical and/or atypical antipsychotic medication.

Initial side effects include sedation. If there is highly excessive sedation in the beginning, a caffeinated cup of coffee is allowed in the morning for such patients. Drooling, not dry mouth, can be a cumbersome side effect. An evening dose of benztropine can decrease hypersalivation associated with this medication. Monitoring vital signs is important in the initial phases of clozapine. Symptomatic tachycardia and orthostatic hypotension can occur. A base line EKG is helpful since patients can have late side effects including myocarditis and sudden cardio respiratory event.

Avoiding large doses given all at once initially can help decrease these non-life threatening side effects. Most often it is prescribed at night, but twice day dosing is often needed. Care in monitoring excess sedation from the morning dose is important since it can lead to non-compliance and relapse.

Monitoring for post-psychotic depression in clozapine patients is critical since depression and suicidality can first present in a new clozapine patient. For the first time, the patient may experience the sense of being free from intense and severe psychotic symptoms, and subsequently get depressed and suicidal. Add-on antidepressant therapy in post psychotic depression is helpful for many patients.

Combination pharmacotherapy using clozapine with mood stabilizers such as lithium or valproic acid, can help impulsive behavior associated with psychotic thoughts and suicidal behavior. Medications such as carbamazepine and benzodiazepines are contraindicated.

Atypical antipsychotic pharmacotherapy with clozapine, such as the combination of risperidone and clozapine, may be needed in extremely ill suicidal schizophrenics. Some partially compliant suicidal schizophrenic patients with severe psychotic symptoms taking clozapine have responded better to the addition of long-acting injectable risperidone to the clozapine.

## Antidepressants and Suicide

Historically somatic therapies for depression consisted of monoamine oxidase inhibitors (MAOIs) such as phenelzine, tranylcypromine, and isocarboxazide; and tricyclic antidepressants (TCAs) such as imipramine, desipramine, nortriptyline, amitriptyline, and doxepin. High suicide risk patients have an available and lethal method of overdosing on the tricyclic antidepressants. There is some evidence that older antidepressants may afford somewhat better protection against suicidal behavior than the newer, safer agents may. Others suggest that some of these older antidepressants may actually increase suicide risk owning to their direct lethality on overdose. Therefore, careful use of these medications is warranted[31].

Selective serotonin reuptake inhibitors (SSRIs) became the most popular treatment of depression in the 1980's with medications such as fluoxetine, sertraline, paroxetine, fluvoxamine, nefazodone, citalopram, and escitalopram. SSRIs act on several different central nervous system serotonin pathways. As a result, many of these SSRIs also became indicated for the treatment not only of mood disorders (major depressive disorders), but also for anxiety disorders (panic disorder, obsessive compulsive disorders, posttraumatic stress disorder, and generalized anxiety disorder) and eating disorders. Additionally, they are much safer than the traditional tricyclic antidepressants with regard to lethality in overdose.

Anecdotal experience suggests that suicides and suicide attempts are not reduced in patients taking SSRIs versus TCAs; only the method of suicide is changed to other means in those taking TCAs.

Even with these recent developments of a variety of new generation antidepressants, many patients are reluctant to take antidepressant mediation for various reasons. The keys to increasing compliance with antidepressant treatment are communicating with patients about what to expect during treatment, prescribing efficacious medications with favorable side effect profiles, and encouraging full remission and recovery.

It is clinically important to complete an adequate trial of any antidepressant at a proper dose and duration. Adherence to treatment, optimizing treatment, diagnostic review, defining response, non-response, or partial response prior to switching, or using conventional or unconventional augmentation strategies is important before concluding that the patient is resistant to treatment[32].

Too often antidepressants are still under-detected, and they are less common than anxiolytics-hypnotics or even antipsychotics when retrieved in post-mortem toxicology samples of patients who complete suicide[33].

There is frequent use of psychotropic medication among suicides; however, few use antidepressants and complete suicide. Many suicides are still misdiagnosed and are not adequately treated[34].

A recent trend in the United States however is evolving. Between 1987 and 1997, there was a marked increase in the proportion of the population who received outpatient treatment for depression. Treatment became characterized by greater involvement of physicians and greater use of psychotropic medications, coinciding with the advent of better-tolerated antidepressants. The proportion of individuals treated for depression that received a prescribed psychotropic medication increased from 44.6% in 1987 to 79.4% in 1997. Antidepressants were the most commonly prescribed medications for the treatment of depression. The increase in antidepressant use was primarily attributable to the newer antidepressant medications available[35].

In 1993 the book, *Listening to Prozac*, by Peter D Kramer, MD contributed to a wider understanding of depression, serotonin, and SSRIs[36].

In a recent series of national population-based reports, studies are suggesting that the potential beneficial effect of antidepressants on suicide is apparent.

In Australia, reviewing the suicides from 1986 to 1990 (the pre-SSRI era) and 1996 to 2000 (after the introduction of SSRIs), strong evidence of a beneficial impact of antidepressant prescribing on suicide rates was noted among both men and women. The largest declines in suicide occurred in the age groups with the highest exposure to antidepressants, with controlling for other factors.

In Sweden, there has been a gradual reduction in suicide rates over the period from 1977 to 1997, with an accelerated decline after 1990 when the SSRIs were introduced. The rate of suicides in the 1990's was inversely related to the rate of antidepressant prescribing in most age and gender groups[37].

In Hungary, rates of suicide declined in parallel with a rapid growth of antidepressant usage, despite steep increases in unemployment and per capita alcohol consumption[38].

The same phenomenon is not observed in all European countries, with no such association being observed in Italy[39]. The United Kingdom reports more than a twofold increase in antidepressant prescriptions for the period 1975 to 1998. They found increases in prescribing in all age and gender groups, but most noticeably a threefold increase in older age groups. Between 1950 and 1998, suicide rates declined in older males and females. However, this decline is offset by a doubling of the suicide rate in males younger than 45 years old.

Before choosing an antidepressant, efficacy must be evaluated. Most antidepressants, including both tricyclic antidepressants and newer antidepressants, have been proven in numerous trials to be efficacious in reducing the symptoms of depression. Although remission rates differ slightly among types of antidepressants, these rates are generally between 35 and 45%. To encourage compliance and understanding, physicians should inform each patient about the efficacy of different antidepressants and allow the patient to have an active role in choosing the medication that is best[40].

A standard trial of an antidepressant should be at least four to six weeks and longer for elderly patients. Signs of remission include a significant decrease in depressive symptoms and suicidal thoughts. An underlying depression that is treated can lead to a better quality of life. The following case represents some of the consequences and outcomes of a depressed patient:

> *A 19-year-old single, white, female runaway was admitted to the psychiatric hospital. Two years ago, she had previously been treated with citalopram for depression with good effect, but the patient stopped it soon thereafter. Eight months ago, she ran away from her rural hometown to work as a prostitute. She complained of depression, sadness, crying, doom and gloom thinking, and suicidal thoughts. She has a history of suicide attempts in the past including wrist slashing and overdosing on over-the-counter medication. The patient became increasingly depressed about the type of work she is doing. She began using amphetamines several times per week. The week prior to admission, the amphetamine intoxication induced severe psychotic symptoms, whereby she brought herself to the hospital. Family history is remarkable for mood disorder on the paternal and maternal sides. Her sibling also has suicidality. Recent psychosocial stressors included job dissatisfaction, lack of social support, and relationship issues. The patient had no active medical problems.*

> *Her mental status exam revealed moderate depression, suicidal thoughts, and poverty of speech. Moderately severe psychomotor agitation was observed. The patient complained of auditory hallucinations, insomnia, loss of appetite, and poor attention and concentration.*

> *The diagnosis was major depressive disorder, recurrent and amphetamine induced psychosis. She received intramuscular ziprasidone at 20 mg upon arrival to the hospital, followed by a 40 mg ziprasidone tablet twice daily for three days bringing complete relief of her psychosis. Then she was started on citalopram at 20 mg per day with an increase to a maintenance dose of 40 mg per day. She tolerated the medication well without side effects. Over the next three days, her mental status improved. She denied suicidal ideations. There were no auditory hallucinations or paranoia. Her mood improved. There was less agitation and anxiety. Her sleeping and appetite improved. Her insight and judgment as well as attention and concentration also improved.*

> *The patient was discharged from the hospital after four days. Her parents came to the hospital to pick her up and take her back home with them.*

> *She was instructed to take the ziprasidone for approximately one month and to continue on the citalopram for approximately six months.*

Other types of antidepressants besides SSRIs include the norepinepherine dopamine reuptake inhibitors (NDRIs) such as bupropion. Bupropion is also prescribed for substance related disorders, nicotine dependence. Bupropion is especially useful for those patients who have had numerous unsuccessful trials of SSRIs. Since it is a norepinepherine and dopamine reuptake inhibitor (NDRI), burpropion's mechanism of action is quite different from SSRIs. A combination of SSRIs with bupropion is a common strategy in treating more severe depressive episodes.

Recently, the development of dual acting serotonin-norepinepherine reuptake inhibitors (SNRIs), such as venlafaxine and mirtazapine effect both the serotonin and norepinepherine pathways in the brain involved in depression. New, dual-acting, potent antidepressants are now available[41].

Switching therapy from an SSRI to a drug of different class may be preferable for patients with mild to moderate depression. There are a number of SSRIs available such as paroxetine, sertraline, fluoxetine, nefazodone, citalopram, and escitalopram, which are all selective serotonin reuptake inhibitors. Some patients who do not respond well to one may respond to another one. Studies have shown that the response rate, when switching from one antidepressant to another, typically ranges from 40 to 60% across many different classes of antidepressants. A decision whether to switch or augment remains a question of clinician preference[42].

Aggressive treatment of depression is important for decreasing suicidal risk, but the anti-suicidal effects of antidepressant medications do not come into play in the short term, perhaps not for six months. No antisuicidal effect of antidepressants is reported. In a long term follow-up, a 2.5 times reduction in suicide in patients hospitalized for a major mood disorder who had received at least six continuous months of treatment is reported.

The Food and Drug Administration recently issued a public health advisory in March 2004 stating that some patients using these popular antidepressants should be watched carefully for signs of worsening depression or suicidal thoughts. This focus is primarily on the risks of the medications in children, but the warning applies to use in both pediatric and adult patients.

In June 2004, I received the first "dear doctor" letter from Wyeth, which reads as follows:

Dear Health Care Professional,

*Wyeth wishes to inform you about important safety information that the U.S. Food and Drug Administration (FDA) has asked the manufacturers of ten antidepressants, including Effexor (venlafaxine HCL) and Effexor XR (venlafaxine HCL), to include in their product information. The Effexor XR prescribing information was amended as follows (the prescribing information for Effexor was similarly updated):*

*Under the **WARNINGS** section:*

***Clinical Worsening and Suicide Risk***

*Patients with major depressive disorder, both adult and pediatric, may experience worsening of their depression and/or the emergence of suicidal ideation and behavior (suicidality), whether or not they are taking antidepressant medications, and this risk may persist until significant remission occurs. Although there has been a long-standing concern that antidepressants may have a role in inducing worsening of depression and the emergence of suicidality in certain patients, a causal role for antidepressants in inducing such behaviors has not been established. **Nevertheless, patients being treated with antidepressants should be observed closely for clinical worsening and suicidality, especially at the beginning of a course of drug therapy, or at the time of dose changes, either increases or decreases.** Consideration should be given to changing the therapeutic regimen, including possibly discontinuing the medication, in patients whose depression is persistently worse or whose emergent suicidality is severe, abrupt in onset, or was not part of the patient's presenting symptoms.*

*Because of the possibility of co-morbidity between major depressive disorder and other psychiatric and nonpsychiatric disorders, the same precautions observed when treating patients with major depressive disorder should be observed when treating patients with other psychiatric and nonpsychiatric disorders.*

*The following symptoms, anxiety, agitation, panic attacks, insomnia, irritability, hostility (aggressiveness), impulsivity, akathisia (psychomotor restlessness), hypomania, and mania, have been reported in adult and pediatric patients being treated with antidepressants for major depressive disorder as well as for other indications, both psychiatric and nonpsychiatric. Although a causal link between the emergence of such symptoms and either the worsening of depression and/or the emergence of suicidal impulses has not been established, consideration should be given to changing the therapeutic regimen, including possibly discontinuing the medication, in patients for whom such symptoms are severe, abrupt in onset, or were not part of the patient's presenting symptoms.*

***Families and caregivers of patients being treated with antidepressants for major depressive disorder or other indications, both psychiatric and nonpsychiatric, should be alerted about the need to monitor patients for the emergence of agitation, irritability, and the other symptoms described above, as well as the emergence of suicidality, and to report such symptoms immediately to health care providers.***

*Prescriptions for Effexor XR should be written for the smallest quantity of capsules consistent with good patient management, in order to reduce the risk of overdose. If the decision has been made to discontinue treatment, medication should be tapered, as rapidly as is feasible, but with the recognition that abrupt discontinuation can be associated with certain symptoms (see PRECAUTIONS and DOSAGE AND ADMINISTRATION, Discontinuing Effexor XR, for a description of the risks of discontinuation of Effexor XR).*

*A major depressive episode may be the initial presentation of bipolar disorder. It is generally believed (though not established in controlled trials) that treating such an episode with an antidepressant alone may increase the likelihood of precipitation of a mixed/manic episode in patients at risk for bipolar disorder. Whether any of the symptoms described above represent such a conversion is unknown. However, prior to initiating treatment with an antidepressant, patients should be adequately screened to determine if they are at risk for bipolar disorder; such screening should include a detailed psychiatric history, including a family history of suicide, bipolar disorder, and depression. It should be noted that Effexor XR is not approved for use in treating bipolar depression.*

*Under the PRECAUTIONS section, Information for Patients subsection:*
*Patients and their families should be encouraged to be alert to the emergence of anxiety, agitation, panic attacks, insomnia, irritability, hostility, impulsivity, akathisia, hypomania, mania, worsening of depression, and suicidal ideation, especially early during antidepressant treatment. Such symptoms should be reported to the patient's physician, especially if they are severe, abrupt in onset, or were not part of the patient's presenting symptoms...[43]*

Often antidepressant treatment alone is not enough in patients manifesting severe acute psychosis, anxiety, agitation, panic attacks, and severe (global) insomnia with co-morbid alcohol use. In these situations, antidepressant treatment may be tragically ineffective. Rather, some sustained, short-term treatment of anxiety may reduce the likelihood of suicide in this group of depressed patients.

Antidepressant polypharmacy refers to the use of more than one medication in the same therapeutic class for the same indication. Prescribing two, three, or even four different antidepressants together, such as fluoxetine and mirtazapine and bupropion; mirtazapine and venlafaxine; or sertraline and imipramine, are examples of antidepressant polypharmacy. Caution is required for the potential of drug-drug interactions.

A fatality associated with combined fluoxetine-amitriptyline therapy was recently reported. The co-administration of fluoxetine at 40 mg and amitriptyline at 150 mg increased the functional daily dose of amitriptyline to 600 to 1050 mg/day, due to a reduction in the clearance of amitriptyline caused by fluoxetine. Such a dose was sufficient to produce toxic levels normally associated with acute overdose[44]. Care and caution is needed when considering combining antidepressants. In addition, it is common to precipitate a manic episode when antidepressant polypharmacy is prescribed.

Antidepressant polypharmacy also may be cost-inefficient. It may predispose the patient to additional, unwanted side effects. For example, adding mirtazapine at night to a high dose of venlafaxine in the morning can induce another complex set of side effects, such as excess sedation and weight gain, although this combination of two dual acting antidepressants can be quite effective in cases that are more resistant. Some antidepressant combination pharmacotherapies, such as fluoxetine and trazodone, are particularly effective. These treatment strategies are often required to treat moderate depression with suicidality.

The potentially fatal serotonin-syndrome can occur, however, after prescribing antidepressant polypharmacy with two SSRIs or SSRI-like medications. The serotonin syndrome is characterized by confusion, fever, hypomania, restlessness, myoclonus, hyperreflexia, diaphoresis, shivering, tremor, diarrhea, coordination delirium, and death. Early recognition and treatment is required. Stopping the SSRI and using diphenhydramine or lorazepam is effective in early management.

In summary, since the introduction of the selective serotonin reuptake inhibitors and other new antidepressants in the early 1990s, there is a major shift in prescribing patterns for this class of medications. Rather than newer agents merely replacing the former market leading class, the tricyclic antidepressants as has happened for other therapeutic groups in medicine such as the antihypertensives, there has been a true increase in usage of antidepressants. There still needs ratable evidence of the beneficial outcomes of suicide risk reduction as there is with lithium in patients with mood disorders.

## Lithium's Antisuicidal Effect

Lithium is antisuicidal in patients with bipolar disorder. Lithium was the first anti-manic treatment discovered, and it represented the birth of the psychopharmacology revolution. Lithium is a salt or rock, a crystal and natural element listed in the periodic table of elements. Lithium still has a stigma attached to it as being a synthetic tranquilizer for severely ill people. *That is only used for seriously sick patients* is a frequent comment by my patients as a first response, yet it remains a safe and effective augmentation strategy for suicidality in bipolar patients.

Lithium has neurotropic effects on the human brain as evident by synaptogenesis, axonal lengthening, and dendrite sprouting.

Lithium is indicated in the treatment of manic episodes of bipolar disorder. Lithium is effective against recurrences of bipolar depression as well as mania. Maintenance therapy prevents or diminishes the intensity of subsequent episodes of bipolar patients with a history of mania. It is quite effective against recurrences of bipolar depression[45].

Despite many pharmacological interventions reported to reduce the risk of suicide among mentally ill patients, especially those with bipolar disorder, the effects of such interventions are inconsistent at best, except with lithium[46].

Lithium is the only medication for which the evidence consistently shows an antisuicidal effect[47]. Lithium's substantial protection against suicide is supported by more compelling evidence than that for any other treatment provided for patients with mood disorders[48]. Evidence of pharmacological prevention of suicide can be found in research on long-term treatment of bipolar and non-bipolar mood disorders with lithium[49].

Studies reporting on suicide and lithium have consistently found lower rates of suicide and suicide attempts during lithium maintenance treatment than without lithium treatment[50]. During long-term lithium treatment, there is a 6.5 fold reduction of suicide, risk of suicides, and life threatening suicide attempts in bipolar patients. Long-term lithium treatment has been associated with a sevenfold lowering of the crude average suicide rate, from 1.78 to 0.25% per year of patients with bipolar disorder[51].

When lithium treatment is discontinued in bipolar patients, there is an increase in suicidal behavior. The risk increases twenty-fold within the first year after discontinuing lithium maintenance treatment[52]. The increase in suicide risk in the first year after lithium discontinuation parallels the clinical finding that morbidity is increased in the first year after lithium discontinuation compared with that in the years before treatment. The risk of both depression and of suicidal act is more elevated after rapid discontinuation. Rapid discontinuation of lithium treatment is a significant risk factor for suicide in bipolar patients. Patients who stop lithium therapy, usually because they were doing well and did not want to continue using it, had a twenty-fold increase in risk of suicidal behavior within the first year without treatment. Therefore, the period immediately after withdrawal of lithium appears to be a high-risk time not only for general morbidity, including depression, but also for suicidal behavior[53].

Lithium is more effective in suicide risk reduction in bipolar patients compared to divalproex or carbamazepine. Suicide and suicide attempts among bipolar patients were more when carbamazepine was prescribed. Mood stabilizer choice and suicide events among bipolar patients in two large HMO's involving over 25,000 patients showed a significantly higher number of in-patient suicide, outpatient suicide attempts, and completed suicides when prescribed divalproex compared to lithium. The 2002 American Psychiatric Association recommends lithium as the first line treatment of bipolar depression, that is, depression with only a past history of mania. Interestingly, an antidepressant for this type of bipolar depression is not recommended[54].

During the time between 1993 and 2001, the number of new lithium prescriptions fell from 653 to 281 in a community geriatric outpatient drug benefit program in Canada. This trend reflects the decrease in prescribing of lithium. Nevertheless, for suicidal patients with mood disorders, it can be life saving. Lithium is more effective in adults than children.

There are several reasons reported for the decline in lithium response rates including changes in the illness, which is a broadening of diagnosis to include psychosis, axis II disorders at earlier age of onset, increased substance abuse, co-morbidity, and more exposure to antidepressants. Changes in the nature of the studies have also influenced prescribing since earlier lithium studies were conducted by investigators skilled in lithium use. There is a misconception that lithium is more difficult to prescribe and has more side effects. Finally, there is decreased residency training in lithium use with a large discrepancy in continuing medical education and corporate marketing by the other popular of anticonvulsant manufacturers.

Pre-lithium labs include the following: 1) an EKG since lithium can be associated with EKG changes such as widening of the QRS complex and bundle branch blocks; 2) a thyroid panel since lithium can induce hypo- or hyperthyroidism; 3) a baseline urinalysis to check the specific gravity, since lithium can induce polydipsia, polyuria, and nocturia; and 4) a baseline CBC since lithium can increase WBCs.

Starting low and going slow is important to increase patient compliance. For example, trying to start 900 mg per day may be too much at once resulting in the patient never have the opportunity to take it again and miss its benefits in suicide risk reduction. I frequently prescribe 300–450 mg per day for one or two days, then increase to 600–900 mg per day, and finally to 1200 mg per day if needed. At that point, I would augment it with another mood stabilizer or atypical antipsychotic. It takes two weeks to build up a steady-state serum lithium level so trying to load or start a patient on high dose lithium may be ineffective.

Adverse reactions to lithium are usually apparent early. I advise the patient to stop lithium if he/she develops any of these three reactions: a rash, heart palpitations, or confusion. Since lithium is not a tranquilizer, if the patient develops confusion, I will stop the medication and reevaluate.

Management of side effects during maintenance treatment is important for the patient. For example, lithium generally will not cause weight gain. It does make the patient thirsty. In addition, the patient needs to be instructed to drink more water when febrile or in any dehydrated state, especially in hot climates, since lithium levels can rise in a dehydrated state and cause toxicity. If the patient is not informed that water should be given, and the patient inadvertently starts drinking high fructose, high calorie fluids, then weight gain is likely. One way to monitor this side effect is to monitor for swelling of the finger with a ring.

Certain drug-drug interactions such as lithium and NSAIDs require special attention. NSAIDs decrease the renal clearance of lithium and high dose NSAIDs can raise lithium levels causing toxicity. Therefore, caution is advised when the patient is also taking ibuprofen, acetaminophen, aspirin, naproxyn, and cox-inhibitors. Caution is also advised with lithium and ace-inhibitors and diuretics.

Monitor lithium levels more closely when adjusting dose or checking compliance or when there are new general medical conditions. Annual CBC, UA, TFTs and EKG tests are advised when monitoring patients on lithium for bipolar disorder. Controlling the amount of lithium dispensed in high-risk suicidal, bipolar patients is advised since it can be fatal in overdose.

## Combination Pharmacotherapy for Treatment Resistant Depression with Suicidality

Some patients with more severe, resistant suicidal major depressive disorder respond inadequately to conventional antidepressant therapy or conventional augmentation pharmacotherpies. As many as 30% of depressed (non-psychotic, non-bipolar) patients may not respond to a variety of standard antidepressant therapy.

As the scope of suicide is increasing, there is an increased risk in mood disorders and a further increase of suicide in treatment resistant, chronic mood disorders. Treatment- resistant depression (TRD) frequently has suicidal thoughts as a prominent symptom[55].

Treatment-resistant depression is defined in psychopharmacology as no response to at least two trials of antidepressants at adequate dose and duration from at least two different classes[56].

For patients with suicidal ideation, unremitting depression can become a precarious clinical situation. Traditional pharmacotherapeutic approaches may not adequately manage clinical signs and symptoms exhibited by patients with non-psychotic unremitting, unipolar, treatment-resistant depression. Symptoms include suicidal thoughts, poor impulse control, near paranoid thinking, marked anxiety and agitation and sleep disturbance. In non-psychotic depressed patients, these symptoms can lead to poor quality of life, recurrent hospitalizations and high risk of suicide[57].

Clinical management of treatment resistant depression includes monitoring adherence, optimization of treatment, diagnostic review, monitoring non-response and partial response, and the use of augmentation strategies[58].

Adherence: one of the first considerations is whether the patient has adhered to the prescribed medication regimen. Patient non-adherence may play a part in apparent treatment resistance in up to 20% of patients considered treatment resistant. Side effects may lead to non-compliance. Careful assessment of side effects and changes in medication, using adjuvant agents or dose adjustments can improve adherence and increase the likelihood of treatment response. The psychiatrist's ability to generate and sustain a therapeutic alliance is important to discussing the downside of taking antidepressants and other matters such as ambivalence about the prospects of having to take medication and the associated stigma of mental illness.

Optimization: full adherence does not ensure response if the antidepressant trial is too short or at too low a dose. Optimizing an ongoing antidepressant trial may mean increasing the dose of the current medication or extending the length of the trial. As many as 20–30% of patients who had an insufficient response to the usual dose of a standard therapy responded to higher doses.

Diagnostic review: no response may be due to misdiagnosis or failure to detect a complicating medical condition. Disorders such as hypothyroidism can render antidepressant therapy ineffective.

Monitoring non-response and partial response: if one antidepressant is not effective, then knowing that the response rate when switching from one to another typically ranges from 40% to 60% across many different classes of antidepressants suggests switching. For example, switching from a failed SSRI to venlafaxine results in a response rate between 33–70%. In non-response, the decision whether to switch or augment remains a question of clinician preference. Unfortunately, a 50% response rate to the second antidepressant means that a significant number of patients who began therapy, about 25% of the group, have developed treatment resistance.

Treatment resistant depressive disorder can be staged, as cancer is staged. One proposed staging criteria for treatment-resistant depression, adapted from Thase and Rush, describes five levels of severity of depression with respect to treatment in different stages.

*Stage 1 is the failure of at least one adequate trial of a major class of antidepressant.*

*Stage 2 is stage 1 resistance plus the failure of an adequate trial of an antidepressant from a distinctly different class.*

*Stage 3 is stage 2 resistance plus the failure of an adequate trial of a tricyclic antidepressant.*

*Stage 4 is stage 3 resistance plus the failure of an adequate trial of a monoamine oxidase inhibitor.*

*Stage 5 is stage 4 resistance plus the failure of a course of bilateral electroconvulsive therapy.*

Conventional augmentation strategies for more severe suicidal depression include adding the following types of medication to an SSRI antidepressant: lithium, thyroid hormone, tricyclic antidepressants, additional antidepressants, stimulants, dopamine agonists, and buspirone.

Adding low dose lithium (300–450 mg per day) can result in significant improvement and in decrease depressive symptoms, including spiraling down into a deep depression or impulsive depressive symptoms. This use of lithium has an effect for non-bipolar depression. Lithium is thought to potentiate serotonergic transmission. Less worry about toxicity at the lower doses and less side effects are reported by the physician and patient.

As an augmentation to antidepressants in unipolar, more treatment resistant depression, low-dose lithium is very effective, especially if the patient also has impulsive suicidality associated with the depressive disorder. Low-dose lithium augmentation is one of the best studied, but one of the least used, augmentation strategies for antidepressant non-responder. In addition, its use in combination with SSRIs or tricyclic antidepressants is reported.

The use of an SSRI plus lithium is the best and most basic example of augmentation of the antidepressant. This combination is particularly effective in suicidal depressed patients who fail to respond to an adequate dose and duration of two different types of antidepressants, such as an SSRI and a TCA. Lithium augmentation of antidepressants for major depressive disorder with suicidality may be the treatment of choice for patients with moderate impulsive suicidal depression, or those with a more refractory history to antidepressant monotherapy.

Augmentation of antidepressants with lithium is one of the most extensively studied augmentation therapies to date. It was first described over twenty years ago. A recent survey, however, shows it is under-prescribed. Most practitioners use lithium as third line options, not first or second line strategies for treatment resistant depression, even though seven of the nine double blind placebo- controlled studies showed a benefit for lithium augmentation with response rates up to 50%.

Low-dose lithium (300 mg/day, 450 mg/day or 600 mg/day) augmentation of antidepressants for depression can limit the annoying side effects of higher dose lithium. In contrast to the higher doses of lithium (1200 mg/day up to 2100 mg/day) used for bipolar disorder in the manic phase, low-dose lithium augmentation to antidepressants offers a unique opportunity to treat impulsive depressive symptoms including suicidality.

The following case is an example of lithium augmentation to an SSRI with a good clinical outcome:

*A 33-year-old, white female with recurrent major depressive disorder taking citalopram 20 mg day prescribed by her OB/GYN, was having increased suicide attempts, becoming more lethal and frequent. She was admitted to the psychiatric hospital for suicidal depression. The patient did not have a history of mania or hypomanic episodes, substance related disorders, or general medical conditions. Her family history was remarkable even though her grandmother suffered from schizophrenia.*

*Her depression was characterized by sadness, hopelessness, agitation, anhedonia, and marked impulsiveness. She had slashed her wrists, overdosed on her father's cardiac medications, and recently tried to run her car off the road. She had insomnia, but no psychosis.*

*The citalopram was increased to 40 mg per day and low dose lithium, at 450 mg per day, was added. Her depressive symptoms resolved, and over the following three years, she had no further suicidal or impulsive thoughts or behaviors.*

The addition of the thyroid hormone, even supraphysiologic doses, to antidepressant therapy was common in the 20th century, but the more modern, trained psychiatrists who rarely do medical history and physical examinations, are cautious about prescribing medical medications without proper medical follow-up. For example, giving a patient with a thyroid nodule that is barely palpable a thyroid hormone could cause hyperplasia and increase the risk and neoplasia. Thyroid hormone is thought to potentiate the noradrenergic system, which may suggest that thyroid supplementation would be more useful when combined with tricyclic antidepressants rather than with SSRIs.

Combining antidepressants requires knowledge of the antidepressants, side effects, the mechanism of action, and drug-drug interactions. For example, it is odd that two, potent, dual acting SNRIs, mirtazepine and venlafaxine, mix for more resistant depressive symptoms. These two, dual-acting antidepressants, the stimulating venlafaxine taken in the morning and the sedating mirtazepine taken at night, can relieve some cases of resistant depression. Two antidepressants can be best combined for the additive effect if different mechanisms of action are employed. An SSRI (fluoxetine) can mix well with an NDRI (bupropion). That combination can further decrease depression and eliminate certain side effects. For example, the addition of bupropion to the SSRI can relieve residual depressive symptoms and counteract SSRI induced sexual dysfunction in many patients.

A recent study suggests that combining citalopram (an SSRI) and bupropion-SR (an NDRI) is more effective than switching to monotherapy. Moreover, that combination treatment is well tolerated with no greater side effect than monotherapy in patients with treatment resistant depression[59].

SSRI polypharmacy, or the combination of two SSRIs, should generally be avoided because the risk of serotonin syndrome is strong. Serotonin syndrome can be life threatening and is characterized by the following: mental status changes including confusion, disorientation, hypomania, restlessness, agitation, myoclonus, hyperreflexia, diaphoresis, shivering, shaking chills, tremor, diarrhea, abdominal cramps, nausea, ataxia, incoordination, and headache. Autonomic dysfunction includes tachycardia, labile blood pressure, and hyperthermia. The serotonin syndrome can be caused by two SSRIs in combination.

The use of stimulants added to antidepressants is controversial. It is generally discouraged in patients with active or a past of substance related disorders. It should be avoided in areas where illicit drug use exists. The psycho-stimulants are considered because they indirectly promote dopamine release in relevant terminal fields of the brain. They also have significant noradrenergic effects.

Although augmenting dopaminergic function has become a strategy for treatment resistant depression (TRD), it has virtually no empirical basis. Most antidepressants have little effect on dopaminergic function; yet dysfunctional dopamine neurotransmission is clearly implicated in symptoms such as anhedonia and psychomotor retardation. In open trials direct dopamine agonists, such as bromocriptine were reported to be useful as an augmentation agent and as monotherapy in depression.

The addition of the non-addicting anxiolytic buspirone can help relieve some co-morbid anxiety symptoms associated with depression, but generally this does not help relieve the suicidality associated with depression.

The anticonvulsant mood stabilizers like valproate or carbamazepine added to an antidepressant does not usually help depression, even though it is more effective for mania or mixed states. Although lamotrigine may help more depressive phases, there is still not enough experience with that anticonvulsant for TRD. Thus, add-on anticonvulsant mood stabilizers generally do not relieve treatment resistant depression.

The addition of benzodiazepines to the antidepressant generally makes the suicidal depression worse. That is, adding long-term use of clonazepam, lorazepam, diazepam, alprazolam, and even zolpidem to an antidepressant for TRD generally makes the depression worse. Since these are hypnotics and minor tranquilizers, they can increase depressive symptoms and cause confusion, memory impairment, forgetfulness, and sleep disturbance. Physiological and psychological dependence can develop and complicate TRD.

The use of antipsychotics in the treatment of depression has a long history[60]. However, until the advent of the newer atypical agents, the use of antipsychotics in mood disorders has been limited to psychotic depression and mania because of the risk of tardive dyskinesia. The use of typical antipsychotics or phenothiazenes such as chlorpromazine and thioridazine, was studied between 1960 and 1976 for use in depressive disorders. In seventeen double-blind trials involving nearly 1700 patients, they were superior to placebo but were consistently associated with a greater incidence of extrapyramidal side effects. The use of phenothiazine antipsychotics in nonpsychotic depression as monotherapy never became widespread; the use of antipsychotic agents in depressive disorders is not a new idea. Further, the combination of a neuroleptic and an antidepressant has been established as a treatment of first choice for the psychotic or delusional forms of major depressive disorder. Likewise, adjunctive therapy with typical, high potent, conventional or typical antipsychotics such as perphenazine and halperoidol, was commonly undertaken in combination with antidepressants for patients with more severe or near-psychotic depressions.

Limitations of the use of conventional antipsychotics in suicidal depression include the worsening of depressive symptoms and the adverse side effects of neurolepic-induced akathisia. Akathisia is associated with an increased risk of suicidality. A particular case of delayed akathisia and suicidal attempts following epidural droperidol infusion is described. Epidural administration of droperidol is used to prevent postoperative nausea and vomiting caused by opioids. A patient was receiving patient-controlled epidural analgesia with a bupivacaine-morphine-droperidol mixture for one and half days following hemorrhoidectomy; he developed paroxysmal adverse reactions of akathisia, dysphoria, and suicidal attempts three days after the initiation of the treatment.

The superiority of the newer antipsychotic medications such as risperidone and olanzapine, in terms of lower rates of extrapyramidal symptoms including akathisia, and lifetime risk of tardive dyskinesia, are now FDA approved for their use in mood disorders, such as bipolar disorder. Clinical trials are being done for their use in treatment resistant depression with suicidality. This allows another option rather than resorting to electro convulsive therapy (ECT).

Novel augmentation strategies have become an important approach for achieving response in treatment-resistant depressed patients with suicidality. They have been particularly helpful in achieving complete remission in partial responders. Some augmentation strategies have been shown to be of value for speeding up initial response.

Recently, psychiatrists have been able to treat depressive disorders more aggressively with safe and better-tolerated psychotropic medication including atypical antipsychotics. There are several case reports that demonstrate adding an adjunctive atypical antipsychotic agent to an antidepressant turns many treatment non-responders with non-psychotic suicidal depression into responders, and the benefits are seen very quickly.

It is not yet known why this approach is effective. Can suicidal thoughts be treated with medications used for a thought disorder? Suicidal thoughts have not traditionally been considered psychotic. Can pervasive, debilitating, severe, and intense suicidal thoughts be considered nearly psychotic? Is the use of atypical antipsychotic medication for extreme, nearly psychotic, suicidal thoughts justified? Alternatively, do atypical antipsychotics safely reduce non-specific mood and anxiety symptoms, such as severe agitation and anxiety in acutely suicidal patients? Do atypical antipsychotics affect those serotonin type 2a receptors in the prefrontal cortex of the brain as described in Chapter 1? The answers are not yet known.

Most research on the use of atypical antipsychotics for mood disorders has focused on the manic episodes of bipolar disorders; there are few, if any, reports for their use in treatment-resistant depression[61]. Two reports augmenting antidepressants with olanzapine and four reports augmenting antidepressants with risperidone are highlighted.

In an eight-week, double-blind study with twenty-eight patients who were diagnosed with recurrent, non-bipolar, treatment-resistant depression without psychotic features, olanzapine plus fluoxetine demonstrated superior efficacy for treating resistant depression compared to either agent alone. Clinical responses were evident by the first week suggesting rapid onset of action. In contrast with the significant response observed with combined therapy, neither fluoxetine nor olanzapine alone was effective in this resistant population. The most frequently reported significant adverse events included somnolence, increased appetite, and weight gain, as well as headache, dry mouth, and nervousness. Both increased appetite and weight gain occurred significantly more frequently among patients treated with olanzapine[62].

Another olanzapine augmentation study involved the olanzapine-fluoxetine combination in treatment-resistant depression. This eight-week, double-blind study had 499 subjects with non-bipolar, non-psychotic, treatment resistant depression who had a history of failing on an SSRI alone, as well as a TCA (nortriptyline). The olanzapine-fluoxetine combination had onset of action within the first week of treatment. This study suggests that the olanzapine-fluoxetine combination is particularly effective in the subset of more treatment-resistant subjects. It represents a promising therapeutic option[63].

Recently, the long-term antidepressant efficacy, tolerability and safety of olanzapine/fluoxetine combination in a seventy-six-week, open-label study were published. This large, open-label study evaluated the combination of olanzapine and fluoxetine in the treatment of patients with major depressive disorder, including those with treatment resistant depression. The findings indicate a robust effect, rapid onset, and sustained maintenance of effect. The five most commonly occurring treatment-emergent adverse events were somnolence, weight gain, dry mouth, increased appetite, and headache. Although such combination treatment is likely to be unnecessary for most cases of major depressive disorder, the olanzapine/fluoxetine combination may represent a possible treatment option for treatment-resistant cases. Alternatively, it would be appropriate in the acute treatment of severe cases where the need for rapid onset is of particular concern, such as in the case of patients hospitalized for suicidality[64].

However, since the side effects of weight gain and sedation with olanzapine are much less with risperidone, low rise risperidone may be a better atypical antipsychotic to augment with an antidepressant in suicidal depressed patients.

Risperidone is a high-potent, atypical antipsychotic that has serotonergic as well as dopaminergic activity. At low doses, risperidone acts as a serotonin type 2a receptor antagonist (See chapter 1). Preclinical data suggests that serotonin type 2a receptor antagonists may enhance the action of serotonin. Four significant case series prescribing low dose risperidone with an antidepressant in treatment resistant depression have emerged.

The first published case series showed risperidone as adjunctive therapy with a selective serotonin reuptake inhibitor improved major depression in treatment-resistant depression with suicidality. These patients had inadequate clinical response to SSRIs alone, severe episodes of major depression, and lack of mania or psychosis. In this report, risperidone was targeted for the suicidal ideation and agitation that was superimposed on depression and anxiety. The improvement with risperidone was rapid[65].

A second case series reports on five, non-psychotic, depressed out-patients with treatment-refractory, prolonged mood disorder who responded to the combination of a MAOI antidepressant (tranylcypromine) and low-dose risperidone. Patients experienced a dramatic and sustained antidepressant response to the combination. Despite the lack of psychosis and previous, less than successful MAOI monotherapy, these patients responded to the combination of tranylcypromine and risperidone. The tranylcypromine and risperidone were started simultaneously in the patients with the most dramatic response[66].

Two other complementary case series reports using risperidone augmentation to antidepressants demonstrate similar remarkable findings.

The Hamilton Rating Scale for Depression (HAM-D) was used to measure the change in depression symptoms in eight outpatients with treatment-resistant depression. Low dose risperidone (0.5 to 1.0 mg) was added to the SSRI, and the measured response was significant and dramatic. The time to response was in as little as one day. All patients remitted in as little as one week. The patients tolerated the low-dose risperidone well without side effects[67]. One patient, who was once scheduled for electro-convulsive therapy, wrote back two months later and stated,

*"I visited your office in a distressed state of mind and utter despair. You prescribed 1 mg risperdal with 30 mg of Paxil and the results were instantly miraculous. I have been able to sleep peacefully and my appetite has returned. I have also been able to cope patiently with the daily anxieties at work and home and actually look forward to a productive routine."*

In the complementary case series of five out-patients suffering from treatment-resistant depression with suicidality, the Clinical Global Impressions scale (CGI) was used to measure the severity of illness and the degree of improvement after three months of treatment with low-dose risperidone augmentation of antidepressants. The dramatic effect noted was not only present, but also safely sustained, for several months up to several years[68]. The first five original cases describe this novel and effective treatment strategy I recently published in the *Journal of Clinical Psychopharmacology.*

*Case 1: The patient is a forty-nine-year-old, divorced, white, female outpatient diagnosed with major depressive disorder without psychotic features. She has had three hospitalizations due to depression with suicidal ideation, intentions, and plans. Twenty years ago, she attempted to commit suicide by arson. Another major depressive episode occurred during the postpartum period. A recent episode was associated with increasing suicidal ideation and plan. She recently wrote a suicide note to her sister. There are no significant general medical conditions or substance related disorders. There is a strong family history of depression. Numerous trials of antidepressants include fluoxetine at 40 to 60 mg per day for seven years, paroxetine at 40 mg per day for eight months, trazodone at 300 mg per day for six months, bupropion at 100 mg per day for two months, all were ineffective. Augmentation with lithium carbonate at 900 mg per day for one month and zolpidem at 10 mg per day for one year proved ineffective. For severe agitation thioridazine, from 25 mg to 150 mg per day, was prescribed, intermittently for over two years without any beneficial effects. She reported that over twenty years, none of the psychotropic medication has been effective.*

*On exam, she exhibited marked anxiety, agitation, insomnia, depression, and suicidal ideation, but no mania or psychosis.*

*Risperidone at 0.5 mg per day was added to fluoxetine at 60 mg and trazodone at 100 mg per day. Over the next two weeks, the risperidone was increased to 1.0 mg without developing any new side effects. Beyond the next several months, the patient reported much improved sleeping and less depression and disorganized thinking. She stated, "I don't have as many suicidal thoughts anymore. I can think now. I guess the medication is working." She has a new companion and recently purchased a new trailer with appliances. Her quality of life continues to improve.*

*Case 2: The patient is 48-year-old, white, female outpatient diagnosed with mood disorder, NOS. She has had numerous hospitalizations for major depression including several suicide attempts, overdosing on psychotropic medication as well as over-the-counter medications (NSAIDS). Twenty years ago, she overdosed on diazepam and attempted to shoot herself, using a gun "to blow her brains out." Another suicide attempt involved trying to walk in front of a semi truck, and recently while intoxicated with alcohol, she wrote an extensive suicide letter. Numerous trials of antidepressant monotherapies, such as sertraline at 150 mg for eight months, were ineffective. Antidepressant polypharmacy such as paroxetine at 40 mg plus bupropion at 450 mg and trazodone at 150 mg per day had been ineffective for over fourteen month. Augmentation with valproic acid at 1250 mg per day for fourteen months was also ineffective.*

*On exam, she reported worsening self- esteem and depression with poor impulse control, insight, and judgment. She recently began having indiscreet sexual affairs with married men. She feels worthless and hopeless. Insight and judgment is poor. There are no signs of mania or psychosis.*

*Risperidone at 1 mg per day was added to the bupropion at 300 mg and valproic acid at 1250 mg per day, while discontinuing the daily dose of paroxetine and trazodone. Over the next five months, her insight and judgment improved. There were no more impulsive behaviors. There was less anxiety and agitation. Her attention and concentration improved, with no further depression or suicidal ideation, intentions, or plans. She reported, "My thinking is much clearer. I feel human again. I can actually sit and read a book." She is working again and has recently married, optimistic and more confident that "finally things are turning around."*

*Case 3: The patient is a 52-year-old, female outpatient diagnosed with major depressive disorder without psychosis. She has had recurrent episodes of depression, the first one being after the birth of her fourth child in the postpartum period. She had a lumpectomy, chemotherapy, and radiation therapy for breast cancer two years ago, and she currently is prescribed tamoxifen. There is no history of mania or substance related disorder. Numerous trials of antidepressants including fluoxetine at 40 mg per day for two months, paroxetine at 20 mg per day for three months, citalopram at 60 mg per day for three months, imipramine at 250 mg per day for twenty-four months were ineffective. The combination of citalopram at 40 mg and imipramine at 150 mg per day was ineffective, too. Augmentation with benzodiazepines including alprazolam at 1.0 mg per day for one month was discontinued due to side effects of forgetfulness, confusion and worsening depression.*

*On exam, there was mild paranoia, but no delusions, hallucinations, mania. Her mood is depressed and affect flat, with poverty of speech and poverty of thought, hypersomnia, and increased appetite with a forty-pound weight gain. She has doom and gloom thinking stating, "Life is not worth living. I would be better off if I were no longer here."*

*Risperidone at 0.5 mg per day was added the paroxetine at 30 mg per day, with an immediate beneficial effect noted. Although the dose was adjusted to 1.0 mg risperidone per day for a total of thirteen months, there was no additional clinical benefit, so it was decreased to 0.5 mg for seven more months, and she did not exhibit any side effects. Over the past several years, the patient's major depressive disorder has been in full remission. Her depression no longer impairs her quality of life. Aside from changing the paroxetine to citalopram and resuming low dose imipramine, the patient continues to exhibit better attention and concentration, a brighter affect, and no further doom and gloom thinking or mild paranoia. She started attending church social events and is now engaging in a new, satisfying, social relationship. She is tolerating the risperidone well without any side effects and does not want to stop it.*

*Case 4: The patient is a 61-year-old, white, female outpatient diagnosed with major depressive disorder without psychosis. Five years ago, she overdosed on amitriptyline and diazepam. Since then, the depression has not remitted. Numerous trials of antidepressants, including high dose mirtazepine at*

*60 mg per day for two months, sertraline at 100 mg per day for two months, doxepin at 200 mg per day for eighteen months, amitriptyline at 200 mg per day for twelve months, and nefazodone at 400 mg per day for six months, have been ineffective. Polypharmacy combinations including trazodone at 200 mg and mirtazapine at 30 mg, also have been ineffective. Augmentation with anxiolytics including flurazepam at 30 mg for seven months and lorazepam at 2 mg for two years, has not provided relief.*

*On exam, there was anhedonia, social withdrawal, poor attention and concentration, suicidal thoughts, flat affect, marked anxiety and agitation as well as sleep disturbance, but no hallucinations or delusions.*

*Risperidone at 0.5 mg per day was added to the trazodone at 200 mg and mirtazapine at 30 mg per day, while the lorazepam was tapered off slowly for 1 month. Risperidone was increased to 1.0 mg per day after six months. The patient did not develop any side effects. Since starting risperidone over eight months ago, the patient denies all depression. There were no further suicidal thoughts and much less anhedonia. Sleeping improved, attention and concentration improved. There was relief of marked agitation and anxiety. Her quality of life remarkably improved. She began doing art-work and entered the work in a local fair. She resumed hobbies such as photography and gardening, and she started a book about her family members.*

*Case 5: The patient is a 59-year-old, married, white, female outpatient diagnosed with major depressive disorder without psychotic features. There is a strong family history of suicide. Specifically, eleven of fourteen offspring in two generations have committed suicide. There are no significant general medical problems or substance related disorders. She has been maintained on lithium carbonate at 900 mg and fluoxetine at 60 mg per day over the past several years without relief. Numerous trials of antidepressants included fluoxetine at 40 mg per day for three years, bupropion at 300 mg per day for four years, paroxetine at 40 mg per day for two months. Augmentation with valproic acid at 750 mg per day for three months and diazepam at 5 mg per day for two months were ineffective.*

*On exam, the patient had chronic suicidal thoughts, recently escalating into intentions and plans. She would not share her plan, but she stated she "put two of her dogs to sleep" and wrote two separate suicidal notes to her family stating, "I'm tired of fighting this depression in and out of the hospital." She wrote a third suicidal note directly to the local county coroner stating "I, and I alone, am responsible for this action. No one is to blame." [note: the patient would not share this information at the time of the examination. It was only revealed many months later]. Marked anxiety and agitation, insomnia, and poor impulse control, insight, and judgment were evident. No delusions or hallucinations were present. There was marked anhedonia. The patient's husband was very concerned.*

*Risperidone at 0.5 mg per day was added to the fluoxetine at 40 mg and lithium carbonate at 900 mg per day. The patient tolerated the medication well, and it was increased to 1.0 mg per day three weeks later. Since the addition of risperidone, the husband reports "it is like a miracle." The patient has a brighter affect, no depression, and no suicidal ideation, intentions, or plans. She ripped up the suicidal notes and can not believe she was thinking that way. She wants to improve her physical appearance. She is doing more with the husband and had recently reestablished family relations. She is concerned about her son who is also suffering from the same condition.*

These cases illustrate novel approaches in treating the most resistant and suicidal depressed outpatients in the psychiatric clinic. The addition of low dose risperidone to antidepressants and/or mood stabilizers resulted in marked and sustained improvement in mood and anxiety symptoms in each of these patients. Patient similarities included age greater than 45 years, gender, and a history of multiple failed antidepressant/mood stabilizing medications with unremitting depression. All patients exhibited suicidal ideation. After the addition of low-dose risperidone, none of these patients reported further suicidal thoughts, intentions, or plans. Patients also reported less agitation and anxiety, better sleep quality, better impulse control, and the demonstrated clearer, less disorganized thinking. All patients were markedly ill, very much improved, and documented by the same outpatient psychiatrist and advanced nurse practitioner for over a three-year period. No patient required hospitalization.

Similar cases of severely suicidal depressed (treatment resistant depression with suicidality) hospitalized patients are described:

*Case 6: The patient is a 46-year-old, white female admitted to the hospital for depression. She was transferred from another hospital after attempting to hang herself while in the general hospital. She was admitted to the general hospital for medical evaluation after a carbon monoxide inhalation with opiate intoxication in a suicide attempt. The patient has a diagnosis of bipolar disorder, with a recent depressive episode. There is a strong family history of suicide in the family. The patient has been seeing a therapist twice a week for several months. The patient has had two previous psychiatric hospitalizations for suicidal depression. Her medical problems include the need for a wheelchair due to damage of muscles of left lower extremity. Other medical problems include recent renal and respiratory failure from the overdose, migraine headaches, hyperlipidemia, and benign breast lesions. Surgery includes history of bilateral salpingo-ophreoectomy, osteomyelitis, and mastoidectomy. She requires urinary self-catheterization for a neurogenic bladder.*

*She has had numerous trials of antianxiety and mood stabilizer medications without relief. She is allergic to citalopram, and has failed multiple trials of lithium, carbamazepine, and divalproex. Haloperidol has not been effective. She had no history of drug or alcohol use.*

*Her depression is associated with sadness, crying, hopelessness, and poor impulse control but not with delusions or hallucinations. She describes at least four episodes of a mood disturbance in the previous twelve months, which is considered rapid cycling.*

*Her mental status showed mildly pressured speech, labile affect, depressed mood, but no delusions or hallucinations, only near paranoia under stress. She exhibited marked agitation, sleep disturbance, and very poor impulse control. The admitting diagnosis was bipolar, type I recent episode depression and borderline personality traits.*

*The hospital course involved discontinuing benzodiazepines. Low-dose risperidone was started at 0.5 mg at night with valproic acid at 1250 mg per day. The patient had a marked improvement. There were no more negative suicidal thoughts. She tolerated the medication well without any side effects. Although issues around pain frequently was a focus of clinical attention, after five days, her mental status examination showed much better activities of daily living, good eye contact, no depression, no anxiety, and no suicidal ideations intentions, or plans. Her affect was brighter. Attention, concentration, and impulse control improved. She complained of less pain.*

*After hospitalization, she returned home with her friend, rather than to a nursing home, and she continues care in the out-patient community clinic. She continues taking her medication, and she has begun regular physical therapy and pain management at a specialized pain clinic.*

*Case 7: The patient is a 29-year-old, white male committed to the psychiatric hospital after being medically cleared from the local hospital. His chief complaint was depression. According to the physician's emergency certificate, the patient was brought into the psychiatric assessment services with three family members who believed that he would kill himself. The patient has recurrent major depressive disorders and dysthymia.*

*He had a serous suicide attempt just two weeks prior. That recent depressive episode was associated with depression several weeks prior to admission. It culminated in a serious suicide attempt with carbon monoxide poisoning in the rural county. Flight ambulance was required to transport him to the hospital for life saving measures. He was on temporary mechanical ventilation. Since then his depression with suicidality has not improved. He states that his suicidal thoughts are easy to act on. He denies any associated psychotic or manic symptoms. Depression is associated with crying, sadness, hopelessness, doom and gloom thinking, anhedonia, erratic eating and sleeping patterns, and impairment in his psychosocial functioning. Dysthymia has been present for twenty years, according to the patient, with recurrent major depressive episodes, moderate without psychotic features. He was recently treated with venlafaxine and paroxetine monotherapies for several weeks at moderately high doses without effective results. Recent stressors include work, family, and relationships. He denies substance abuse or alcohol use prior to this suicide attempt. He also denies being intoxicated during the attempt, however, his blood alcohol level prior to admission was 0.08.*

*At age twenty-five and twenty-seven, the patient had been treated at a local private psychiatric hospital for recurrent suicide attempts. He has a history of inpatient substance abuse treatment for alcohol dependence.*

*Medical problems include hypertension that required clonidine therapy. He suffered a mild head injury from a motor vehicle accident four months ago with no associated seizures or other neurological deficits. The patient has a history of renal artery stenosis for which he is under the care of a primary care physician. The patient is allergic to penicillin.*

*His mental status exam on admission showed an anxious, but cooperative patient. There was no agitation. Sleep and appetite have been poor. Mood was depressed. Affect was flat. Thinking revealed mild poverty of thought, with no delusions or hallucinations. There was marked doom and gloom thinking. Insight and judgment were poor. Impulse control was poor. He scored 23 out of 30 on the mini mental status examination.*

*The admitting diagnosis was major depression disorder, moderate, without psychosis, and most likely treatment resistant with marked suicidality.*

*The hospital course was relatively uneventful. He agreed to start rather aggressive pharmacotherapy. In particular, he was started on sertraline and low-dose risperidone. He could not take lithium due to active renal disease and his history of non-compliance and intolerance to other mood stabilizers. Although this was an off-label indication, the patient agreed to the trial. He responded rapidly and effectively without any adverse effects in less than one week. His suicidal thoughts were relieved, and depression was in remission in less than one week. His appetite and sleeping improved. Affect was brighter, and he felt better "for the first time in my life."*

*This brief five-day hospitalization and treatment proved quite effective.*

*He was released from the hospital on Christmas Eve, with a one-month supply of medications including sertraline and risperidone. The patient will follow up at the community mental health clinic for continuing outpatient psychiatric aftercare, including group therapy and medication management. He will follow up medical issues with his primary care physician. The prognosis is good, and he should remain in remission and abstain from any alcohol use.*

These cases may also represent aggressive treatment of severe anxiety and agitation with an atypical antipsychotic medication in treatment resistant depressed suicidal patients, emphasizing the importance of treating acute risk symptoms. This concept is especially relevant since antidepressants for example exert little antisuicide effects until treatment is established for six months. It shows that patients who fail to improve or show worsening symptoms, especially anxiety and agitation, should be considered for immediate treatment. Aggressive novel combination pharmacotherapy in treating symptoms of agitation and anxiety in depressed patients may provide an opportunity for clinicians to intervene and prevent suicide in the short term.

Several biochemical reasons explain how the combination of atypical antipsychotics and antidepressants seem to be effective in treatment-resistant suicidal depression. They can be understood in relation to the antipsychotic medication effects on the serotonin, dopamine, norepinepherine and other neuroreceptors in central nervous system.

Atypical antipsychotics and antidepressants in combination increase the release of more norepinepherine and dopamine in the prefrontal cortex compared to either alone. Serotonergic properties are also important. The novel serotonin dopamine antagonist, risperidone, has predominantly serotonergic properties at low dose (0.5 to

1.0 mg/day) by acting mostly as a serotonin type 2 receptor antagonist. Prescribed with that intention, it has a marked effect on the serotonin type 2a receptor and enhances the action of serotonin in the prefrontal cortex of the brain, most often associated with suicide.

Risperidone augmentation to antidepressants in treatment-resistant depression is being further studied during severe major depressive episodes often associated with suicidality. Large and controlled clinical trials to validate findings in these case report series are being completed to determine if it is a safe and effective treatment strategy in view of the high morbidity and mortality in treatment-resistant depressed patients.

The ARISe-RD, augmentation with risperidone in resistant depression, clinical trial is a large international study designed to evaluate the efficacy, safety, and maintenance effect of risperidone augmentation to SSRI monotherapy in patients with unipolar treatment resistant depression[69]. Interim results from the open label phase of the study conclude there is a high non-response rate with citalopram monotherapy to validate the concept and meet the definition of treatment resistant depression. Also improvement with risperidone augmentation was robust, rapid (by day 4), and progressive. Moreover, remission was achieved with risperidone augmentation in more than 50% of patients. There was significant improvement in quality of life, even over a relatively short study period. Risperidone augmentation was associated with an improvement in self-rated sexual functioning in females. There was no increased risk of movement disorders. Subsequent data from the double-blind relapse prevention phase of the study will provide further information on the long-term benefit-risk profile of risperidone augmentation to SSRIs in treatment-resistant depression[70]. The unique serotonergic properties of low dose risperidone, less than or equal to 1.0mg per day, highlights this neuroleptic agent with strong 5-HT2A antagonism. It is frequently combined with SSRIs and is quite well tolerated in a vast majority of cases in patients with bipolar depression, psychotic depression, and treatment resistant depression with suicidality. These results were recently presented at the Collegium Internationale Neuropsychopharmacologicum, the oldest international group dedicated to the advancement of psychopharmacology, during the June 2004 convention in Paris, France.

Ziprasidone, another novel, high potent atypical antipsychotic with strong serotonergic properties, may be similarly effective as an augmentation to selective serotonin reuptake inhibitors (SSRIs) for SSRI-resistant major depressive disorder. The pattern of 5-HT2 receptor occupancy of low plasma level of ziprasidone (20 ng/ml) with little D2 receptor occupancy is a similar pattern seen with low dose risperidone[71]. Ziprasidone has potent affinity for the 5-HT1A receptor. It being a strong 5-HT1A (not 5-HT2A) receptor agonist (not antagonist) sets it apart from other atypical antipsychotics. These strong serotonergic properties seem to be involved in depression and suicide. In a recent study, a significant improvement in depressive symptoms by week 1 occurred with the addition of ziprasidone to the antidepressant regimen. One in every two patients with treatment resistant depression responded when ziprasidone was added to their antidepressant regimen. Overall, one in every four patients experienced complete remission by the end of the six-week trial. It was concluded that ziprasidone augmentation should be among the options considered after a patient does not respond to an adequate SSRI trial[72].

However, in medically ill or geriatric patients, care and caution of such combination pharmacotherapy as described is warranted. Knowledge about the different receptor binding profiles of low- versus high-dose risperidone and drug-drug interactions (ie…paroxetine increases risperidone) is essential in safely using such novel combination pharmacotherapy in patients with treatment resistant depression with suicidality. One case describes a serious outcome if the dose of the risperidone is not fixed and low. The development of serotonin syndrome in an elderly patient taking paroxetine and risperidone resulted in a fatal outcome.

*An 86-year-old man presented himself to the emergency room after several days of increased confusion and generalized weakness. His medical history included hypertension, hyperlipidemia, depression, and dementia. His medications included quinapril at 40 mg BID, simvastatin at 20 mg HS, paroxetine at 10 mg, and risperidone at 0.25 mg. The patient's confusion worsened, and he underwent changes resembling delirium. After being placed in a geri chair, he became extremely agitated. Next, he was treated with escalating doses of risperidone at 0.5 mg BID with 0.5 mg every six hours as needed. He alternated between extreme agitation and unresponsiveness. The patient died on day five, at a time when he was taking risperidone 2–3 mg per day in addition to his other medications.*

The patient's presentation is consistent with serotonin syndrome, likely precipitated by the combination of paroxetine and risperidone. Despite these rare case reports, the pharmacological armamentarium available to help clinicians treat acute and chronic suicidality associated with mental disorders is broad and continues to grow.

Other somatic treatment for depression exists when depression fails to respond to any medication, medication combination, and/or psychotherapy. This non-pharmacotherapy, FDA approved treatment widely available in the United States is ECT (electro-convulsive therapy). I have not had to refer any of my suicidal patients for ECT throughout my ten years of clinical practice.

Yet another new treatment with promise for resistant depression is daily, prefrontal repetitive transcranial magnetic stimulation (rTMS) given over several weeks. Instead of using electrical energy to induce a seizure, rTMS uses magnetic fields to non-convulsively stimulate the brain. A handheld electrical coil is positioned on the scalp of an awake and alert patient. The coil is powered by capacitors that send an electrical current pulse through the coil. The electrical current creates a magnetic field that passes unimpeded through the skull to the brain. The magnetic field pulse induces electric fields in the brain that depolarize the neurons. rTMS is generally tolerated very well without any cognitive side effects. It can produce transient headaches that usually respond to simple analgesics like acetaminophen. The biggest safety concern with rTMS involves the possibility of producing a seizure. Since the introduction of safety guidelines five years ago, however, there have been no reported inadvertent seizures. Patients are free to drive home and even return to work after a treatment. The most important concern with a new treatment is whether it actually works. Controversy exists over whether rTMS is effective for depressive symptoms. Four meta-analyses have been performed on the twenty published trials, and they have shown rTMS to be effective in reducing depressive symptoms. The few studies so far that has directly compared rTMS with ECT have found them to be equally effective in treating nonpsychotic depressed patients. There are no specific studies using rTMS for suicidality. Currently rTMS has not been approved for the treatment of depression by the U.S. FDA[73].

# CHAPTER 3 END NOTES

(1)  Clark NG. Consensus development conference on antipsychotic drugs and obesity and diabetes. *Diabetes Care* 2004; 27:596-601.

(2)  Meyer JM. A retrospective comparison of weight, lipid, and glucose changes between risperidone and olanzapine treated inpatients: metabolic outcomes after 1 year. *J Clin Psychiatry* 2002; 63:425-433.

(3)  Ananth J, Johnson KM, Levander EM, Harry JL. Diabetic ketoacidosis, neuroleptic malignant syndrome and myocardial infarction in a patient taking risperidone and lithium carbonate. *J Clin Psychiatry* 2004; 65:724.

(4)  Selemon LD, Lidow MS, Goldman-Rakic PS. Increased volume and glial density in primate prefrontal cortex associated with chronic antipsychotic drug exposure. *Biol Psychiatry.* 1999; 46:161-172.

(5)  Ananth H, et al. Cortical and subcortical gray matter abnormalities in schizophrenia determined through structural magnetic resonance imaging with optimized volumetric voxel-based morphometry. *Am J Psychiatry.* 2002; 159:1497-1505.

(6)  Marder SR. Antipsychotic medications. In: Schatzberg AF, Nemeroff CB, eds. *Textbook of Psychopharmacology.* 2nd ed. Washington, DC: American Psychiatric Press, Inc; 1998:309-321.

(7)  Conley RR, Tamminga CA, Bartko JJ, et al. Olanzapine compared with chlorpromazine in treatment-resistant schizophrenia. *Am J Psychiatry.* 1998; 155:914-920.

(8)  Davis JM, Chen N. Are second-generation antipsychotics a homogeneous group? *Primary Psychiatry.* 2002; 9:54-62.

(9)  Viner MW, Schroeder S, Kamper P. A practical classification of current atypical antipsychotics. *Primary Psychiatry.* 2000; 7:84-88.

(10)  Conley RR, Mahmoud R. A randomized double-blind study of risperidone and olanzapine in the treatment of schizophrenia or schizoaffective disorder. *Am J Psychiatry.* 2002; 158:765-774.

(11)  Csernansky JG, Mahmoud R, Brenner R. A comparison of risperidone and haloperidol for the prevention of relapse in schizophrenia. *N Engl J Med.* 2002; 346:16-22.

(12)  Schatzberg AF, Cole JO, DeBattista C. Antipsychotic drugs. In: *Manual of Clinical Psychopharmacology.* 3rd ed. Washington, DC: American Psychiatric Press, Inc; 1997:113-180.

(13)  Love RC, Conley RR, Kelly DL, et al. A dose-outcome analysis of risperidone. *J Clin Psychiatry.* 1999; 60:771-775.

(14)  Hong KS, Cheong SS, Woo JM, et al. Risperidone-induced tardive dyskinesia [letter]. *Am J Psychiatry.* 1999; 156:1290.

(15)  Pies RW. Antipsychotics. In: *Handbook of Essential Psychopharmacology.* Washington, DC: American Psychiatric Press, Inc; 1998 113-210.

(16)  Weiden P, Aquila R, Standard J. Atypical antipsychotic drugs and long-term outcome in schizophrenia. *J Clin Psychiatry.* 1996; 57(suppl 11):53-60.

(17)  Ganguli R, Brar JS, Ayrton Z. Weight gain with atypical antipsychotic medications. Presented at the Annual Meeting of the American Psychiatric Association, May 30-June 4, 1998; Toronto, Ontario, Canada.

(18) Wirshing DA, Wirshing WC, Kysar L, et al. Novel antipsychotics: comparison of weight-gain liabilities. *J Clin Psychiatry*. 1999; 60:358-363.

(19) Tran PV, Dellva MA, Tollefson GD, et al. Extrapyramidal symptoms and tolerability of olanzapine versus haloperidol in the acute treatment of schizophrenia. *J Clin Psychiatry*. 1997; 58:205-211.

(20) Alphs LD, Anand R. Clozapine: the commitment to patient safety. *J Clin Psychiatry*. 1999; 60(suppl 12):39-42.

(21) Fleischhacker WW. Clozapine: a comparison with other novel antipsychotics. *J Clin Psychiatry*. 1999; 60(suppl 12):30-34.

(22) Wirshing DA, Marshall BD Jr, Green MF, et al. Risperidone in treatment-refractory schizophrenia. *Am J Psychiatry*. 1999; 156:1374-1379.

(23) Stahl SM. Essential Psychopharmacology. Cambridge, UK: Cambridge University Press; 1996: 272-273.

(24) Hand TH, Hu XT, Wang RY. Differential effects of acute clozapine and haloperidol on the activity of ventral tegmental (A10) and nigrostriatal (A9) dopamine neurons. *Brain Res* 1987; 415:257-269.

(25) Hippius H. A historical perspective of clozapine. *J Clin Psychiatry*. 1999; 60 (suppl 12):22-23.

(26) Viner MW, Escobar JI, Werick T. Clozapine plus psychoeducation in treatment refractory schizophrenia. *Neuropsychopharmacology* 1994; 10(3S/Part 2) 207S.

(27) Novartis Pharmaceuticals USA. Press Releases. FDA Committee Recommends Approval for Clozaril to Treat Suicidal Behavior. Available at: http://www.pharma.us.novartis.com/newsroom/pressReleases/releaseDetail.jsp?PRID=403Accessed November 15, 2002

(28) Glick ID, Zaninelli R, Hsu C, Young FK, Weiss L, et al. Patterns of concomitant psychotropic medication use during a 2-year study comparing clozapine and olanzapine for the prevention of suicidal behavior. *J Clin Psychiatry* 2002; 65:679-685

(29) Meltzer HY, Alphs L, Green AI, et al. Clozapine treatment for suicidality in schizophrenia: International Suicide Prevention Trial (InterSePT). *Arch Gen Psychiatry*. 2003; 60:82-91.

(30) Viner MW, Escobar JI. An apparent neurotoxicity associated with clozapine. *J Clin Psychiatry*. 1994; 55:38.

(31) Barbui C, Campomori A, D'avanzo B, et al. Antidepressant drug use in Italy since the introduction of SSRIs: national trends, regional differences and impact on suicide rates. *Soc Psychiatry Psychiatr Epidemiol*. 1999; 34:152-156.

(32) Lin EHB, Von Korff M, Katon W, et al. The role of the primary care physician in patients' adherence to antidepressant therapy. *Med Care*. 1995; 33:67-74.

(33) Isacsson G, Holmgren P, Druid H, et al. Psychotropics and suicide prevention. Implications from toxicological screening of 5281 suicides in Sweden 1992-1994. *Br J Psychiatry*. 1999; 174:259-265.

(34) Henriksson S, Boethius G, Isacsson G. Suicides are seldom prescribed antidepressants: findings from a prospective prescription database in Jamtland county, Sweden, 1985-1995. *Acta Psychiatr Scand* . 2001; 103:301-306.

(35) Olfson M, Marcus SC, Druss, B, et al. National trends in the outpatient treatment of depression. *JAMA*; 2002; 287:203-210.

(36) Kramer PD. *Listening to Prozac*. 1993 Viking Penguin Books USA Inc. New York, New York

(37) Carlsten A, Waern M, Ekedahl A, Ranstam J. Antidepressant medication and suicide in Sweden. *Pharmacoepidemiol Drug Saf* 2001; 10:525-530

(38) Rihmer, 2001 as cited in: Hall WD, Mant A, Mitchell PB, et al. Association between antidepressant prescribing and suicide in Australia, 1991-2000; trend analysis. *BMJ* 2003; 326:1008

(39) Barbui C, Campomori A, D'Avanzo B, et al. Antidepressant drug use in Italy since the introduction of SSRIs: national trends, regional differences and impact on suicide rates. *Soc Psychiatry Psychiatr Epidemiol* 1999; 34:152-156

(40) Thase ME, Entusah AR, Rudolph RL. Remission rates during treatment with venlafaxine or selective serotonin reuptake inhibitors. *Br J Psychiatry* 2001; 178:234-241.

(41) Anttila S, Leinonen E. Duloxetine. Eli Lilly. *Curr Opin Investig Drugs*. 2002; 3:1217-1221.

(42) Howland RH, Thase ME. What to do with SSRI nonresponders? *J Pract Psychiatry Behav Health*. 1999;

5:216-223.

(43) Camardo J. Dear Healthcare letter Professional letter Wyeth®, June 3, 2004.

(44) Preskorn SH, Baker B. Fatality associated with combined fluoxetine-amitriptyline therapy. *JAMA*. [letter to editor]. 1997; 277:1682.

(45) Fava M, Rosenbaum JF, McGrath PF, et al. Lithium and tricyclic augmentation of fluoxetine treatment for resistant major depression: a double-blind, controlled study. *Am J Psychiatry*. 1994; 151:1372-1374.

(46) Baumann P, Nil R, Souche A, et al. A double-blind, placebo-controlled study of citalopram with and without lithium in the treatment of therapy-resistant depressive patients: a clinical, pharmacokinetic, and pharmacogenetic investigation. *J Clin Psychopharmacol*. 1996; 16:307-314.

(47) Tondo L, Ghiani C, Albert M. Pharmacologic interventions in suicide prevention. *J Clin Psychiatry*. 2001; 62(suppl 25):51-55.

(48) Baldessarini RJ, Tondo L, Hennen J. Treating the suicidal patient with bipolar disorder. Reducing suicide risk with lithium. *Ann N Y Acad Sci*. 2001; 932:24-38.

(49) Goodwin FK, Ghaemi SN. The impact of mood stabilizers on suicide in bipolar disorder: a comparative analysis. *Primary Psychiatry*. 1999; 6:61-66.

(50) Tondo L, Baldessarini RJ. Reduced suicide risk during lithium maintenance treatment. *J Clin Psychiatry*. 2000; 61(suppl 9):97-104.

(51) Baldessarini RJ, Tondo L, Hennen J. Antisuicidal effects of lithium in manic-depressive disorders. *J Clin Psychiatry*. 1999; 60(suppl 2):77-84.

(52) Baldessarini RJ, Tondo L, Viguera AC. Effects of discontinuing lithium maintenance treatment. *Bipolar Disord*. 1999; 1:17-24.

(53) Suppes T, Baldessarini RJ, Faedda GL, et al. Risk of recurrence following discontinuation of lithium treatment in bipolar disorder. *Arch Gen Psychiatry*. 1991; 48:1082-1088.

(54) Goodwin FK. Update of treatment for bipolar disorder. Paper presented at: The Annual Meeting of the American Society of Clinical Psychopharmacology, November 2-3, 2002. San Francisco, CA.

(55) Fava M, Davidson KG. Definition and epidemiology of treatment-resistant depression. *Psychiatr Clin North Am*. 1996; 19:179-200.

(56) Thase ME, Rush AJ. Treatment-resistant depression. In: Bloom FE, Kupfer DJ, eds. *Psychopharmacology: The fourth generation of progress*. New York, NY: Raven Press; 1995: 1081-1097.

(57) Nicholas LM, Golden RN. Managing the suicidal patient. *Clin Cornerstone*. 2001; 3:47-57.

(58) Thase ME. What role do atypical antipsychotic drugs have in treatment-resistant depression? *J Clin Psychiatry*. 2002; 63:95-103.

(59) Lam RW, Hossie H, Solomons K, Yatham LN. Citalopram and bupropion-SR: Combining versus switching in patients with treatment-resistant depression. *J Clin Psychiatry*. 2004; 65:337-340.

(60) Sachs GS. Treatment-resistant bipolar depression. *Psychiatr Clin North Am*. 1996; 19:215-236.

(61) Keck P, McElroy SL, Strakowski SM. Anticonvulsants and antipsychotics in the treatment of bipolar disorder. *J Clin Psychiatry*. 1998; 59:74-81.

(62) Shelton RC, Tollefson GD, Tohen M, et al. A novel augmentation strategy for treating resistant major depression. *Am J Psychiatry*. 2001; 158:131-134.

(63) Dube S, Shelton RC, Paul S, et al. Olanzapine-fluoxetine combination in treatment-resistant depression. Poster presented at: Annual Meeting of the American College of Neuropsychopharmacology. December 9-13, 2001. Honolulu, Hawaii.

(64) Corya SA, Andersen SW, Detke HC, Kelly LS, VanCampen LE, et al. Long-term antidepressant efficacy and safety of olanzapine/fluoxetine combination: a 76 week open-label study. *J Clin Psychiatry*. 2003; 64:1349-56.

(65) O'Connor M, Silver H. Adding risperidone to selective serotonin reuptake inhibitor improves chronic depression. *J Clin Psychopharmacol*. 1998; 18: 89-91

(66) Stoll AL, Haura G. Tranylcypromine plus risperidone for treatment-refractory major depression. *J Clin Psychopharmacol*. 2000; 20:495-496.

(67) Ostroff RB, Nelson CJ. Risperidone augmentation of selective serotonin reuptake inhibitors in major depression. *J Clin Psychiatry.* 1999; 60:256-258.

(68) Viner MW, Chen Y, Bakshi I, et al. Low-dose risperidone augmentation of antidepressants in nonpsychotic depressive disorders with suicidal ideation. *J Clin Psychopharmacol.* 2003; 23:1-4-106

(69) Rapaport M, Canuso C, Turkoz, I, Loescher A, Lasser RA, Gharabawi G. Preliminary results from ARISe-RD (Augmentation with risperidone in resistant depression) trial. Poster at the 156th Annual Meeting of the American Psychiatric Association, San Francisco, California, USA, May 17-22, 2003.

(70) Rapaport M, Canuso C, Turkoz I, et al. Preliminary results from ARISe-RD (augmentation with risperidone in resistant depression ) trial. Presented at the 43rd annual meeting of the New Clinical Drug Evaluation Unit; May 27-30, 2003. Boca Raton, Fla.

(71) Mamo D, Kapur S, Shammi CM, Papatheodorou G, Mann S, et al. A PET study of dopamine D2 and serotonin 5-HT2 receptor occupancy in patients with schizophrenia treatment with therapeutic doses of ziprasidone. *Am J Psychiatry.* 2004; 161:818-825.

(72) Papakostas GI, Petersen TJ, Nierenberg AA, Murakami JL, Alpert JE, et al. Ziprasidone augmentation of selective serotonin reuptake inhibitors (SSRIs) for SSRI-resistant major depressive disorder. *J Clin Psychiatry.* 2004; 65:217-221.

(73) Kozel AF, George MS, Simpson KN. Decision analysis of the cost-effectiveness of repetitive transcranial magnetic stimulation versus electroconvulsive therapy for treatment of nonpsychotic severe depression. CNS Spectrums. 2004; 9:476-482.

# CHAPTER 4

## Suicide in General Clinical Practice

## Pediatric and Teen Suicide

SUICIDE IN INFANCY and childhood is rare, probably reflecting difficulty in planning and carrying out a suicide plan, limited availability of lethal means and illegal substances, and greater dependence on adults. In six to twelve year-old children, suicide is not only associated with feelings of hopelessness and worthlessness and preoccupations with death, but also the unique wish to die believing that the concept that death is temporary and pleasant[1].

Youth suicide is indeed a global emergency. It is estimated that the number of suicide attempts in the United States among fifteen to twenty-four year-olds is believed to exceed one million annually. About 2,000,000 child and adolescent suicide attempts occur annually, resulting in close to 700,000 emergency room visits, and approximately 2,000 deaths per year[2].

Suicide is the third ranking cause of death youth in the US. The annual rate between 1950 and 1994 has increased more than fivefold in the United States, from 2.7 to 13.8 per 100,000[3]. A recent report issued by the Idaho Department of Education noted that nearly one in twelve of the state's high school students had attempted suicide during the previous year[4].

Current USA data indicate one death by suicide every two hours and three minutes is occurring in youths. Youths aged 15–24 account 14.1% of 2002 population and comprised 12.7% of suicides. 4010 youth suicides occurred in the USA in 2002. This averages 11 per day[5]. Each suicide corresponds to 100–400 attempts of varying levels of lethality and intent. Suicide attempts are 3 times more frequent in females than males[6]. From 1980 to 1997, the rate of suicide among persons aged 15–19 years increased by 11%, and among persons aged 10–14 years by 109%.

Suicide is the third leading cause of death, behind unintentional injury and homicide, for young people ages 15–24 years old. More teenagers and young adults died from suicide than from cancer, heart disease, AIDS, birth defects, stroke, pneumonia and influenza, and chronic lung disease combined as reported for the year 1998. Firearm-related suicide is the leading method among persons aged 15–19 years. The risk for suicide among young people is greatest among young white males. Nevertheless, suicide rates increased most rapidly among young black males between the years 1980 and 1995[7].

Suicide increasing among persons aged 10–14 years underscores the urgent need for intensifying efforts to prevent suicide among persons in this age group. It is now the second leading cause of death in Nevada teens, greater than deaths from motor vehicle accidents[8].

It should be emphasized that suicidal behavior and severe depression in the parent contributes to pediatric suicide. Offspring of a parent who had attempted suicide are six times more likely to attempt suicide than offspring of non-attempters; that suggests a familial transmission, most likely related to impulsive aggression including suicidal behavior, exists[9].

Approximately 7% of youths attempt suicide at least once before age 25 and 41% make more than one attempt. Suicide risk factors specific to youth, other than actual Axis I primary psychiatric disorders and substance related disorders, include the following:

1) previous suicide attempts
2) absence of parental support or single parent families, especially if the father is missing 3) past or current physical or sexual abuse, antisocial and narcissistic personality traits
4) school problems, lack of social acceptance, interpersonal problems, unemployment, poverty, availability of firearms, early marriage, and unwanted pregnancy
5) various forms of limited problems solving or coping skills[10].

Childhood sexual traumatization is highly associated with teen suicide and may be a common pathway to serious high suicide risk and mental illness. One study found that the odds of a sexually abused patient attempting suicide was more than ten times that of a patient who had not been sexually abused. Sexual traumatization in childhood, especially in cases of incest or prolonged sexual abuse, is also highly associated with subsequent development of both major depression and borderline personality disorder. Childhood sexual abuse is highly associated with completed suicide in patients with borderline personality disorder.

Physically abused children manifest significantly higher levels of depressive symptoms and suicidality. Physically abused children exhibit more depression and suicidality than children neglected or not abused at all[11].

Lack of adequate nutrition or food insufficiency is associated with increase risk of suicide in children, but this is not necessarily related to low family income. Families who sometimes or often did not have enough food to eat include children and adolescents in the family. These food insufficient children are significantly more likely to have dysthymia, thoughts of death, a desire to die, and suicide attempts. There is a strong association between food insufficiency, depressive disorder, and suicidal symptoms in U.S. adolescents[12].

Childhood homelessness is associated with suicidal ideation. Childhood homelessness of at least one week without family members and periods of homelessness longer than six months is associated with suicidal ideation[13].

Interpersonal difficulties associated with maladaptive parenting and abuse, are important risk factors for suicide attempts in early adulthood. One study reported parental psychiatric disorders are significantly associated with suicide attempts in the child[14].

Lack of parental attachment and emotional disconnection from parents, associated with repeated experiences of conflict and lack of communication in the home, increases the risk of suicidal adolescents. The impact of attachment issues in child development with both parents and peers can be inadequate, resulting in the adolescent feeling inadequate, isolated, and unsupported. In addition, without those interpersonal relationships adolescents report a life that has little meaning or a life without connection, leading to suicidal ideation and behaviors.

Children and adolescents in foster care are likely to have high rates of suicidal behavior given their elevated exposure to risk factors traditionally associated with suicide, such as child maltreatment, parental psychopathology, and alcohol/substance abuse. Despite the increased risk, the prevalence of suicidal behavior in youth in foster care has not been carefully examined. Adolescents entering foster care are now in the CATCH program in New York, which is a collaborative program with the Department of Mental Health and Columbia University to assess mental health needs of youth entering foster care.

Before puberty, common signs of depression include somatic symptoms such as abdominal pain, headaches, and irritability, whereas adolescents are more likely to express feelings of depression and exhibit suicidal behavior. Girls and boys are equally at risk for depression until puberty, when girls begin to outnumber boys and the presentation begins to resemble adult depression.

The prevalence of depression in youth age 18 and younger is 8.3%, and the rate increases with the patient's age. Depression in children and adolescents is associated with an increased risk of suicidal behaviors. In childhood, boys and girls appear to be at equal risk for depressive disorders, but during adolescence, girls are twice as likely as boys to develop depression.

Suicidality may manifest itself first during childhood and adolescence. Parents report observing remarkable behavioral and social changes in their children in the months preceding suicide, including a declining grade-point average, a change in attitude, social withdrawal, problems with temper, increased substance use and conflicts with teachers. Recent parental divorce also contributes to teen suicide, since the family usually serves as a protective and potentially buffering factor.

Girls have an increased risk of suicide attempts significantly more often and at a much younger age than the males. Furthermore, the girls who experience sexual abuse may then suffer significantly more anxiety disorders compared to adolescent boys. This higher rate of anxiety in female adolescent suicide attempters most likely results because of that sexual abuse[15].

Girls thinking about suicide are related to peers, in particular, to relationships with friends. A girl's relationships to friends plays a significant role, compared to little such impact on suicidal thoughts among boys. Girls are nearly twice as likely to think about suicide if they had only a few friends or were isolated from their peers. Girls are more likely to consider suicide if their friends were not friends with each other. Close friendships appear to be more important for adolescent girls, and problems with these relationships have major impacts on girls' mental health. Friendships play a larger role for girls than for boys. Girls who feel isolated and friendless were at as great a risk for considering suicide as were girls who knew someone who had committed suicide. Teachers and parents need to look for adolescents, especially girls, who do not seem to be socially connected to their peers or who have friends who do not get along.

Girls, with the constellation of eating disturbances and aggressive behavior, have an associated increased risk of drug use and attempted suicide. These eating disturbances such as binge-eating, purging, and dietary restrictions, are associated with aggressive behavior, as observed in one study of Midwest girls in grades 6 through 12. In this group, eating disturbances and aggressive behavior had a tendency to occur with and contribute to suicide[16].

Girls have a different development of substance related disorders compared to boys, and this trend may contribute to increasing suicidality. Girls have different motivation, risk factors, and vulnerability than boys towards the development of substance related disorders. Girls develop substance related disorders faster than boys do. Girls report using substances to lose weight, improve mood, increase confidence, reduce inhibitions, relieve stress, and reduce boredom; whereas boys are more likely to use drugs for sensation-seeking purposes. Girls who develop substance related disorders and an increased risk of suicide are more likely to be depressed, have eating disorders, and to be physically or sexually abused. These girls are more likely to smoke, drink, and/or use drugs than girls who do not experience these problems. Girls become intoxicated faster with the same or less amount of alcohol. Girls are more susceptible to alcohol related liver and heart disease and brain damage from ecstasy use. In addition, girls who drink coffee are more likely to be smokers and more likely to consume alcohol[17].

Girls with suicidal depression in particular seem to experience more hopelessness than suicidal depressed boys. Suicidal depressed girls who are more frequently hopeless and have longer duration of depression, are significantly more despondent. It is possible that among girls, the longer duration of major depressive symptoms will account for why they are more hopeless.

Dating violence against adolescent girls is now becoming a major public health concern. This intimate partner violence affects approximately one in five adolescent girls, who report being physically and/or sexually abused by a dating partner. With this, there is an associated increase risk of substance abuse, unhealthy weight control behavior (use of laxatives and or vomiting), sexual risky behaviors (first intercourse before the age of 15 years), pregnancy, other serious health risk behaviors, and suicide[18].

Single, pregnant girls are at increased risk of suicide. In a study of 120 pregnant adolescents in Brazil, suicidal ideation, suicide, and depression showed a significant correlation with single girls without boyfriends and little social support. Symptoms including poor attention and concentration, anxiety, depression, preoccupations, obsessions, compulsions, tiredness, and worries concerning body functions are associated with suicidal ideations. These heterogeneous symptoms associated with suicidality do not differ during gestational trimesters[19].

For boys, if depression is accompanied by conduct disorder and alcohol or other substance abuse, there is an increased risk of suicide.

Boys are less likely to attempt suicide if they attend schools in which the friendship network is dense and interlocked. Dense friendship networks seem to help prevent suicide attempts in boys, but friendship does not seem to affect suicidal thoughts as it does in girls.

Boys tend not to share their thoughts about suicide with friends, but they may admit when they are planning to attempt suicide. In a school where there are a lot of interlocking relationships, there are many people who may hear a suicidal boy talking and help him get the support he needs. Boys may not tell people what they are thinking about, but they may talk about what they might do.

For boys who tend to cluster more in groups, close relationships do not seem to have as important impact on suicide than as on girls. Friendships have essentially no major effect on whether boys consider suicide.

Boys with suicidal behaviors are associated with substance misuse including alcohol and solvent misuse. These observations can help understand how suicide rate, depression, conduct disorder, crime, and substance misuse in boys ages 8–18 have increased and may be linked. Adding access to firearms may explain the increase in suicides. There is a particular increase risk of suicidal behaviors among adolescent boys if the depression is accompanied by conduct disorder and substance related disorders. Male suicide attempters show higher rates of alcohol disorders. There is an additional finding insomnia emerges as one of the most significant risk factors noted in up to 71% of depressed suicidal boys[20].

Sexual orientation can play a role in youth suicide. There is a strong link between adolescent sexual orientation and suicidal thoughts and behaviors. The effect of sexual orientation on suicidal thoughts is mediated by critical youth suicide risk factors including depression, hopelessness, alcohol abuse, recent suicide attempts by a peer or family member, and experiences of victimization. These findings provide evidence that sexual minority youths are more likely than their peers to think about and attempt suicide[21].

Homosexuality can lead to social stress or identity conflicts with a consequent increase of suicidal behavior. Gay, lesbian, and bisexual young people are at increased risks of major depression, generalized anxiety, conduct disorder, nicotine dependence, other substance related disorders, multiple disorders, suicidal ideation, and suicide attempts. In one study, a twofold increase risk of suicidal ideation associated with a homosexual or bisexual orientation is noted. A significant increased risk of attempted suicide associated with homosexuality or bisexuality was found in females. There is a higher rate of suicide attempts (39%) in young homosexuals and bisexuals that are 5–10 times above expected rates (20%). Suicidal behavior is associated with low self-esteem, higher levels of hopelessness, and suicidal behavior in someone close. Among homosexual or bisexual young people, less satisfying homosexual friendships were an additional risk factor for suicidal behavior[22]. Gay Lesbian Bisexual Unsure (GLBU) people have high rates of non-fatal suicidal behavior. A frequently cited precipitant of Gay Lesbian Bisexual Unsure non-fatal suicidal behavior is the personal and interpersonal turmoil associated with coming to terms with one's sexual identity. There is a greater empathy of GLBU individuals toward suicidal persons, independent of the precipitant of the suicidal act, which may imply a greater acceptance of suicidal behavior as a way to cope with adversities.

Imitation of suicide events among teens is another independent risk factor for suicide in youths[23]. Although an extremely personal decision, suicide, may be influenced by social forces, peer pressure, including imitation. A prominent example of imitation youth suicide is from a novel by Goethe in 1774 in which the hero, Werther, killed himself after being rejected by a girl he loved. His fictional death was followed by imitation by many youths in real life, hence the term "Werther effect," which describes suicide by romantic imitation.

Today, suicide by imitation appears to be influenced by diffusion of information through the mass media. Examples include the following: the clustering of teenage suicides after television news stories[24]; evidence from Japan about the effect of the media on youth suicide; imitative subway suicides in European youth[25]; and "the Kurt Cobain suicide crisis" in America[26]. The American Foundation of Suicide Prevention published an expert panel on recommendations to the media, which included studies of stories and headlines in media about suicides leading to copycat suicide attempts[27]. Imitation suicide is not limited to print or video. Music can contribute to suicide. At least 150 suicides were committed in Hungary during the 1940's with the song "Gloomy Sunday" being played on a turntable at the time of the death. It is, therefore, hypothesized that the song had some connection with the decision to die, and as a result, the song was banned from being played in both the U.S. and Britain for several years. Billy Holiday later recorded the song in the U.S. In 2003, the movie "Gloomy Sunday" was released in the U.S., and the movie chronicles the tumultuous history of the song. The original author of the song, later in life, overwhelmed with grief over his link to the numerous suicides, also committed suicide.

Any teen exposed to a friend's suicide is most likely to suffer from a new onset of major depressive disorder within the first month after the event. Efforts to get students involved in starting a campaign in their schools to prevent suicide are underway in order to help sensitize the friend around someone who is suicidal to be aware of the warning signs. Teacher's guides can be used in the classroom or on retreats with intent of sensitizing students regarding issues of self-esteem, coping, anger management, and suicide prevention. Teens with a family history of major depressive disorder, past history of alcohol abuse, interpersonal conflicts with friends and family, and those who feelings of accountability for their friends' suicides should be monitored closely during the first month for the development of major depression and suicidality[28].

Certain personality traits of adolescents are more associated with suicidal ideation. Neuroticism is a significant predictor of depression and suicidal ideation. In a group of hospitalized teens, neuroticism was associated with more readmissions within a year for suicidal ideation and suicidal behavior. In addition, self-criticism, rather than other traits such as dependency, self-oriented perfectionism, or socially prescribed perfectionism, was strongly associated with depression, hopelessness, and suicidality[29].

Contrary to popular belief, married teenagers have been found to have high suicide rates. Legalized abortion may lower suicide risk through decreasing the number of unhappy marriages among immature youth. By decreasing the number of forced teenage marriages and unions considered at risk for failure, the legalization of abortion caused a drop in female suicide after 1973: high abortion rates were predictive of low teenage marriage rates.

A representative study of youth and young adult suicide done at the Institute of Forensic Medicine of Paris between 1998 and 1996 examined the socio-demographic, clinical characteristics, autopsy, and toxicological findings among 392 teen suicide cases. Two hundred and sixty victims (66%) were males. The mean age was 22 years in both sexes. Ninety-two percent of the subjects were single. Forty percent were students. One third had previously attempted suicide. Thirty-five percent used to take psychoactive prescription drugs, and some of them had been under the care of a mental health professional at the time of suicide. In 40% of the cases, a suicide note was found near the body. Depression (in 70% of victims), schizophrenia (in 10%), mood disorders, parent-child relational problems, partner relational problems, adolescent antisocial behavior and borderline personality disorder were found to be the most frequent diseases and stressors involved in the suicides. The suicide was rarely an accidental reaction to stress. It was constantly preceded by situational distress, which led to suicidal ideas if the adolescent failed to cope with problems. The most frequent method of suicide was poisoning followed by jumping from a height, gunshot, subway death, and hanging/asphyxia. Among firearms, a handgun was more likely to be used than rifles. Tranquilizers were the most frequent psychoactive drugs used for suicide followed by antipsychotic drugs, antidepressants, and barbiturates[30].

Vulnerability to suicide in the young is strongly associated with unrecognized depressive states, substance abuse, eating disorders, and personality disorders. More than half of the parents reported, in another study, that their child who committed suicide had a psychiatric disorder. In one group, 37% reported a mood disorder, including bipolar disorder, 20% reported a substance related disorder, and 10% reported schizophrenia.

Another report of suicidal behavior in adolescent psychiatric inpatients demonstrated that the significant predictors of suicidal behavior in these patients were depression, alcohol abuse, past suicidal behavior, and aggressive behavior[31].

These studies demonstrate the complex multiaxial diagnostic issues suicidal patients have, and they increase insight about pediatric suicide. The highest risk of suicide occurs in the presence of multiple co-morbid conditions, particularly combinations of mood or psychotic disorders with abuse of alcohol or drugs[32].

Without co-morbid substance abuse, suicide rates are lower.

The two major psychiatric disorders commonly associated with suicide in children and adolescents include mood disorders and substance related disorders.

A number of epidemiological studies have reported that up to 2.5 percent of children and up to 8.3 percent of adolescents in the U.S. suffer from depression. An NIMH sponsored study of 9–17 year olds estimates that the prevalence of any depression is more than 6 percent in a six-month period, with 4.9% having major depression.

Depression in children and adolescents is associated with an increased risk of suicidal behaviors.

Among adolescents who develop major depressive disorder, more than as seven percent may commit suicide in the young adult years. Consequently, it is important for health care providers and parents to take all threats of suicide seriously. While the recovery rate from a single episode of major depression in children and adolescents is quite high, episodes are likely to recur[33].

Although a very recent trend of decreased substance abuse among teens is reported since its peak in the 1990s both the rate of adolescent suicide and the rate of adolescent substance related disorders, in general, have increased significantly. An early pattern of substance abuse, in particular, is a risk factor associated with suicide in children. In one study of rural seventh and eighth grade students, suicidal behavior including suicidal thoughts and suicidal plans were most often associated with the use of tobacco, alcohol, and inhalants[34].

Primary psychiatric disorders in children and adolescents associated with suicidality include mood disorders, oppositional defiant disorder, posttraumatic stress disorder, anxiety disorders, sleep disorders and developmental disorders.

Suicidal depressed children have a higher lifetime risk of co-morbid oppositional disorder. Suicidality is less often associated in children with autism and severe and profound mentally retardation. Children and adolescents with developmental disorders exhibit a wide range of self-destructive behaviors. Interestingly, suicidal ideation and gestures have been underreported in this population. Nearly one-half of such patients can experience either suicidal ideations and threats or suicidal attempts. This behavior is encountered in pediatric patients with developmental disabilities[35].

Whereas sleep terrors and sleepwalking in childhood are related primarily to genetic and developmental factors, their persistence and especially their onset in adolescence may be related to psychological factors. Adolescents with sleep terrors and sleepwalking have an increased prevalence of other sleep disorders, neurotic traits, psychiatric disorders, and suicidal thoughts[36].

Anxiety, as part of an anxiety disorder or itself contributes to suicidality in depressed adolescents. Adolescents with panic attacks are three times more likely to have expressed suicidal ideation and two times more likely to have made suicide attempts than were adolescents without panic attacks in a group of 13–14 year olds. Self-rated suicidality correlates with both increased rates of anxiety and depression. A high rate of anxiety in adolescent female suicide attempters is noted in several reports. Anxiety is an independent risk factor for suicidality in adolescents[37].

The most common psychiatric disorder in children and adolescents leading to suicide is major depressive disorder. For youths with major depression, the risk of suicide is significantly higher than in the general population. Depressive disorders are the most common disorders among adolescent suicide victims, ranging from 49 to 64%[38]. Mood disorders in children and adolescents include the depressive disorders such as major depressive disorder (unipolar depression), dysthymic disorder (chronic, mild depression), and bipolar disorder (manic-depression). These mood disorders can have far-reaching effects on the functioning and adjustment of young people.

The onset of major depressive disorder is occurring earlier in life today than in the past decades. An early-onset depression often persists, recurs, and continues into adulthood, and this indicates that depression in youth may also predict more severe illness in adult life. As many as 2.5 % of children in the U.S. suffer from depression.

Depression in children and adolescents is associated with an increased risk of suicidal behavior. Among adolescents who develop major depressive disorder, nearly eight percent may commit suicide in the young adult years[39]. Among both children and adolescents, depressive disorders confer an increased risk for illness and interpersonal and psychosocial difficulties that persist long after the depressive episode is resolved which leads to an increased risk for substance abuse and suicidal behavior. Unfortunately, pediatric psychiatric disorders often go unrecognized by families and physicians alike. It may take a specialist in child psychiatry to make an accurate diagnosis.

Signs of depressive disorders in young people often are viewed as normal mood swings typical of a particular developmental stage. In addition, health care professionals may be reluctant prematurely to label a young person with a mental illness diagnosis. Yet early diagnosis and treatment of depressive disorders are critical to healthy emotional, social, and behavioral development.

It may be difficult to imagine a child suffering from chronic depression for several years, even before suffering a major depressive episode. Dysthymia is that less severe, yet typically more chronic, form of depression. It is diagnosed when depressed mood persists for at least one year in children or adolescents and it is associated with an increased risk for developing major depressive disorder. Treatment of dysthymia may prevent deterioration into more severe illness. This milder more chronic form of depression includes depressive symptoms for more days than not, for at least one year with no two-month period of remission. It should be noted that 70% of pediatric dysthymia patients develop major depressive disorder. In addition, double depression, a major depressive episode (acute), can be superimposed upon dysthymia (chronic), increasing the suicidal risk further.

The incidence of major depressive disorder increases from preschool through puberty and adolescence. Prepubertal major depression is equally common in males and females, but by adolescence, females outnumber males two to one. Pediatric major depression is common in the general population. Pediatric mood disorders have an increasing prevalence and a decreasing onset age with distinctive presentations. Girls and boys appear to be at equal risk for depressive disorders, but during adolescence, girls are twice as likely as boys to develop depression. Children who develop major depression are more likely to have a family history of the disorder, often presenting as a parent who experienced depression at an early age. The diagnosis of major depressive disorder in a child is clinically challenging for several reasons, including the fact that the way symptoms are expressed varies with the developmental stage of the youngster.

Signs and symptoms of pediatric major depression include irritability, pervasive symptoms of sadness or loss in pleasurable activities, various changes in sleep, appetite, or weight, feeling worthless or guilty, and impaired concentration which occur as well as suicidal ideation. These symptoms persist most of the day, nearly every day for at least two weeks.

Manifestations of pediatric major depression include somatic complaints such as headache and stomach pain. Irritability is a symptom often overlooked in pediatric depression. School refusal and separation anxiety, as well as academic deterioration and new behavioral problems are common. Finally, a preoccupation with suicide or death is noted[40]. Untreated pediatric depression is associated with substantial morbidity, including reduced academic performance, substance abuse, interpersonal problems, social withdrawal, and a poor quality of life. It also increases the risk of suicide.

With its early onset, pediatric depression is considered a more malignant illness than adult-onset depression because of its effect on development, potential for recurrence, and chronicity into adulthood[41].

Co-morbidity in pediatric major depression is common, especially with oppositional defiant disorder. Co-morbidity is associated with more severe and longer depressions, worse short-term outcome, and more frequent suicidality. One study found a group of high-lethal attempters had major depressive episode and attention deficit disorder. Other co-morbid conditions include disruptive behavioral disorders, but substance abuse is the most common co-morbid disorder leading to suicide in children and adolescents. An emphasis on co-morbid chronic general medical conditions, such as diabetes mellitus should not be overlooked. Children with co-morbid, chronic medical illness experience hopelessness, depression, and suicidality.

At least 30% of pre-pubertal depressed patients subsequently go on to develop bipolar disorder. In fact, twenty to forty percent of adolescents with major depression develop bipolar disorder within five years after depression onset[42]. Bipolar disorder in adulthood is a frequent outcome in pediatric depression. A bipolar outcome in pediatric depression is suggested by the following characteristics: 1) depression with acute onset; 2) an atypical depression, including psychotic depression; 3) a family history of mood disorder; 4) a pharmacological induced hypomania; and 5) attention deficit hyperactive disorder with mood instability and mood liability.

Although rare in young children, bipolar disorder can appear. Nearly one fourth of bipolar children attempt suicide[43]. Evidence exists to indicate that bipolar disorder beginning in childhood or early adolescence may be a different, possibly more severe form of the illness than older adolescent- and adult-onset bipolar disorder. When the illness begins before or soon after puberty, it is often characterized by a continuous, rapid-cycling, irritable, and mixed symptom state. Medical conditions that may mimic pediatric bipolar mania include temporal lobe epilepsy, hyperthyroidism, closed or open head injury, multiple sclerosis, systemic lupus erythematosus, alcohol-related neurodevelopmental disorder, and Wilson's disease, a rare progressive disease caused by defective copper metabolism. Medications that may increase mood cycling include not only antidepressants, but also aminophyline, corticosteroids, and sympathomimetic amines such as pseudoephedrine.

Child and adolescent bipolar disorder may co-occur with disruptive behavior disorders, particularly attention deficit hyperactivity disorder (ADHD), conduct disorder, and oppositional defiant disorder. It may have features of these disorders as initial symptoms. For example, clinical findings common to both ADHD and bipolar disorder include distractibility and hyperenergetic symptomatology[44].

Childhood or adolescent bipolar disorder may frequently be a co-morbid condition with not only disruptive behavior disorders such as ADHD, oppositional defiant disorder, and conduct disorder but also substance related disorders, psychotic, and anxiety disorders[45]. In a group of adolescent inpatients with bipolar disorder, as many as 70% of patients had co-morbid ADHD, 40% had co-morbid substance related disorders; 30% had clinical anxiety; and 10% had Tourette's syndrome. That study highlights the frequent occurrence of co-morbid psychiatric disorders in adolescents with bipolar disorder[46].

A child or adolescent who appears to be depressed and exhibits ADHD-like symptoms that are very severe, with excessive temper outbursts and mood changes, should be evaluated by a psychiatrist with experience in pediatric bipolar disorder, particularly if there is a family history of the illness. This evaluation is especially important since psychostimulant medications often prescribed for ADHD may worsen manic symptoms. Psycho-stimulants frequently used to treat ADHD or ADHD-like symptoms can worsen manic symptoms in a child or adolescent with bipolar disorder. Earlier bipolar disorder onset in stimulant-exposed adolescents has been reported. Clinical observations in pediatric bipolar disorder include the observation that although many patients are initially prescribed stimulants for ADHD, ultimately they are diagnosed with bipolar disorder years later[47]. Treatment for mood disorders in children and adolescents often involves short-term psychotherapy, medication, and/or targeted interventions involving the home or school environment. Such an effective targeted intervention may involve a rapid-response outpatient treatment model leading to reduced hospitalizations among suicidal adolescents[48]. Even after psychiatric hospitalization, many suicidal youth remain untreated or under-treated because of poor adherence to recommended pharmacological and/or psychosocial treatments. Because treatment adherence is known to be poor among oppositional, aggressive, and antisocial youth and because conduct problems and depression are often co-morbid, the relationship to these externalizing symptoms and suicidality on treatment adherence is significant.

There remains, however, a pressing need for additional research on the effectiveness of psychopharmacological treatment for mood disorders in youth. Not until recently have effective medications been developed. Older medications have proven rather ineffective until recently. For example, although a tricyclic antidepressant can be used for enuresis in a patient who is a minimum age of six, the tricyclic antidepressant lacks efficacy in pediatric major depression. Available studies generally do not support the efficacy of tricyclic antidepressants or monoamine oxidase inhibitors for depression in youth. In contrast, recently there are some controlled studies showing efficacy of SSRIs for pediatric major depression.

Currently, the National Institute of Child Health and Human Development (NICHD) in consultation with the Food and Drug Administration and pediatric research experts, is testing psychiatric medications in children as part of the Best Pharmaceuticals for Children Act. These medications are being studied in children because they are often prescribed for children. This process then allows the Health and Human Services agencies to sponsor pediatric studies of off-patent drugs approved for use in the U.S. that have not been tested in children. These studies will provide useful information about certain medications used in children[49].

Safe and better-tolerated pediatric psychopharmacologic approaches to treat mood disorders in children and adolescents include the use of selective serotonin reuptake inhibitors. SSRIs have been shown to be safe and effective for pediatric use. The United States Food and Drug Administration recently approved fluoxetine (Prozac, Eli Lilly) for the treatment of major depressive disorder in children and adolescents. Fluoxetine may be prescribed to children as young as eight years old. It is the first of its kind to receive approval for treatment of depression in children. Clinical trials with fluoxetine in children indicated that it produced significant effect compared to placebo. Side effects such as nausea, fatigue, nervousness, and difficulty of concentration were similar to those observed in adults[50].

Stimulating antidepressants may induce mania. This adverse reaction should be monitored for carefully. Because antidepressants are believed to have the potential for inducing manic episodes in patients with bipolar disorder, there is a concern about using antidepressants alone in this population. Therefore, patients should be adequately screened to determine if they are at risk for bipolar disorder before initiating antidepressant treatment.

Risk factors for causing SSRI induced mania in children and adolescents during treatment of depression include a family history of bipolar disorder, psychomotor retardation, atypical depression (such as with psychotic features), and acute onset.

Recently, other SSRIs besides fluoxetine have been found effective for major depression in numerous pediatric clinical trials. Sertraline, paroxetine, and venlafaxine have been studied in pediatric depression and pediatric anxiety disorders. Warnings that antidepressants can paradoxically increase suicidality emphasize the need for close and careful clinical monitoring. Health care providers should carefully monitor patients receiving antidepressants for possible worsening of depression or suicidality. To determine what intervention is indicated, they should also carefully evaluate patients in whom depression persistently worsens or emergent suicidality is severe, abrupt in onset, or not part of the presenting symptoms.

Reports of anxiety, agitation, panic attacks, insomnia, irritability, hostility, impulsivity, akathisia (severe restlessness), hypomania, and mania are reported in adult and pediatric patients being treated with antidepressants not only for major depressive disorder, but also for other indications, both psychiatric and non-psychiatric. Although the FDA has not concluded that these symptoms are precursors to either worsening of depression or other emergence of suicidal impulses, there is serious concern that patients who experience one or more of these symptoms may be at increased risk for worsening depression or suicidality. Furthermore, if a decision is made to discontinue treatment, these medications should be tapered rather than stopped abruptly. Thus, health care providers should instruct patients, families, and caregivers to be alert for the emergence of agitation, irritability, and other symptoms described, as well as the emergence of suicidality and worsening depression. They should report such symptoms immediately to their health care provider.

The recent concern as to whether antidepressants are potentially related to suicidal thinking or behavior for children with major depression is addressed in the United States and United Kingdom. SSRI associated behavioral activation and suicidal ideation in children and adolescents were reported anecdotally, as case reports, in the early 1990's[51] and more recently[52].

The U.S. Food and Drug Administration reported in October 2003 that it had completed preliminary review of reports for eight antidepressants—citalopram, fluoxetine, fluvoxamine, mirtazapine, nefazodone, paroxetine, sertraline, and venlafaxine—with regard to the issue of suicidality. The FDA stated at that time that the data does not clearly establish an association between the use of these medications and suicidal thoughts or actions by children. However, it was also noted that it is not possible to rule out an increased risk of these adverse events for any of the medications at this point. A significant problem with any retrospective analyses of these studies to further investigate any potential relationship between antidepressants and suicidality is that they were not designed to assess suicidality. Furthermore, the focus on a potential link between antidepressants and suicide in children and adolescents with depression misses the fundamental point that depressed youths are at a significant risk of having suicidal thoughts, attempting suicide, and committing suicide. The illness itself can lead to suicide-related outcomes, rather than any form of treatment.

The FDA has requested that the manufacturers of ten antidepressant medications include on their labels stronger warnings about the need to monitor adult and pediatric patients for symptoms of worsening depression and the emergence of suicidal ideation. The new warnings also alert prescribers, patients, and caregivers to the emergence of symptoms that are known to be associated with antidepressants in some patients including the following: anxiety, agitation, panic attacks, insomnia, irritability, hostility, impulsivity, akathisia, hypomania, and mania. Although a causal link has not been established between the emergence of such symptoms and either worsening of depression or suicidal impulses, medications may need to be discontinued when such symptoms are severe, abrupt in onset, or not part of the patient's presenting symptoms. The FDA wants the new warnings on the labels of fluoxetine, sertraline, paroxetine, fluvoxamine, citalopram, escitalopram, bupropion, venlafaxine, nefazodone, and mirtazapine. The warnings also cite the potential of antidepressants for inducing manic episodes in patients with bipolar disorder. The first episode of bipolar disorder is often a depressive one; thus if one treats this with antidepressants, the potential for invoking a manic episode exists, especially if treating with an antidepressant alone. Therefore, the warning will remind physicians to obtain a patient's personal and family history before prescribing antidepressants to try to make sure the depression is not the onset of bipolar disorder. Although the FDA is investigating the relationship between the medications and behaviors in pediatric patients, the same concerns exist for adult patients. The behaviors of concern, including suicidality, agitation, irritability and severe restlessness, have long been concerns in the adult population as well. Thus, it seems wise to include all patients in the proposed warnings. The agency has not concluded that any of the medications induce suicidal thoughts or behavior. However, the FDA's preliminary review of twenty-four pediatric studies of nine antidepressants, which included more than 4,000 pediatric patients, raised suspicions of a possible association between their use and increased suicidal ideation and suicide attempts. The review could not establish causality, but the association is strong enough for the FDA to initiate labeling changes and to require the issuing of stronger warnings to clinicians regarding possible risks of these medications, without recommending that their use be contraindicated. However, venlafaxine is now not recommended in depressed pediatric patients in the United States.

In the United Kingdom, the MHRA (Medicines and Healthcare Products Regulatory Agency) acted on the paroxetine findings by issuing a directive and label change contraindicating use for depression in children. The MHRA also contraindicated venlafaxine after the manufacturer found a signal of suicidality in the data review requested by the FDA. The MHRA then announced that sertraline, citalopram, and escitalopram are also contraindicated for treatment of pediatric major depression in the United Kingdom.

Only fluoxetine remains approved for the treatment of pediatric depression in both the United States and the United Kingdom for demonstrating superiority to placebo in the pediatric supplemental studies.

Reports of suicidal ideation induced by antidepressants are poorly described and problems in tracking these kinds of symptoms occur. However, careful monitoring of patients is always advised, especially when initiating or changing doses. We should be very careful when giving these powerful medications to children.

Despite these new warnings, these medications remain the treatment of choice for many patients and are widely prescribed. For example, in 2002, about 2.7 million prescriptions for SSRIs and atypical antidepressants were written for children aged 1–11 years. An estimated 8.1 million prescriptions were written for children aged 12–17 years, according to one data source. Despite the stronger warnings, antidepressants remain important in the fight against childhood psychiatric disorders. In a large population based, retrospective study examining the prevalence of ambulatory prescription antidepressant use in children who were commercially insured between 1998–2000, the trend, as a sample of more than 300,000 children aged 18 years and younger, is that antidepressant use soared for preschool girls and boys. The number of children using antidepressants increased from 5,880 in 1998 to 9,013 in 2004. Overall antidepressant use in children aged 18 years and younger in the United States jumped by 49%—from 160 prescriptions per 10,000 children (1.6%) in 1998 to 240 prescriptions per 10,000 children (2.4%) in 2002. Antidepressant use doubled among preschool girls and increased by 64% among preschool boys. The total growth in antidepressant prescription use was higher among girls (68%) than boys (48%)[53].

Is treating depression in children lowering the suicide rate? One published study reports the relationship between changes in antidepressant treatment and suicide in adolescents from 1990–2000, examining the relationship between trends in antidepressant use and suicide rates in youths aged 10 to 19. In particular, a 1% increase in use of antidepressants by adolescents was associated with a decrease of 0.23 suicides per 100,000 adolescents per year. There was a significant negative relationship for changes in regional rates of overall antidepressant treatment and changes in the regional suicide rates. These findings support the need to improve identification and pharmacological treatment of youths with major depression. It is critically important that children with major depression receive adequate treatment.

However, there currently are public concerns about the use of medication to treat youths. Caitlin McIntosh, 12, hanged herself with shoelaces weeks after starting treatment for depression with an SSRI. Matt Miller, 13, hanged himself in his bedroom closet after taking his seventh SSRI dose. Michael Shivak, 11, slashed his wrists in class while taking an SSRI. These adolescents' parents testified at an FDA hearing on February 2, 2004 about possible increased risk of suicidality with SSRI pharmacotherapy[54].

Although there is no guarantee that pharmacotherapy will actually prevent suicide in children and adolescents with depression, medication can often be life saving in this age group. Sherri Walton said her daughter, Jordan, 14, has achieved "enormous benefit" from taking SSRIs for obsessive-compulsive disorder. Suzanne Vogel-

Scibilia told the same FDA panel she is convinced that her two children with psychiatric disorders lead full lives because of SSRIs.

For the clinician, the risks and benefits should be weighed when considering prescribing SSRIs in children. Prescribing SSRIs safely in youth include the following five main points:

- First: Monitor for suicidality. As part of the medication informed consent process, discuss with parents the potential for suicidal behavior. Discuss antidepressant side effects, which may include impulsivity. So already aggressive and impulsive children require even more special attention as addressed in the individualized treatment plan.
- Second: Rule out bipolar depression and mixed episodes, that are often characterized by marked irritability, before prescribing antidepressants. Some clues to bipolar disorder include early-onset depression.
- Third: Minimize side effects. Although children can tolerate moderately high SSRI dosages, there is not a clear dose response relationship. But the side effects are dose-dependent[54]. Most frequent SSRI side effects are nausea, diarrhea, decreased appetite, headaches, restlessness, tremor, and insomnia. Rare side effects include ecchymoses. Reduced growth, possibly related to growth hormone suppression, has been reported in four boys treated with SSRIs[55].
- Fourth: Prevent drug interactions. Since SSRIs are rarely used as monotherapy in pediatric patients and using two or more medications is the rule, rather than the exception, awareness of the potential impact of combining SSRIs with other agents is important. Since the half lives of sertraline and citalopram in children is relatively short (14–16 hours), some researchers suggest giving those SSRIs twice daily[56].
- Fifth: Avoid withdrawal. The withdrawal syndrome following abrupt cessation of paroxetine, venlafaxine, or fluvoxamine is well known, and its irritability and depression-like symptoms, along with flu-like symptoms, can be quite distressing for patients. Thus, make decisions thoughtfully when discontinuing SSRIs and plan to taper for one to two weeks.

The recommended antidepressant dosage for fluoxetine in children is 5 to 20 mg once daily and in adolescents, 10 to 60 mg once daily[57].

Pharmacological treatment of pediatric mood disorders is clinically challenging. In pediatric bipolar depression, the SSRIs are seven times more likely to help than no medication, but the SSRI itself is three times more likely to induce mania than no medication at all. In addition, for depressive symptoms in pediatric bipolar disorder, selective serotonin reuptake inhibitors (SSRIs) are seven times more effective than tricyclic antidepressants or no medication at all. The emphasis is that using antidepressant medication to treat depression in a person whom has bipolar disorder may induce manic symptoms, especially without a mood stabilizer.

The novel approach of augmentation of antidepressants with mood stabilizers and/or atypical antipsychotics is being further studied. Early reports suggest some role for these medications. For manic symptoms of pediatric bipolar disorder, the anticonvulsant mood stabilizer divalproex can be quite effective, and it seems more effective in pediatric bipolar disorder than carbamazepine or lithium. Adjunctive quetiapine to divalproex for severe adolescent mania seems very promising. More clinical trials evaluating the safety and efficacy of mood stabilizers and atypical antipsychotics for pediatric bipolar disorder are currently underway[58].

Precautions and warnings need to be considered in these special patient populations. For example, young female patients prescribed divalproex should be monitored carefully, since studies conducted in Europe involving women with seizure disorders who were treated with valproate before the age of 20 developed increased testosterone levels and polycystic ovarian syndrome. Increased testosterone led to polycystic ovary syndrome with irregular or absent menses, obesity, and abnormal growth of hair.

Despite the new knowledge, pediatricians and parents have been understandably reluctant to have young people treated with psychotropic medications. Only in the last few years, researches have been able to conduct randomized, placebo-controlled studies with children and adolescents with major depressive disorder. Physiologically, children are not mini-adults. Thus, practicing evidence-based medicine requires separate empirical research for pediatric conditions. Despite some efforts by the National Institute of Mental Health and the pharmaceutical industry, research in pediatric psychopharmacology lags decades behind evidence-based treatment in adults.

Interview with parents of forty-nine youth between 13–21 years old who completed suicide in Utah revealed high rates of psychiatric diagnoses. Antidepressants were detected in only 20%; mood stabilizers in only 4%; antipsychotics in only 2%; and medication for ADHD in only 2% of these suicide victims. One might expect therapeutic levels of the psychotropic medication. Yet, the medical examiners' toxicology reports detected no psychotropic medications among the blood samples, even though the parents reported that the suicide completers had been prescribed psychotropic medications. More often than not, inadequate treatment of pediatric psychiatric disorders in suicides is confirmed in postmortem studies by detecting psychotropic medication drug levels in blood or tissue samples from suicide victims. The medical examiner's toxicology department during autopsy usually does this procedure. Frequently, little, if any, psychotropic medications are detected in the serum of any of the suicide completers.

It is very important for parents to understand their child's depression and the treatments that may be prescribed. Physicians can help by talking with the parent and child about questions or concerns, reinforcing that depression in youth is not uncommon and reassuring them that appropriate treatment can lead to improved functioning at school, with peers, and at home with family. In addition, referring the youth and family to a mental health professional and to the information resources can help to enhance recovery. Much education with the patient, family, caregivers, and providers is needed to increase awareness of treatment available. It may be that youths perceive taking psychotropic medications as an absolute failure. Clinicians need to emphasize how important it is for children with psychiatric problems to take their medications, and help them work through the stigmas and understand the barriers to treatment. The physician can dispel the myth that taking the medication is going to make them suicidal or that by prescribing medications, you are increasing suicide risk in any shape.

If youngster appears to have suicidality, then a comprehensive diagnostic evaluation by a mental health professional is warranted. This evaluation should include interviews with the youth, parents, and, when possible, other informants such as teachers and social service personnel; even within the general population of adolescents, rates of suicidal ideation and suicidal behavior are high. Many teen suicide prevention programs such as the Columbia University TeenScreen Program in New York, the SAMSHSA teen suicide prevention project, the Signs of Suicide (SOS) suicide prevention program in Georgia, Massachusetts and Connecticut, and TEEN-LINE in Los Angeles are ideal programs. Most teen programs in suicide prevention are school-based. Some focus on suicide prevention with the focus on help-seeking behavior and reducing stigma driven barriers to help. Then the ultimate goal is reducing suicidal acts. The use of the internet is becoming a popular strategy since it can be a user-friendly medium, providing safe and secure, nonjudgmental information through a referral and online counseling and offering safe, reliable information and help. Kidscrisis.com is an example of such interactive website.

Finally, other strategies are used for suicide risk reduction in teens, such as reducing the availability of lethal methods. It is known that suicidal youth are 3.5 times more apt to carry firearms than nonsuicidal youth. In the United States, the restriction of handgun availability appears to have had an impact upon suicide rates in younger adolescents. In England, there is now a restriction on the number of acetaminophen tablets that can be sold in a package. This as another way to attempt to reduce the lethality of a popular suicide method. Thus, the availability of handguns or other lethal equivalents may in and of itself confer lethality to what would otherwise be a transient self-destructive impulse.

If a youngster already attempted suicide, there is a heightened risk for suicide within the following three months, so families can be involved and do interventions for the suicidal children. As the individual continues to grow and develop from childhood and adolescence into young adulthood, new issues and perspectives about suicidality form and need further elaboration to gain a better understanding into suicide risk reduction.

The second leading cause of death among college students is suicide. During the college years, many mental illnesses reach a clinical threshold that gets attention and requires clinical care, and numerous psychosocial stressors can appear. On Saturday, March 6, 2004, Diana Chien became the fourth New York University student to commit suicide during the academic year. She jumped from a twenty-four-story building. The controversial aspect was that the *New York Post* printed a photograph of Chien in mid-fall on its March 10th cover with dramatic headlines about the suicide. Psychiatrists now staff the counseling centers of many universities and colleges, but better screening and detection, as is occurring in high school, is underway. Social hopelessness is associated with stress, depression and suicidal ideation among college students[59]. Comprehensive suicide prevention programs are designed specifically for the college community. The problems leading up to suicidal behavior, risk factors, stressors and environmental contributors that are particularly relevant to the college environment and campus community highlight the programs.

## Women and Suicide

Depression and suicide in women can be best understood in the context of the shifting reproductive hormonal environment. Disorders, such as premenstrual dysphoric disorder, postpartum depression, puerperal psychosis, perimenopausal and postmenopausal mood disturbance, are associated with increased suicidality.

Depression occurs more often in women than in men. The higher rates of major depressive disorder are nearly double that for men with a prevalence 21.3%[60]. The clinical signs and symptoms of depression in women may differ from men. Pre-menopausal women are more likely to present with atypical or reverse androgenous symptoms of depression such as excessive sleeping, carbohydrate craving, hyperphagia, or weight gain[61]. Women also tend to report a greater number of depressive symptoms and a greater degree of distress associated with these symptoms[62]. Women are more likely to report symptoms such as anxiety or functional impairment particularly as related to family and marital roles[63]. Women more often present themselves as depressed and suicidal at the outpatient clinic, seeking and more easily accepting help from friends or professionals. Women are more likely to experience seasonal depression and depression associated with stressful life events[64, 65]. Depressed suicidal women have more co-morbid anxiety and eating disorders[66].

Additional risk factors for women, such as past childhood abuse or previous mood disorder during the early reproductive years, are associated with a greater risk of a depressive disorder developing in women[67].

In general, suicide attempts occur more often in women than men. Women have a lower rate of completed suicide compared with men[68]. Usually, women use less violent and highly lethal means. In Eastern countries, however, where self-poisoning with pesticide is a common non-violent but lethal method, women commit suicide at least as frequently as men do.

Taking into account that mood disorders are approximately twice as common in women as in men, in addition to genetic and psychosocial factors, repeated dysphoric premenstrual or postpartum events might contribute to the greater lifetime prevalence of mood disorders in women. Mood disorders linked to hormonal changes occur during premenstrual, postpartum, and perimenopausal periods. During reproductive events, exposure to and withdrawal from progesterone, more specifically from the centrally acting metabolites of progesterone termed neurosteroids, could modulate receptors, including GABA and serotonin functioning in a fashion similar to chronic stress, increasing the vulnerability to depressive disorders. Factors indicating dysregulation of serotonergic activity include the helpful effect of SSRIs in many women with mood disorders. Estrogen, in addition, modulates neurotransmission at multiple points in the serotonin pathway, including serotonin uptake, synthesis, receptor transcription and density, and response to serotonergic stimulation.

## Menarche, Menstrual Cycle, and Suicide

In a study of high-school girls, later age of onset of menses (menarche) and irregular menstrual cycles are significantly associated with depressive disorders. Secondary amenorrhea is associated with depressive disorders and eating disorders. Moreover, polymenorrhea is associated with eating disorders. Both disorders, depressive disorders and eating disorders, are associated with a substantial increased risk of suicide[69].

Within the menstrual cycle: the menstrual phase (day 0–4), the luteal phase (day 15–28, after ovulation), and the follicular phase (day 4–14, after menstruation but before ovulation), there are differences with respect to an increased risk of suicide specific to the phases. The follicular phase, the time when sex drive is greatest, is the phase of the menstrual cycle associated with the most increased risk of suicide. Increased suicide attempts in women during the follicular phase of the menstrual cycle are reported[70].

Premenstrual dysphoric disorder (PMMD) is severe premenstrual syndrome. PMDD occurs in the luteal phase. Premenstrual dysphoric disorder previously referred to as late luteal-phase dysphoric disorder is recently more extensively investigated. Not only is PMDD more severe than PMS, but it is also more strictly defined, with an emphasis on mood and behavioral symptoms, the cyclic nature of the symptoms, and functional impairment. Clinically, the symptoms completely remit with the onset of menses.

Intermittent antidepressant treatment limited to the luteal phase for women suffering from PMDD appears promising. Use of the medication during the luteal phase only, as opposed to daily continuous treatment throughout the menstrual cycle, may be a better option since such a dosing schedule may reduce risk for certain treatment-emergent side effects. However, it is critical to guarantee that patients who elect luteal phase versus continuous treatment are not experiencing an episode of depressive illness for which intermittent therapy would be inappropriate[71]. Many times a patient has major depressive disorder and a premenstrual worsening of depressive symptoms. Treatment approaches include doubling the dose of the SSRI during the premenstrual phase as described in the following clinical vignette:

> *A 22-year-old, white female with major depressive disorder is in remission taking fluoxetine at 20 mg per day for three years. She tolerates the medication well without side effects. During the premenstrual phase of her monthly cycle, she experiences increasing depression, carbohydrate cravings, excess sleeping, and depressed mood with increasing doom and gloom thinking and transient suicidal thoughts. There is no co-morbid general medical condition or substance related disorder. The patient increased the fluoxetine to 40 mg per day premenstrually, and then decreased the dose back down to 20 mg per day for the other three weeks of her monthly cycle. Her remaining symptoms are in remission and she continues to be symptom-free with improved quality of life.*

Symptoms of a primary mental disorder may be exacerbated during the premenstrual phase of the menstrual cycle. That is, a premenstrual patient with a primary psychiatric disorder (psychotic, mood, anxiety, etc.) can have an exacerbation of the primary psychiatric disorder during the premenstrual phase. This may result in an increased risk of suicidal behavior during that time of the monthly menstrual cycle. For example, a depressed premenstrual female patient may have severe depressive symptoms with increasing suicidality. Furthermore, one study demonstrated that premenstrual exacerbation is a risk factor for suicidal behavior in patients with panic disorder independent of major depression. Patients with premenstrual exacerbation of panic disorder had more active suicidality than patients with panic disorder without premenstrual exacerbation[72].

## Pregnancy and Suicide

Although pregnancy may be a time of emotional well being for some women there is no protection during pregnancy from new-onset depression or relapse of depression. The rates of mood disturbance in pregnant women are, in fact, comparable to those seen in non-pregnant women[73]. Risk factors for depression in pregnant women include a history of major depressive disorder, young age, limited social support, number of children, marital conflict, and ambivalence about pregnancy[74]. Due to a misconception that women are protected from depression during pregnancy, the disorder may be under-diagnosed and under-treated. As many as 75% of euthymic pregnant women with a history of depression who reduced or discontinued antidepressant medication during pregnancy relapsed into depression[75]. When assessing the risks and benefits of taking psychotropic medication during pregnancy, women and their physicians should be aware that the abrupt discontinuation of psychotropic drugs could lead to serious adverse effects such as suicidal ideation[76].

Pregnant patients, not necessarily related to gestational trimester, can become suicidal if there is any associated depression, lack of concentration, anxiety, preoccupations, obsessions, fatigue, worries concerning body functions and compulsions, or little social support. Suicide in pregnancy is strongly associated with HIV. Women who are both pregnant and HIV positive may be at a particularly high risk of suicidal behavior[77]. Substance-dependent pregnant women with posttraumatic stress disorder report more suicide attempts along with more previous drug treatments, more lifetime major mental illness and personality disorders, and higher lifetime rates of sexual abuse compared to similar patients without posttraumatic stress disorder[78].

Suicides, as well as accidents and homicides, are not usually considered due to the pregnancy, yet they may be indirectly related to the pregnancy[79]. Given their desperate situation with an unwanted pregnancy, some women opt for an unsafe abortion, which can lead to their death, but other women can go so far as to commit suicide[80]. In third world countries such as Mexico, Bangladesh, or those in the Caribbean, unwanted pregnancy especially affects adolescent women, single women, and women over 40 years of age. Suicide during pregnancy is more common than perceived. Suicide during pregnancy historically has been classified along with homicide, or pregnancy related deaths by anything such as snakebites, fires, or airplane crashes. A study of suicides in Sweden for the period 1925–1944 found that 7.7% of women committing suicide had been pregnant. The investigators proposed that unwanted pregnancy was the principal reason for these suicides, owing to the limited choices women faced when confronted with an unwanted pregnancy. Of note, another study did not show an association between induced abortion and suicide in a study of suicides after pregnancy[81]. Deaths from pregnant women because of suicide are underreported due to the difficulties in collecting data[82]. One study in Mozambique noted that the magnitude of the problem of violence related maternal death including suicide compared equally to deaths due to pregnancy-induced hypertension[83].

The decision to treat depression during pregnancy must be based on considering the risks associated with untreated depression, as well as the possible risks associated with exposure to medication. The U. S. Food and Drug Administration approves no antidepressant currently specifically for use during pregnancy. However, various amounts of reproductive safety data are available regarding antidepressants. Of the newer antidepressants, information regarding outcomes following prenatal exposure to SSRIs is available; with the greatest amount of information, supporting the reproductive safety exists for fluoxetine[84]. One scenario in the perinatal period is to use SSRIs and low dose typical antipsychotic medication such as haloperidol if discontinuing mood stabilizers such as lithium, valproic acid, and carbamazepine.

Neonates exposed to SSRIs or SNRIs late in the third trimester have developed complications requiring prolonged hospitalization, respiratory support, and tube feeding. Precautions should be taken into consideration when treating pregnant patients for depression. Such complications can arise immediately upon delivery. Reported clinical findings have included respiratory distress, cyanosis, apnea, seizures, temperature instability, feeding difficulty, vomiting, hypoglycemia, hypotonia, hyperetonia, hyperreflexia, tremor, jitteriness, irritability, and constant crying. These features are consistent with either a direct toxic effect of SSRIs and SNRIs or, possibly, a drug discontinuation syndrome. It should be noted that in some cases the clinical picture is consistent with serotonin syndrome. Thus when treating a pregnant woman with SSRI's or SNRIs during the third trimester, the physician should carefully consider the potential risks and benefits of treatment.

The following case report is an example of issues clinicians need to address in psychotic pregnant patient at risk of suicide and infanticide:

*The patient is a twenty-seven year old white female with chronic paranoid schizophrenia who was not taking her medication clozapine. She reports she has been pregnant for six months and that she is in "labor."*

*The patient was committed to the psychiatric hospital for inability to care for herself. She is a poor historian, uncooperative in answering questions. She presented to the local ER the day prior to admission with abdominal pain. She was assessed by the OB/GYN physician, placed on a monitor and found to have no contractions. She stated her nephew had punched her in the stomach repeatedly. She reported she got into an argument with her mother and brother and that they also assaulted her. "My* nephew killed my baby and ate it." Her mother reports that the patient grabbed her sisters hair and was pulling it. She also had anger outbursts and started punching a wall. She has not been on medication (clozapine) since her pregnancy. She was an inpatient at this psychiatric hospital three months prior and went AWOL.

The patient stated she was having contractions every three minutes, her focus. She stated she still was in labor and needs to be checked. She stated she "has the spirit of Michael in me." Michael is a previous child, currently 6 years old. She stated she received a thirty thousand dollar car loan in the mail and believes that her mother and brother stole that money. She has paranoid delusions believing family members are trying to take her money and lock her up. She denied suicidal, homicidal, or infanticide ideation. She feels depressed, has had erratic sleeping and eating patterns and increased energy.

The patients past psychiatric history involves two recent in patient hospitalizations, three months prior to this admission and two years before that. She has tried numerous antipsychotic trials for her paranoid delusions, including most conventional oral and long-acting, injectable antipsychotics and recently atypical oral medications. She responded well to clozapine after a six-month hospitalization nearly two years prior. She had her first psychotic break as a teenager. She has been non-compliant and significantly partially compliant with oral medications. The conventional depot neuroleptic caused extrapyramidal side effects. She has a history of suicide attempts, and she becomes quite impulsive when active positive psychotic symptoms occur, such as command auditory hallucination in conjunction with depressive episodes. She reported episodes of depression; she has had significant substance abuse in the past including methamphetamine. Urine drug screen prior to admission was normal.

The past medical history is significant for asthmatic bronchitis. She denied any allergies. She had one prior normal vaginal delivery of a healthy baby boy six years ago.

The developmental and social history is significant for the patient being divorced. She has one previous child. She had been living alone in the community actively six months pregnant. She has two years of college education. She did odd jobs such as painting houses. Her mother raised her. Parents divorced when she was age five. She has a mentally ill sister and mother. Her dad is somewhat supportive, has remarried, and attempted to help her in the past.

The mental status exam revealed the patient's appearance as markedly disheveled. She was uncooperative; her affect was blunted and inappropriate to thought content. Mood was depressed. Speech was normal rate, pitch and tone. Thought content was remarkable for severe, Schneiderian, first-rank symptoms including thought broadcasting, thought insertion. There was marked thought blocking. Although the patient denied auditory hallucinations, she appeared to be responding to internal auditory stimulation as evidenced by mumbling talking to herself, staring into space. She believed the devil was on her shoulder, showing abnormal mannerisms such as rotating her head to the right, frequently associated with hallucinatory experiences. She would stare at the door and mumble to herself. Impulse control was fair. She denied suicidal or homicidal ideations, intentions, or plans. She denied thoughts of self-mutilation or harming herself or the baby. She was easily distracted, with poor attention and concentration. The Folstein Mini Mental Status examination for cognitive deficits was normal. Insight and judgment was poor. She stated, "I need to be discharged immediately to buy a truck and get groceries."

Her admitting diagnosis was schizophrenia, chronic paranoid with acute exacerbation due to non-compliance with oral medication and six-month active pregnancy.

The patient's hospital course was complicated. Trying to weigh the risks and benefits of medicating this patient with possible adverse effects on the fetus was constantly reviewed. Initially, she was offered low dose haloperidol, 0.5 mg at night. However, she was afraid that the haloperidol would harm the baby, and she would not take that medication. She did start her prenatal vitamins, and eventually she began cooperating more with her prenatal care after numerous prompts. One month later, we initiated a denial of rights for the patient to receive psychiatric medication against her will *for her ongoing psychosis. It was approved, but upon further review, the risk of adverse reaction to the fetus versus the benefit of decreasing psychosis was weighed. Since the patient was cooperating with her prenatal care and did not exhibit any infanticide thoughts, suicidal thoughts, homicidal ideation, or poor impulse control, but remained delusional, it was decided not to force medication at the time. Although haloperidol and lorazepam, low dose, oral medication was offered, the patient took the medication only one or two times.*

*A second opinion with the medical staff was scheduled two weeks later to get input and opinions from numerous physicians regarding this patient's care. The conclusion of that meeting was that appropriated care was being provided. I.e, it was not necessary to force medication with daily injections at that time. I rescinded the denial of rights order for reasons outlined above.*

*The patient continued to do well on the psychiatric unit, despite having active ongoing psychosis. She cooperated with her prenatal care. She was eating and sleeping well. She was participating in one-on-one education regarding her pregnancy, and she did not exhibit any suicidal, homicidal, or infanticidal ideations, intentions, or plans. She had episodes of anxiety and agitation a few times a week, demanding she be discharged from the hospital.*

*There was no development of depression, but mild anxiety increased. During the eighth month of pregnancy, low dose risperidone and low dose benztropine were ordered, but she was again afraid to take the medication. She had responded somewhat to oral risperidone in the past but was non-compliant with the oral medication. She continuously stated that haloperidol caused her to suffer from parkinsonism. A consultation for the long acting injectable form of risperidone was obtained and approved. The patient agreed to take the medication. She received the first injection of 25 milligrams, while eight months pregnant, after the risks and benefits were weighed. The reason this was started at this time was that it was suspected that the patient would become even more delusional during the post partum period. Since this long-acting, injectable form of risperidone was new at the time, it was not well studied for its use in pregnancy.*

*Beginning treatment during the eighth month of pregnancy commenced. By three weeks prior to delivery, she changed her mind and did not want further long-acting injectable atypical antipsychotic medication. In addition, she agreed to take fluoxetine, not during pregnancy, but only after delivery, because she was afraid it would cause blindness in the baby. She was getting near delivery one week prior, using a semi-recliner chair and a special hospital bed. She remained on bed rest except for bathroom and meals. Her vital signs remained stable during this time. She began labor and was suddenly transferred to the local hospital delivery room.*

*Mental status at the time of discharge revealed the patient in a psychotic delusional state with inappropriate affect and ambivalent thinking with auditory hallucinations. But there were no suicidal or homicidal ideations, intentions, or plans. She had poor insight and judgment, but there was no depression, and she was oriented.*

*The patient subsequently delivered a healthy baby boy. She was transferred back to the psychiatric hospital, with child protective services involved. Upon return from the hospital, she became agitated and impulsive, and she had insomnia and delusions. She started oral risperidone and a denial of rights for long acting injectable atypical antipsychotic was obtained.*

*She started taking the medication, at a dose of 37.5 mg intramuscularly every two weeks Delusions decreased. For moderate depressive symptoms, she started fluoxetine 20 mg per day. She was discharged to a group home. She will be seen in the outpatient psychiatric clinic for follow up.*

## Suicide After Miscarriage

About 10–20% of clinically recognized pregnancies end in miscarriage and psychiatric consequences, including depression, develop. There is an increased risk of suicide associated with depressive symptoms after miscarriage, especially among impoverished minority women. For example, Hispanic women have significantly greater mean depression scores, younger age, severity of depression, number of previous reproductive losses, and lower socioeconomic status than did white women. Married women had less depression than did divorced or single women after miscarriage.

The awareness of the link between voluntary pregnancy termination and suicide is better known. Post abortion emotional distress is difficult to recognize and to provide appropriate treatment for. The emotional needs center on the woman who struggles with the feelings of grief, shame, and guilt, or of being judged by others. Social taboos can stifle discussion of abortion related feelings. After an abortion, some women may suffer symptoms of loss and isolation that may place them at risk for despair and suicide.

## Postpartum Depression and Suicide

Depression during the postpartum period remains one of the most frequently observed complications in modern obstetrics[85], unlike postpartum blues which is relatively benign with symptoms remitting by about the tenth postpartum day. Nonpsychotic postpartum depression is less common than postpartum blues, with signs and symptoms similar to those seen in other depressed patients, depressed mood, anhedonia, low energy, guilty ruminations, and suicidal ideation[86]. Postpartum depression may present from twenty-four hours to several months after delivery. While postpartum depression is well known to the public and medical community, it is often overlooked or ignored by patients and caregivers[87]. Increased risk of postpartum depression, including suicidal thoughts, is depressive symptoms during pregnancy, marital discord, inadequate social support, and stressful life events. A history of psychiatric illness and a previous history of postpartum illness increases suicidal risk in these patients. Left untreated, postpartum depression is associated with health risks to the mother as well as to the child in terms of cognitive, emotional, and social development[88]. Maternal depression in the postpartum period may have adverse effects on maternal infant attachment and long-term infant cognitive development[89].

Treatment of postpartum depression may consist of pharmacotherapy. Fluoxetine[90], sertraline[91], and venlafaxine[92] have demonstrated efficacy for postpartum depression. For patients who are particularly concerned about the possibility of detrimental effects caused by the trace amounts of psychiatric medication evident in the serum of breastfed infants whose mothers use these compounds, an alternative to consider is the use of infant formula instead of breast-feeding. The risk of untreated depression must be considered.

## Postpartum Psychosis and Suicide

Postpartum psychosis is a rare disorder, and it is considered a psychiatric emergency. It is associated with the most severe symptoms and generally requires inpatient treatment compared with non-psychotic postpartum depression and postpartum blues. The onset can be as early as the first forty-eight to seventy-two hours postpartum, with the majority of women developing symptoms within the first two weeks after delivery. Symptoms may include restlessness, irritability, depressed or elated mood, disorganized behavior, delusions, and hallucinations. Puerperal psychosis has been associated with bipolar disorder, and it is often treated similarly to manic psychosis, with mood stabilizers, antipsychotic medications, or both[93]. Untreated puerperal psychosis has been associated with infanticide and considerable maternal morbidity[94], including increased suicide[95]. Therefore, aggressive treatment is necessary to ensure maternal and neonatal well being.

## Peri and Postmenopause and Suicide

Another time of change of female reproductive biology, the transition to menopause, and its association with risk for depression and suicide remains unclear[96]. Menopause is frequently associated with physical symptoms and psychosocial transition in a woman's life. An increased rate of recurrence, mood fluctuations, and the emergence of depressive symptoms, but not necessarily of a new onset major depressive disorder, have been associated with perimenopause. The combination use of hormone replacement therapy and antidepressant therapy has been a therapeutic option. Despite the evolving data supporting an antidepressant effect of certain forms of estrogen—transdermal estradiol appears to be effective in the treatment of depression in perimenopausal women—the role of hormone as a therapeutic intervention will be scrutinized much more following recent reports from the Women's Health Initiative. This study suggests that postmenopausal women treated with estrogen and progestin may face a higher risk of serious health effects. Antidepressants such as SSRIs have been quite effective in relieving peri and postmenopausal depression. Adequate treatment of postmenopausal depression is important to prevent further deterioration into late life depression and suicide.

In summary, women can have increased risk of suicide depending on her phases during the life cycle. Certain periods are particularly risky to develop increased suicidality.

## Men and Suicide

There are important specific gender considerations in approaching the suicidal patient[97]. Both suicide and depression are different in men and women. Recognizing the differences in the clinical presentation of suicidality in men and women may enhance the clinician's ability to reduce suicides.

Aside from common risk factors for depression in both sexes including stressful life events, family history of a mood disorder, and persistent psychosocial stressors, suicide has traditionally been a male behavior since medieval times in western societies. The male to female ratio of annual suicide rates per 100,000 in the United States was recently reported as 18.7 to 4.4 or 4.25. There is the rather consistent sex ratio of suicide at about four male to one female. Men attempt suicide less often then women. However, men have a higher completion rate of suicide. Worldwide suicide rates have increased over the past three decades mainly among men. The annual suicide rates per 100,000 rose from 16.2 to 18.7 in men[98].

While men have a lower prevalence of major depressive disorder compared to women, (12.7%) and perhaps less chronic, recurrent depressive episodes, other factors most likely play an important role accounting for a high suicide completion rate in males.

Men may have a genetic susceptibility specific to both suicidal ideation and suicide attempt that is not explained by the inheritance of common psychiatric disorders. Both suicidal ideation and suicidal attempt are influenced by additive genetic effects in a study of 3372 twin male pairs after controlling for the inheritance of psychiatric disorders[99].

Men have attempts that are more lethal. In addition, male attempted suicides by violent methods show a clear asymmetry in seasonal distribution, with a peak in spring months and a trough in autumn months. Examples of more lethal attempts involve the use of a firearm, hanging, carbon monoxide poisoning, drowning, suffocation, or jumping from a great height[100]. Examples of less lethal attempts may involve superficial wrist slashing. Drug overdoses and poisoning may be less violent, but they vary in their toxicity and lethality. Risk of a fatal outcome of a suicidal act is least with weak intent and the use of a low lethality method, such as an overdose involving a harmless medication. Risk is highest with firm intention of dying and use of a highly lethal method[101].

Men use means that are more lethal, and they are thus more likely to kill themselves[102]. Men with suicidality often have more co-morbid alcoholism and other substance related disorders. Male alcoholics show a spring peak of suicide as opposed to other diagnostic groups, suggesting a seasonal distribution of suicide in alcohol-dependent males[103].

Loss of a close personal relationship, often a domestic partner, is common during the last year of life among alcoholic men completing suicide. Domestic violence appears to typify many of their domestic relationships, particularly among younger men and men with early onset alcoholism[104].

It is thought that men become suicidal in response to impersonal problems, such as work or health problems. Yet, problems in interpersonal relationships are the most frequent precipitating event of suicide for both men and women. For example, in a report of 66 male cases of suicide ages between 18 and 53 in Canada, the last major event before suicide was a consequence of a highly painful event of rejection by a loved one. The suicide is provoked by the incapacity to respond to the loved one's demands for changing behavior. The person usually has associated severe psychopathology or drug and alcohol addiction. This last major event before suicide takes place in the context of severe ongoing difficulties.

There is a need for suicide prevention services in domestic violence situations. Murder followed by suicide in domestic violence situations, for example, is not well understood in American society. During the past five years, South Carolina has ranked number one three times for women murdered by their partners, yet ranked 28th for suicide. This study found that male perpetrators of violence against others were more likely to engage in murder-suicide. Domestic violence may be a function of power and control; others believe men who murder their wives may be experiencing depression. Depression and suicide in men often results in isolation from others, including the unwanted separation from an intimate partner who has left or is threatening to leave.

Furthermore, mental illness and suicide of a spouse could have a huge impact on the other spouse. The suicide risk is increased in spouses whose partners suffer from a psychiatric disorder or who have committed suicide. In a large, Danish population study, it was found that the risk of suicide was increased in people whose spouse had been first admitted two years earlier, had committed suicide, or died by other causes. Thus, there is an increased risk of suicide among people whose marital partner has been admitted with a psychiatric disorder or has died by suicide or other causes. Studying suicide in relation to spousal psychiatric illness is an area recently explored.

The loss of a partner seems to have a stronger impact on men than women. In fact, young male widows have a high risk of suicide. National data suggest that as many as 1 in 400 young adult widowed men aged 20–35 years will die by suicide in any given year, compared with 1 in 9000 married men in the general population.

The traditional male role increases male vulnerability to premature death due to coronary heart disease, violence, accidents, drug and alcohol abuse, and suicide. The male vulnerability is promoted by the traditional masculine role, which promotes maladaptive coping strategies such as emotional inexpressiveness, reluctance to seek help, and a perceived reduction in social role opportunities that can lead to social exclusion[105]. Men less often keep regular monthly outpatient clinic appointments to seek help, perhaps believing it is a sign of weakness[106]. Barriers to seeking help include stigma of mental illness. Methods to decrease these barriers include specific help-seeking behaviors and enhancing a targeted person's willingness to seek help.

More occupational hazards such as working near phone lines, active military combat, and more devastating effects of unemployment can contribute to higher risk for suicide in men.

Testosterone is high in men with violent, aggressive behavior. The importance of testosterone in male suicide attempters was measured in cerebrospinal fluid, but results demonstrated lower cerebrospinal fluid testosterone levels than aggressive, violent patients in other studies. These results suggest that suicide attempts may be mediated by different biological variables than aggression[107].

## General Medical Conditions and Suicide

Contact with primary care providers in the time leading up to suicide is common. More patients see the primary care provider (75%) than a mental health care professional (33%) within the year prior to suicide. Within one month of suicide, an average of 45% of suicide victims had contact with primary care providers compared to 20% having contact with mental health services[108]. As many as 20% of older patients commit suicide the same day of contact with primary care providers[109].

*An older man with a history of osteoarthritis, who was recently divorced, was seen at the family physician's office complaining of worsening somatic symptoms, such as fatigue and joint pain. On exam, there was no joint tenderness or worse range of motion. The primary care physician prescribed a common analgesic. At home later that day, the patient was found hanging in the bathroom with a suicide note nearby*—this scenario is not as uncommon as most would believe.

While it is not known what degree contact with primary care and mental health care providers can prevent suicide, the majority of individuals who die by suicide do make contact with such providers. Careful questioning and prompt treatment of depression may save lives and reduce suicide risk in the primary care setting. Both patients and clinicians are reluctant to broach the subject, and it may be overlooked[110]. Physicians can open a dialogue with patients so that those who need treatment receive it before they resort to suicide. Since suicide can be encountered across all disciplines of medicine, physicians in particular have a unique opportunity to intervene, diagnose and treat such patients. One way to understand suicide and general medical conditions is to appreciate first, how a patient with mental illness presents himself to the medical clinic, hospital or emergency room. A patient with a primary mental disorder and/or substance-related disorder, so called a dual diagnosis, usually has a third group of risk factors leading to increased morbidity and mortality including suicide, their general medical conditions.

In one of my published studies involving 208 consecutive patients admitted to a hospital in Southern Nevada in the late 1990's, the average number of general medical conditions a patient had while presenting with psychiatric illness was 2.5, compared with 3.5 conditions a patient had while presenting with substance related illness. Patients with both primary mental illness and substance related disorders had an average of 4.5 general medical conditions. The percent of the general medical conditions that were considered severe was only 10% in patients with primary psychiatric disorders, 20% in patients with substance related disorders, and 30% in patients with both primary psychiatric disorders and substance-related disorders.

Applying this model to cardiac disorders for example, I noted a patient with depression (mental disorder) might be diagnosed with stable angina pectoris. A patient with cocaine and alcohol abuse (substance related disorder) may have unstable angina. However, the same type of patient with both depression and polysubstance dependence, a dual diagnosis, may present with an acute myocardial infarction.

In a second example of this observation in obstetrics and gynecology, I noted a patient with psychosis presenting with symptomatic cervical cancer. In addition, a patient with heroin and cocaine dependence was presenting an infected episiotomy with persistent vaginal bleeding. However, in the same type of patient with psychosis and heroin-cocaine dependence, dual diagnosis may present at some point as a three-month, high-risk pregnancy with jaundice, hepatitis B & C, and AIDS.

A third example applied to endocrinology in a patient with mental illness presenting with diabetes mellitus. A similar patient with substance abuse may present with uncontrolled diabetes mellitus. But a similar patient with both mental illness and substance abuse, dual diagnosis, may present with diabetic ketoacidosis and impending coma, a triple diagnosis.

The common theme illustrated in the examples above is that it seems as though the severity of the general medical condition gets worse and is associated with more morbidity, mortality, and unexplained death. The study demonstrates the need for physical examinations in patients suffering from dual diagnosis. These triple diagnosis patients compromise a substantial risk of unexplained and premature deaths including deaths due to suicide [Author's note: in retrospect, most of the death reviews I reviewed, including suicides, were noted to have this as a common trend. Most of the patients reviewed had suffered from this triple diagnosis.].

This concept is illustrated in a study of suicidal ideation and suicide attempts in patients suffering from a number of general medical conditions, after controlling for primary mental illness and substance related disorders. Whereas 16.3 % of individuals, in a representative sample of U. S. young adults ages 17–39 described suicidal ideation at some point in their lives, 25.2% of individuals with a general medical condition and 35.0% of those with two or more medical illnesses reported lifetime suicidal ideation. Similarly, whereas 5.5% of respondents had made a suicide attempt, 8.9% of those with a general medical condition and 16.2% of those with two or more general medical conditions had attempted suicide. Thus, a significant association is found between the number general medical conditions and suicidality[111].

Another way to increase understanding between suicide and general medical conditions is to know relationships between suicides across many different types of general medical conditions. Suicide is increased in patients with general medical conditions even after controlling for co-morbid substance related disorders and primary psychiatric disorders.

## Neurological Disorders and Suicide

Aside from acquired ventral prefrontal cortex injuries, known to be associated with disinhibition and an increase in impulsive behaviors including aggression and suicide attempts, there are a wide variety of neurological disorders associated with increased suicidal risk: epilepsy (seizure disorders) , sensory disorders (pain disorders and migraines with aura), motor nerve disorders (Huntington's disease), multiple sclerosis, traumatic brain and spinal cord injuries, and cerebrovascular diseases (stroke).

Identification and aggressive treatment of psychiatric problems, especially depression, as well as reduction of modifiable suicide risk factors among patients with neurological illness are needed to reduce the risk of attempted and completed suicide in these patients. The risk of attempted or completed suicide in neurological illness is strongly associated with depression, feelings of hopelessness or helplessness, and social isolation. Additional suicide risk factors in persons with neurological illness include cognitive impairment, relatively young age, moderate physical disability, recent onset or change in illness, lack of future plans or perceived meaning in life, recent personal, occupational, or financial losses, and prior history of psychiatric illness or suicidal behavior. Mental disorders including substance dependence, psychotic disorders, anxiety disorders, and some personality disorders may also contribute to increased risk of suicide among persons with neurological illness[112].

Pain is the most common symptom for which patients seek medical help. Pain implies damage to the person, either physical or psychological, and chronic pain, if untreated, will itself damage the person. Suicidal intent in patients with acute and chronic pain shows a relationship between suicidal ideation to the experience of pain, pain-related disability, and pain coping efforts. Depressed patients report higher levels of pain. There is an increased prevalence of depression in specific pain disorders including phantom limb pain[113], migraine[114], facial pain[115], chronic lower back pain[116], tempomandibular disorders[117], fibromyalgia[118], and irritable bowel syndrome[119]. Thus, when individuals with chronic pain report suicidal intent, it is imperative that measures are implemented immediately and the patients depression is treated aggressively[120]. The tricyclic antidepressants have an analgesic effect due to central blockage of monoamine uptake, enhancement of descending inhibition, adrenergic blockade of nerve sprouts, NMDA receptor antagonistic effects, opioid modification, and sodium channel blockade. The first of another new generation of antidepressants will be approved for pain and depression based on these properties and their clinical safety and efficacy in recent clinical trials, which adds to the treatment options for patients.

Suicide is considered to be one of the most important causes of death contributing to the increased mortality of persons with seizure disorder (epilepsy). An epileptic seizure is an episode of uncontrollable abnormal motor, sensory, or psychological behavior caused by hyperactive, hyper-synchronous abnormal brain electrical activity. The risk of suicide in seizure patients seems to increase with high seizure frequency and with the use of multiple antiepileptic drug polytherapy or anticonvulsant polypharmacy. Epilepsy patients who committed suicide in one study had the following associations: early onset (during adolescence), psychiatric illness, and inadequate neurological follow-up. Severity was not necessarily a factor[121]. Some epilepsy patients, particularly those with a history of depression, are at increased risk of post-ictal suicidal ideation. Psychiatric co-morbidity is common among people with epilepsy. For example, the rate of mood disorders, especially major depression, has consistently been reported to be elevated, and the risk of suicide has been estimated to be ten times higher than in the general population. Epilepsy is a risk for depression, and a history of depression is associated with a four to sixfold increased risk of developing epilepsy. The idea of common pathogenic mechanisms involving the occurrence of one in the presence of the other is being evaluated. In addition, depression may be iatrogenic, that is induced with various antiepileptic drugs used to treat the seizure disorder or after surgical treatment of intractable epilepsy.

Anticonvulsant medications are frequently indicated for both seizures and mood stabilization in bipolar patients. As described earlier, these anticonvulsants (divalproex, carbamazepine, lamotrigine, and tigabine) are not proven effective for suicide risk reduction in bipolar patients, so caution is advised when using anticonvulsants in a depressed patient with seizure disorder. Frequently, an antidepressant is needed with the anticonvulsant instead of lithium monotherapy.

Huntington's disease is an inherited, autosomal, dominant genetic disorder of chromosome 4 that damages neurons involving the frontal lobe. Patients with Huntington's disease often present with profound psychiatric symptoms including self-injurious behavior and suicidal ideations. Even non-gene carriers have a very high frequency of attempted suicide. The relatives also have high frequencies of psychiatric disorders, suicide or suicide attempts. With the use of testing programs, the importance of focusing on suicide risk of participants is essential[122].

Multiple sclerosis, a progressive chronic inflammatory disease of the white matter of the brain, involving destruction of the myelin sheath of the central nervous system neurons, is associated with depressive symptoms and suicidality. In particular, shorter and more severe episodes of illness are most correlated with depressive symptoms. A study suggests that depressive symptoms occur more often in multiple sclerosis than in other chronic medical illness[123]. In an examination of suicidal intent in 140 patients with multiple sclerosis, the severity of major depression, alcohol abuse, and living alone were strongly associated with suicidal intent. A third of suicidal patients with multiple sclerosis had not received psychological help. Two-thirds of patients with current major depression, all suicidal, had not received antidepressant medication. Thus, suicidal intent is a potentially treatable cause of morbidity and mortality in multiple sclerosis[124].

Cerebrovascular disease, including ischemic stroke, is associated with increased suicide. Stroke patients have double the risk for suicide. During the first fifteen months after a stroke, the risk of suicide increases and it is most associated with recurrent strokes, depressive symptoms, more disabling strokes, and right-sided strokes[125]. Although the risk of suicide increases during the immediate period three months to fifteen months after the stroke, the risk of suicide appears to decline with time after a stroke, being greatest within the first five years[126]. A rare report of suicide in a patient with symptomatic carotid artery occlusion has been reported[127].

Ophthalmologists need to be aware of the suicide risk in patients suffering the emotional impact exerted by sight loss. When compared with a hearing-impaired control group, impaired sights alone can acutely affect otherwise psychologically healthy individuals. Blindness, as well as sight restoration, is reported to induce both temporary and longer-term psychopathology. In some cases, readjustment may not occur, and suicide may result[128].

## Cardiac Disorders and Suicide

Congenital cardiac malformations include the following: tetralogy of Fallot with pulmonary atresia and aorto-pulmonary collateral arteries, Eisenmenger syndrome, and functionally univentricular cardiac anatomy. Congenital cardiac malformations associated with persistent cyanosis in adult survivors can lead to an inability to interact socially and increase risk of depression with suicidality. Evidence suggests a relatively high incidence of depression in these adults at median age 36 years old. In the classification of the New York Heart Association, depression was associated with older age (40 versus 33 years old), worse functional state and unemployment, but it was independent from the severity of cyanosis, the level of the hematocrit, the saturation of oxygen, and previous surgical treatment[129].

Expanding scientific evidence supports the relationship between depression and cardiovascular disorders. Depression increases patient vulnerability to both cardiac events and mortality[130]. Depression increases the risk for cardiac mortality. That is, cardiac mortality risk is a higher in patients suffering major depression. Moreover, the excess cardiac mortality risk is more than twice as high for major depression as it is for minor depression[131].

The relationship between depression and cardiac disease emphasizes that psychiatric disorders (depression) can affect physical conditions (cardiac disease). Psychiatric disorders can affect not only the prognosis of general medical conditions, but also the diagnosis and treatment as well. A depressed patient may not have the energy or desire to leave the household to go to the doctor and delay diagnosis, be less likely to get general medical care, and often present with more advanced stages of general medical conditions.

Patients with depression are less likely to follow recommendations to reduce cardiac risk during recovery from a myocardial infarction. Those with major depression also reported taking medications as prescribed less often than those without. Hospitalized patients who have symptoms of at least mild to moderate depression or to have major depression and/or dysthymia report lower adherence to a low fat diet, regular exercise, reducing stress, and increasing social support[132].

A review of patients with congestive heart failure and depression, suggest that the identification and treatment of depressed CHF patients may significantly improve level of functioning in these patients[133].

After an acute myocardial infarction, coronary artery bypass grafting, and percutaneous transluminal coronary angioplasty, male and female patients both suffer impaired quality of life. The quality of life measured one month and one year after the cardiac event showed differences. Women tended to experience more impaired general health, feelings of arrhythmia, anxiety, depression, low self-esteem, and sex life disturbances compared with men who have the same cardiac disorder[134].

The type of psychotropic medication used to treat suicidal patients with cardiac disease requires special considerations. When prescribing psychotropic medication in patients with cardiac disease, choice of medication is important. For example, in post myocardial infarction patients, special care in selecting psychotropic medication that does not contribute to hypertension, arrhythmias, lipids and liver enzyme changes, and thrombosis is imperative, as outlined in the HALT study.

Choosing psychotropic medication in a cardiac patient includes consideration that the medication does not exacerbate hypertension and tachycardia, does not cause weight gain or hyperlipidemia, and does not have significant drug-drug interactions with cardiac medication.

These are important clinical issues to consider when safely and effectively treating patients with depressive disorders and cardiac disease. A recent study focused on the treatment of depression in cardiac patients; in particular, it addressed antidepressant therapy for major depressive disorder in patients with acute myocardial infarction or unstable angina. Compared to placebo, sertraline at 50 to 200 mg/day did not significantly affect left ventricular ejection fraction, ventricular premature complexes, QTc interval, or other cardiac measures. Depressive symptoms improved, as reported in the SADHART (Sertraline Antidepressant Heart Attack Randomized Trial) study. This study inaugurates a series of studies intended to address the impact of antidepressant therapy on cardiovascular risk[135]. Sertraline did not exacerbate hypertension or increase heart rate, like venlafaxine does. It did not cause weight gain or affect lipid levels, like mirtazepine does. It is only a weak inhibitor of liver enzymes, so it does not interfere with the metabolism of beta-blocking cardiac medications like fluoxetine, paroxetine and bupropion do.

## Respiratory Disorders and Suicide

Asthma patients have an increased likelihood of panic attack and suicidal ideation. In a sample of primary care patients, physician diagnosed asthma is associated with self-reported panic attacks and suicidal ideation, but not depression[136]. Asthma was associated with a more than fourfold increase in the likelihood of a suicide attempt in another study examining the association between the presence of a general medical illness and suicidality in a representative sample of U. S. young adults ages 17–39[137]. Other disorders, such as bronchogenic carcinoma, have been associated with increased suicidality even after controlling for co-morbid substance related disorders and primary psychiatric disorders. The suicidal patient may require a tracheostomy and artificial respiration via mechanical ventilation after a suicidal act such as hanging or overdose. Pneumonia is a frequent co-morbid general medical condition.

Knowledge of drug-drug interactions can aid the clinician in treating depression in patients with respiratory diseases. For example, the addition of a first line, simple antidepressant, fluovoxamine at 50 mg per day, to a depressed elderly female patient with asthmatic bronchitis taking theophylline at 600 mg per day had caused hemodynamically unstable supraventricular tachyarrhythmia requiring two large-bore central lines for intravenous hemodynamic support. This complication was most likely a result of the fluvoxamine increasing serum aminophylline levels to a toxic level, which subsequently caused the arrhythmia.

## Endocrine Disorders and Suicide

Obesity, as defined by body mass index (BMI), is associated with major depression, suicide attempts, and suicide ideation, but it affects women and men differently. In women, there is increased body mass index; whereas decreased body mass index in men is associated with the probability of past-year major depression, suicide attempts, and suicide ideation as reported in adult U.S. general population sample[138].

In a study of suicide attempts and ideation in Bipolar type I patients it was noted that suicide attempters had a significantly higher BMI than nonattempters. Obesity correlated with important clinical features of patients with bipolar I disorder. Obese patients experience a greater number of lifetime depressive and manic episodes, present with more severe and difficult to treat mood symptoms, and are more likely to develop recurrence of mood symptoms, a depressive recurrence in particular. The finding that there is a relationship between suicide attempts and BMI clearly suggests that suicide risk is yet another aspect of poorer outcome in patients with high BMI. Obese patients are more likely than non-obese patients to have a co-morbid anxiety disorder, more likely to have been treated with antidepressants. These observations in bipolar patients suggest that obesity may well independently increase the risk of suicide through its severe psychosocial consequences, including discrimination and stigmatization in multiple areas of daily life, and its negative impact on general physical well-being and functioning, quality of life, self-esteem, and psychological well-being[139].

Diabetic patients with depression and other depressed patients with general medical conditions are less likely to follow treatment recommendations such as a diet and medication regimen. Deaths due to hyperglycemic and hyperosmolar coma in diabetics are usually disease-related. There are cases of intentional ingestion of a sugar solution in patients with diabetes known to be depressed with suicidal intention[140]. Other case reports of intentional suicidal acts involving large doses of insulin (greater than 2000 units) or overdosing on oral hypoglycemic agents (metformin) are reported in medical journals. Insulin syringes are used for intravenous or subcutaneous injection of illicit substances in suicidal acts involving overdose in mentally ill patients. Psychotropic medications can exacerbate or worsen certain diabetes, taking a controlled diabetic into an uncontrolled diabetic state or causing an uncontrolled diabetic to suffer diabetic ketoacidosis, coma, or death[141]. Weight gain, insulin resistance, and abnormal lipid profiles from psychotropic medications can fuel the metabolic syndrome[142]. In addition, recent weight loss in a diabetic patient may actually signal worsening diabetes. Care and caution are needed when choosing psychotropic medication for diabetic suicidal patients. Frequent monitoring of the blood pressure, weight, blood glucose, and lipid profiles is now recommended when prescribing psychotropic medication[143].

Estrogen therapy for severe persistent depression in women remains a controversial clinical issue due to safety issues. However, several studies have demonstrated useful efficacy. Testosterone in men and women, sex hormones, and gender differences in suicide is another area of research. The use of depot Provera, a long-acting, injectable female hormone in sexually aggressive men with high testosterone can decrease sexually aggressive impulses and urges, but it needs to be combined with psychotropic medication to treat the mental illness as well.

Hypothyroidism can lead to metabolic and psychiatric symptoms, most notably depression, and it may blunt the effectiveness of antidepressants. A patient with hyperthyroidism, a potentially life threatening condition, may present a mixed dysphoric, agitated, depressed state. Finally, lithium can induce hypo- or hyperthyroidism, so suicidal patients with mood disorder taking lithium need to be monitored carefully for the development of any adverse effects on the thyroid gland.

The hypothalamic-pituitary-adrenal neuroendocrine axis is another area of research in suicide. Stress-induced, increased cortisol secretion may play a role in the development of violent suicidal behavior. Violent suicidal behavior is associated with increased cortisol secretion[144]. These patients have higher urinary cortisol levels, supporting the idea that suicidal behavior is associated with depressive disorders that are commonly induced by social stressors in persons with a trait-dependent vulnerability. Higher cortisol levels were found in adolescents after a suicidal attempt, especially in females with depressive disorders in the presence of psychosocial and environmental problems, and elevated risk level of repeated suicidal attempt[145].

Complex endocrinopathies such as the HAIR-AN syndrome, which is the combination of hyperandrogenism, insulin resistance, and acanthosis nigricans, can present with suicidal, psychotic, treatment-resistant depression.

In a report, it was noted that the severe psychiatric symptoms resolved with ovarian suppression treatment using oral contraceptives only.

> *A 37-year-old, divorced female with refractory depression, reported her first episode of depression at age 9–10 with the onset of menses. She tried to kill herself at ages 11 and 17. The only time she remembered not being depressed was when she was using oral contraceptives. She first was prescribed them for oligomenorrhea at age 14. She has suffered from oligomenorrhea on and off ever since. The next time she took oral contraceptives was in her early twenties while she was married. She stopped taking them after she had her son. An outpatient psychiatrist had been treating her for the last ten years. Three years before presenting with refractory depression, she developed psychotic depression and suicide attempts that required in patient psychiatric care. Five years prior she gained 40lbs and developed hirsutism, acne, and a low-pitched voice. Eight months prior, she was diagnosed with acanthosis nigricans, which is a dark hyperpigmentation of the epidermis in body folds. An endocrinologist evaluated her for oligomenorrhea, obesity, and hirsutism, and he prescribed 0.25 mg of dexamethasone per day to inhibit androgen production, regulate menses, and reduce facial hair. Twelve weeks prior to admission, she experienced severe depression. Her psychiatrist treated her with bupropion, amitriptyline, buspirone, and lithium while continuing the same dexamethasone treatment. She developed abnormal glucose tolerance tests and elevated insulin levels. All psychotropic medications and dexamethasone were stopped. A diagnosis of HAIR-AN syndrome (hyperandrogenism, insulin resistance, and acanthosis nigricans) was made. She was prescribed oral contraceptives only, and within several weeks, her mood improved. Two months later, she was clinically stable, and had lost 25 lbs.*

That case report highlights neuroendocrine causes of suicidal depression[146].

In summary, many endocrine disorders are associated with suicidality. Assessing for endocrinopathies can lead to a better understanding of the biology of suicide.

## Renal Disease and Suicide

The psychological adjustments to the presence of organ failure and the dependence on a machine to sustain life, the impact of end stage renal disease requiring chronic dialysis therapy on the lifestyle of the patient with renal disease is significant. Management of dialysis patients requires input from not only nephrologists, but also psychiatrists. A psychiatric evaluation is recommended in the initial evaluation of all prospective dialysis patients. In their treatment, one should consider what prophylactic steps should be taken to avoid the occurrence of a variety of psychiatric symptoms in patients suffering with real failure including delirium, psychosis, depression, anxiety, sexual dysfunctions, uncooperative behavior and suicidality. A very rare case of suicide in and elderly woman by stab wound of a fistula for hemodialysis access is reported. Although the incidence of suicide attempts in people undergoing hemodialysis is increased, suicide means do not usually include stab wounds of the arteriovenous access. Medications have an important role in the treatment of suicidality in patients with renal failure[147]. Titrating of the medication in a patient with renal insufficiency slowly and carefully is required for extra safety.

## Rheumatologic Disorders and Suicide

Systemic lupus erythematosus (SLE) is an acute and chronic inflammatory process of unknown etiology that involves multiple organ systems. It is the prototype autoimmune disorder, which is eight times more common in females than males. Factors associated with anxiety depression and suicide ideation in female outpatients with SLE in a Japanese study included a lack of understanding SLE at the beginning of treatment which lead to anxiety and depression; human relations among family members contributing to depression; and high daily steroid dosage contributing to anxiety. All of which significantly correlated with suicidal ideation[148].

Suicidal SLE patients often have a history of neuropsychiatric SLE presenting with depression and appreciable disease activity at the time of the suicide attempt. In a study of 300 patients with SLE identified to have attempted suicide or completed suicide, five patients made seven attempts at suicide over a twenty year follow-up period: one of them was fatal. All of those attempting suicide had a history of neuropsychiatric SLE presenting with depression. They made suicide attempts soon after the onset of neuropsychiatric SLE, at median time of 12.5 months. Two patients had appreciable disease activity at the time of the suicide attempt. Lymphopenia was present in five suicide attempts. Anti-SSA/Ro antibodies were detected in three patients. All patients apart from one responded to standard treatment for depression; the remaining female patient made two subsequent suicide attempts, with a fatal outcome. Greater awareness of the risk of suicide in patients with psychiatric manifestations of systemic lupus erythematosus may help to reduce the risk of suicide[149].

Neuropsychiatric SLE is a major cause of morbidity and mortality. One case involved an adolescent female who developed acute neuropsychiatric SLE presented with an acute delusional depression with suicidal ideation. Despite high dose corticosteroid therapy, these symptoms persisted. Within seven to ten days of initiation of paroxetine (an SSRI) and fluphenazine (a high-potent typical antipsychotic medication), the symptoms of depression improved and suicidality remitted. Psychosis resolved with longer treatment. Undoubtedly, that treatment with psychotropic medication was treating a psychiatric complication of the underlying disease. That case report supports the notion that some severe neuropsychiatric symptoms can be reversed without reliance upon immunosuppressants. It is that early adjunctive treatment with paroxetine and fluphenazine for steroid-resistant neuropsychiatric SLE that might spare a subset of patients the toxic effects and complications of immunosuppressants[150].

Rheumatoid arthritis (RA) is associated with depression. Marked social difficulties with this general medical condition contribute to the development of major depressive disorder in patients suffering from rheumatoid arthritis independent of disease state[151]. Suicides in persons suffering from rheumatoid arthritis, compared to osteoarthritis or no arthritis, show females to be significantly over-represented among those who committed suicide, over 52%. Co morbid depressive disorders preceded suicides in 90% of the female RA patients. Before their suicide, 50% had experienced at least one suicide attempt. The method of suicide was violent in 90% of the RA females[152]. Patients with major depressive disorder and rheumatoid arthritis participated in a study demonstrating the safety and efficacy of the selective serotonin reuptake inhibitor for the treatment of depression complicating rheumatoid arthritis[153].

The simultaneous use of non-steroidal anti-inflammatory drugs (NSAID) such as naprosyn, ibuprofen, acetaminophen, and SSRIs may induce bleeding and bruising tendencies. Furthermore, NSAID can interact with lithium and result in lithium toxicity, a little known drug-drug interaction. The risks and benefits of using lithium in patients who use excess amounts of NSAID should be considered, and this should be reviewed with the patient in the informed consent process.

## Infectious Disease and Suicide

Sexually transmitted diseases (syphilis, gonorrhea, clymadia and others) are associated with increased suicide in homeless adolescents who have unprotected sex, multiple sex partners, non-heterosexual orientations, intravenous drug use, and depression[154].

Almost 9% of individuals who committed suicide at the turn of the century in New York City were HIV-positive. HIV-positive patients have a seven to thirty-six times increase in risk for suicide. In nearly 150 such patients, as many as 44% had attempted suicide[155]. Significantly, more attempters than nonattempters were females, who had more lifetime histories of depressive episodes and antidepressant treatment and reported family histories of suicidal behavior. Suicide attempters also were younger than non-attempters were, had higher neurotic traits, and had experienced more emotional, physical, and sexual abuse and more emotional and physical neglect. Factors that did not differentiate suicide attempters from non-attempters in this group included ethnic background, marital status, employment status, and type of abused substance. Although the high rate of attempted suicide may be related to the study population and is common to other suicidal populations, the high rate of attempted suicide should prompt clinicians to do early intervention and aggressive treatment of depression[156].

In another study, over 90% of all HIV-positive suicide victims in New York City between 1991–1993 were aged 25–54, and almost 90% were men. In addition, increased levels of suicidal ideation in symptomatic HIV-positive men are frequently reported. Persons who are aged mid-life and older and are living with HIV-AIDS continue to experience significant emotional distress and thoughts of suicide in later life, suggesting a need for targeted interventions to improve mental health and prevent suicide[157].

The rate of HIV infection is significantly elevated among persons with serious mental illness including schizophrenia and mood disorders. The combination can result in difficult to manage patients.

*A 42-year-old, white male with schizoaffective disorder, narcissistic, borderline and antisocial personality traits, and HIV-AIDS was maintained briefly on fluoxetine and fluphenazine until he became non-compliant with his psychiatric and antiviral medications in the community, and his family feared for his safety. As a result, he had increased confusion, delusions and hallucinations, insomnia, suicidal and homicidal ideations, affective instability, poor impulse control, and aggressive sexual behavior. At one point while in the hospital, he would throw his infected urine across the unit. He was frequently found wandering into other patient's rooms. He required continuous observation. The hospital course was prolonged, frequently requiring seclusion and restraints. Finally, he was stabilized on a combination of long-acting, injectable medications: fluphenazine decanoate for psychosis and depot provera for sexually aggressive behavior. He began attending the county AIDS clinic, became compliant with his HIV medications, and is now living independently in the community with close supervision by the service coordinator.*

*A 35 year old, white male in patient in a psychiatric hospital with schizoaffective disorder and HIV-AIDS would hear voices telling him to deberately slash his wrists and squirt blood all over the hospital unit and on other patients trying to infect them. He was taking haloperidol at 80 mg/day among other psychotropic medication. I was called one night on call to see the patient. He had superficial and deep bleeding lacerations on his wrists, bilaterally. The age of the wounds was not known, but because of the increased risk of spreading his infection, I sutured them. He was subsequently charged with illegal behavior, sent to prison, and ultimately murdered there by other inmates with metal shackles.*

Besides viral infections, other infectious diseases are associated with suicide. The treatment for tuberculosis has been associated with a rare, drug-induced, adverse effect to the antitubercular medication, isoniazid. A case report of suicidal psychosis secondary to isoniazid is described[158].

### Gastrointestinal Disorders and Suicide

Major depressive disorder may be associated with extensive dental disease, and people may seek dental treatment before becoming aware of their psychiatric illness. Major depressive disorder frequently is associated with a disinterest in performing appropriate oral hygiene techniques, a cariogenic diet, diminished salivary flow, rampant dental caries, advanced periodontal disease, and oral dysesthesias. Dentists aware of these signs and symptoms have an opportunity to recognize patients with occult major depressive disorder[159].

Peptic ulcer disease is associated with anxiety disorders. Previous reports suggest a link between chronic anxiety and peptic ulcer disease. Generalized anxiety disorder was associated with a significantly increased risk of self-reported peptic ulcer disease[160]. Anxiety has been demonstrated to be an important indicator of suicidality.

Identified more than a decade ago, hepatitis C virus (HCV) is the leading cause of chronic liver disease, cirrhosis, and hepatoceullar carcinoma, and it is the primary indication for liver transplant. This common chronic blood-borne infection affects approximately 3.8 million people in the US. The peak prevalence of chronic HCV is in the fourth and fifth decades of life. Although the infection resolves in 15% of patients, it becomes chronic in 85% of those infected[161]. The treatment involves about forty-eight weeks of pharmacotherapy with interferon, IFN or IFN alfa-2b, monotherapy. For patients who have received IFN monotherapy and have experienced a relapse, an increased dose of IFN or a combination product of IFN alfa-2b and ribavirin has been found to be effective[162].

Primary mental disorders and substance related disorders are more prevalent in patients with chronic hepatitis C infection. This creates a critical clinical dilemma, since the treatment of hepatitis, C itself can induce suicidal depression and suicidal ideation with IFN-alpha and ribavirin in a patient with hepatitis C is another example of a drug induced adverse effect inducing suicidality[163]. Because suicidal depression is sometimes associated with IFN therapy and occurs at even higher rates when IFNs are administered with ribivarin, many patients with a history of depressive illness have not been considered candidates for any IFN formulation[164].

If a patient, however, is compliant with psychotropic medication prescribed by a psychiatrist in an outpatient clinic setting as described below, then such treatment can be used with mentally ill patients.

*A 45 year old, white male, with a remote history of intravenous drug abuse, diagnosed with bipolar disorder (recent episode depressed, moderate without psychotic features), and maintained on lithium and olanzapine, was recently diagnosed with HCV. Pharmacotherapy including interferon Alfa-2b, 3 million units SQ three times a week for forty-eight weeks, was prescribed. The patient was in a depressive phase of his mood disorder. A trial of bupropion at 100 mg per day was added to his lithium at 1200 mg/day. He tolerated this initial dose well. After the addition of ribavirin to interferon, the bupropion was increased to 100 mg every morning and 100 mg bupropion every day at noon. In addition, trazodone at 50 mg every night was added.*

*His depressive symptoms remained in remission, despite his relapse of HCV and need for increased medication. Despite developing fatigue, rash, cough, and irritability, he did not have worse depressive symptoms and completed his course of treatment for hepatitis C.*

This case demonstrates that depressed patients can be treated for HCV if close monitoring by a psychiatrist and dose adjustment in psychotropic medications parallel the clinical course of treatment for the hepatitis C.

Inflammatory bowel diseases such as ulcerative colitis and Chron's disease are affected when co-morbid depression exists. As many as 55% had an undetected depressive disorder. These depressive symptoms contributed to poor health-related quality of life, regardless of the severity of the condition[165].

## Dermatologic Disorders and Suicide

Suicide, suicidal depression, and psychotic depression is a potential complication of a simple acne medication. If a vulnerable, high-risk, suicidal teen patient is simply prescribed an acne medication, a fatal outcome can result. The acne medication is an example of drug-induced suicidality.

In the Physicians Desk Reference, there is a warning for Accutane (isotretinoin). It requires the psychiatric disorder warning that states; "Accutane may cause depression, psychosis and rarely, suicidal ideation, suicide attempts, suicide, aggressive and or violent behaviors. Discontinuation of Accutane therapy may be insufficient, further evaluation may be necessary. No mechanism of action has been established for these events. Physicians should read the brochure, recognizing psychiatric disorders in adolescents and young adults." Dermatologists should do patient education about depression and suicide as part of the informed consent process.

## Cancer and Suicide

The use of effective chemotherapy, radiation therapy, and surgery has made many cancers curable or amenable to palliation, when can prolong a patient's life, extending meaningful survival. Even effective palliation requires close observations for the treatment of complications of malignancy, including emotional distress.

Malignancies are especially associated with suicide. Cancer patients have a twenty-fold greater risk of suicide than the general population. Psychopathological states that can lead to irrational decisions about suicide in terminal illness include delirium, psychotic disorders, despair, or grandiosity associated with mood disorders.

Depression has a negative prognostic factor in breast cancer outcomes as it does for other general medical conditions[166]. Furthermore, depression is by far the most common disorder encountered in terminally ill patients, and it is often associated with suicidal thoughts and acts. Patients with a terminal medical illness like cancer who are depressed may not receive adequate information on which to base an informed decision due to their impaired mental capacity, and they can become suicidal[167].

Hopelessness associated with terminal cancer is common, and it is an important clinical marker of suicidal ideation in this vulnerable patient population. Many factors increase vulnerability to suicide in cancer patients. Uncontrolled pain and other physical symptoms, psychological distress, and existential suffering are related to suicide[168].

Suicide risk is increased significantly within the first five years following newly diagnosed cancer, especially primary malignancies of the reproductive tract with remote metastasis at the initial diagnosis. The highest suicide mortality in this Japanese study was observed between the third and fifth months after cancer diagnosis. Most of these suicides occurred soon after discharge from the hospital. The most common method used was jumping and hanging. Clinicians should closely assess a cancer patient's psychological distress and potential risk of suicide before approving discharge from the hospital[169].

Cancer patients may reject suicidal intention if adequate pharmacological and psychosocial supports are offered. The use of psychotropic medication in patients referred to a psycho-oncology service showed over 75% of patients were prescribed psychotropic medication by the oncology team, general practitioner, and psychiatrist. This overall prescribing of a higher rate of antidepressants suggests that psychological distress is being increasingly recognized[170].

## Late-life Suicide

Seniors have among the highest rates of suicide across all age groups in the United States and worldwide. U. S. mortality data indicate that adults 65 years and older complete suicide at a rate nearly 50% higher than that of the national average (approximately 15.6 versus 11.0 per 100,000) and that suicide rates increase with advancing age. Data from the National Center for Health Statistics (NCHS) reveal that this rate almost doubles their population representation in the United States, averaging one suicidal death by a senior every one hour and thirty-five minutes[171].

The National Institute on Aging estimates that older adults may represent nearly 20% of the U. S. population by 2030 at 70 million. Thus, there is a pressing need to identify vulnerability and protective factors associated with late-life suicidal ideation and behavior in order to inform assessment and treatment considerations with seniors at risk of suicide.

Suicide rates vary greatly with age. Gender and ethnicity factors also need to be included with age to gain a broad understanding of late-life suicide. The elderly population has the highest suicide rates in almost all countries in the world, and it is the quickest growing segment of the population.

Some countries such as Hungary, follow the pattern that suicide rate increases with age in both genders, while others such as the U.S., show suicide rates increases with age only in men. The elderly, 65 and over, make up 12.4% of the U.S. population in 2001, yet they represented 17.6% of suicides. Men account for about four out of five completed suicides in this age group. The suicide rate of white, Chinese-American, Japanese-American, and Filipino-American men increases with age. In contrast, the middle-aged group of African-American, Hispanic, Native American and Alaskan Native men has the highest suicide rate. Because of the gender and ethnic differences in the United States, the suicide rate by age 80 ranges from 3/100,000 among African-American women to 60/100,000 among white men.

There is a clear trend for suicide rates to increase with age. The largest relative increases in suicide rates occur among those 80–84 years of age. An average global suicide rate for men is 25 suicides per 100,000 men, in comparison with the rate of 70 suicides per 100,000 men 75 years and older. White men age 65 and older are the most likely to commit suicide accounting for 20% of the cases. The prevalence of late life depression is influenced by the setting, less in the community and more in nursing homes, and medical inpatients and outpatients. These epidemiological data may help to understand risk and protective factors, but they cannot guide the evaluation of individual patients.

Stressful events or situational changes might be expected to be demoralizing or to precipitate depression. One might wonder why depression is not ubiquitous. In fact, the prevalence of major depression, as systematically assessed in an epidemiological catchment area study is lower in geriatric patients in the community than in the general adult population[172]. Consistent with the finding that worry about chronic or disabling medical illness is the most common stress associated with depression in this age group, nursing home residents and medically ill individuals have markedly higher rates of major depression, ranging from 9% to 42%[173].

Suicidal elderly patients present with a heterogeneous group of mental disorders. As many as 71.4% of the elderly who died by suicide suffered from mood disorders, and 35.7% had a substance related disorder[174].

Older patients tend to use more highly lethal means, are less impulsive, and have high suicide intent. Although they have a later onset of depressive episodes, they are not necessarily more depressed, either subjectively or objectively, and do not have a history of more episodes of depression. They are not more aggressive. Thus, elderly patients at the time of first depressive episode and first suicide attempt may have different biological and clinical characteristics (such as less impulsivity and more intent) and, consequently, higher risk for lethal suicidal behavior than those with earlier onset. More than one-quarter of older adults have access to a gun in their homes, a situation that has the potential to lead to suicide in high-risk patients. Firearms account for 80% of suicides among elderly men. In 1992, guns replaced poisoning as the most common method of suicide in elderly women. Suicide is the leading cause of death of handgun buyers in the first year after purchase, and the suicide rate after handgun purchase is highest in women and people aged 75 years.

The associated increased risk of completed suicide in elderly patients with mental disorders includes the following: a fourfold increase for anxiety disorders, a nine fold increase for single episode major depression, an eleven fold increase for psychotic disorders, a forty-threefold increase for substance abuse, and a fifty-nine fold increase for recurrent major depression[175].

Recurrent major depression is the most common diagnosis in elderly suicide attempters and suicide completers. Other identified risk factors for suicide attempts and completed suicides in late-life include past history of suicidal behavior, substance abuse, hopelessness, and certain personality characteristics such as rigidity and lack of openness to new experience[176].

The diagnosis of depression in the elderly is sometimes difficult because many elderly patients do not report sad mood, and they have more somatic symptoms and co-morbid medical illness that could explain some symptoms they present to the primary care physician. More than 50% of depressed adults in a primary care setting do not report sad mood. If patients do not feel sad or have depressed mood, they may not recognized that their discomfort is caused by depressive illness, and if they report the symptoms to their doctor, the diagnosis of depression will be more difficult. Older depressed patients tend to have more somatic symptoms than their younger counterparts do[177].

Depression in older patients is common in primary care practices, with over 40% of physicians reporting that depression in the elderly is one of the most common problems they see in their patients[178]. Primary care physicians and nurse practitioners may be the only ones to see the red flags associated with suicide in elderly patients because most elderly suicide victims never come to the attention of psychiatrists. Many older adults who commit suicide have visited a primary care physician very close to the time of the suicide: twenty percent on the same day, forty percent within one week, and seventy percent within one month of the suicide[179]. These findings point to the urgency of enhancing both the detection and the adequate treatment of depression as a means of reducing the risk of suicide among the elderly.

Primary care providers should be well prepared to diagnose and treat depression in the older patients. The majority of physicians in primary care practices appear to be fairly confidant in their ability to diagnose, treat, and manage the depressive symptoms of their elderly patients. However, elderly patients are less likely to receive a diagnosis of depression than non-elderly patients during office visits to primary care physicians. One study found that after controlling for a patient's presentation of symptoms, elderly patients were 57% less likely to receive a diagnosis of depression than non-elderly patients were during office visits to primary care physicians[180]. Despite efforts to improve the recognition and treatment of late life depression, efforts from organizations such as the Agency for Health Care Policy and Research's evidence based guidelines, the American Psychiatric Association's clinical practice guidelines, and the National Institutes of Health's consensus development conference on depression in late life, the diagnosis and treatment of late life depression remains low. Furthermore, rates of mental health specialty care are low in this population.

Monitoring for more depressive illness, physical illness burden, and functional limitations is important. Among elderly persons, seventy-five percent of those with probable depression receive no treatment for their depressive symptoms[181]. Even when a patient's depression is recognized and diagnosed and treatment is received, the care patterns are often sub-optimal.

Symptoms of late life depression include loss of energy, loss of appetite, insomnia, aches, and pains, as well as loss of interest or pleasure, hopelessness, worthlessness, guilt, and suicidal thinking. The common presenting complaints include loss of energy, poor appetite and sleep, and vague aches and pains, all of which can easily be mistaken for medical illness; in fact, may older patients have co-morbid medical illness that could explain some of their somatic symptoms. The symptoms that help to clarify the diagnosis of depression and are central to the disorder include the following: loss of interest in work and activities, loss of pleasure, and affective and ideational symptoms such as hopelessness, worthlessness, guilt, and suicidal thinking. These symptoms are more specific for depression and are not likely to accompany medical illness[182].

The role of medical co-morbidity is controversial, as medical illness in general is frequent among the elderly. Some studies show that medical illness has an overestimated role. Other studies find particular conditions such as visual impairment; neurological illness, and malignant disease, are most associated with suicide risk, more often in men. Fear of serious physical illness and perceived health status, anticipatory anxiety, and poor sleep quality, as well as a change in functional status and pain may be better correlates of suicidality than physical illness itself.

Physical illness may contribute to suicidality in another way. Physicians are less likely to discuss suicidal feelings with patients in poor physical health. If depression is detected in the elderly patient, suicidal feelings should also be evaluated[183].

Symptoms of depression may cause or exacerbate physical disability in older individuals and may do so largely than other common chronic diseases such as hypertension, arthritis, heart disease, and diabetes. The World Health Organization estimated that major depressive disorder was the fourth leading cause of disability in 1990, and it is projected to become the second leading cause of disability, behind heart disease, in the coming decades. Depressive symptoms are associated with greater impairment and a decreased quality of life among patients with coexisting chronic illnesses, such as emphysema, cancer, and diabetes. When depression coexists with other medical conditions, the resulting disability appears to be additive.

Depressive symptoms may also exacerbate cognitive impairment in elderly persons, leading to further limitations in independent functioning. As a result, there is an increased need for care giving and supervision from family members. Depressive symptoms in elderly persons are independently associated with significantly higher levels of informal care giving, even after the effects of major coexisting chronic conditions are adjusted.

Consequences of late life depression also include poor quality of life, diminished sense of well being, impairment in activities of daily living, and poor outcome of medical illness. The relationship between depression and medical illness has recently received considerable attention. Depression increases mortality and worsens the course of medical illness. For example, depression increases the risk of myocardial infarction[184]. Alternatively, patients with myocardial infarction are at increased risk for depression, and myocardial infarction patients with depression are more likely to die[185]. Risk of depression is also increased after stroke, and stroke patients who are depressed have worse outcomes. These risks are not limited to cardiovascular disease, having been seen with several medical disorders such as breast cancer.

Less severe forms of depression are also common among the elderly, and they are associated with an increased risk of developing major depression. A number of patients suffer depressive symptoms that do not meet the criteria for a formal diagnosis of major depression. These symptoms are being recognized as common and important in elderly patients especially in those with co-morbid general medical conditions. One report estimates that over 20% of older Americans suffer from minor depression, dysthymia, or adjustment disorder with depressed mood[186]. Dysthymia can lead to major depression and suicide.

Social isolation and living alone is important to consider when assessing suicidality in elderly patients. The absence of a relative or friend to confide in is strongly associated with late life suicide[187]. Suicide rates among the elderly are highest for those who are divorced or widowed. Spousal bereavement increases the likelihood of physician visits. Thus, recently widowed patients may benefit from early interventions that are readily implemented[188]. Women, whether living alone or with someone else, are more likely than men to have contacted their primary care physician and to have been known to psychiatric services. Women seem to have a higher tendency to utilize services and ask for help. Children who urge an elderly parent to get help are more likely to have an impact on mothers than on fathers. Men who live alone are much more likely than women to have a debilitating physical illness, and they are less likely to have contacted their primary care physician or obtain any psychiatric services. Widowed older men should have routing screening about suicidal ideation, and this should be an essential component of the clinical assessment[189]. Negative expectancies regarding the prospect of ever experiencing satisfying interpersonal relationships, global hopelessness, and depression are particularly associated with suicide ideation among seniors. Thus, there is an important interpersonal component to late-life suicide. There is a social-cognitive vulnerability factor for suicidal elderly patients. Interpersonal cognitive interventions including life review, problem-solving therapy, cognitive behavioral therapy and interpersonal psychotherapy have some evidence of their efficacy in potentially ameliorating late-life suicidal ideation[190].

Suicide is a consequence of untreated depression. Major depression is a significant marker of suicide in late life and it increases the risk of suicide. Elderly patients who attempt suicide in late life are at a very high risk for completed suicide. However, the suicide risk of older men may be more difficult to detect than the risk of older women because they are less likely to have had a history of previous attempts. For example, 70% of elderly men who die by suicide did not have a prior attempt[191]. Older age is significantly associated with more determined and planned self-destructive acts, less violent methods, and fewer warning signs of suicidal intent[192].

High symptomatic levels of depression, complicated grief and anxiety, poor sleep quality, and lower levels of perceived support are also associated with suicide in late-life depression. Most importantly, since elderly depressed patients may be more determined to commit suicide, have well planned acts and intentions, and have fewer warnings of suicidal intent, an acute intervention in the midst of a suicidal crisis may be less effective in elderly[193].

Beliefs that the geriatric patient's depression is understandable interfere with treatment. If an older patient were facing declining health, loss of a loved one, or a move to a nursing home, his or her family and clinicians might conclude "Wouldn't you be depressed?" However, if the depression persists, causes suffering, and impairs functioning, treatment should be considered even if the precipitants seem understandable. Depression is not a normal part of aging.

Symptoms of depression may cause or exacerbate physical disability in older individuals, and they may do so largely than other common chronic diseases.

Compared to younger depressed adults, older individuals may be more likely to report anhedonia, or markedly diminished interest or pleasure in usual activities, and somatic complaints such as fatigue and pain. These specific depressive symptoms may be less likely to be detected or treated by health care providers[194].

Even when an elderly patient's depression is recognized and diagnosed, and treatment is received, the care patterns are often sub-optimal. Among elderly depressed patients who actually do receive treatment, less than one-third receive adequate treatment[195]. Patients over 65 years of age are less likely to receive adequate dosages of antidepressants as compared with younger patients. Elderly patients are less likely to receive the antidepressant for an adequate duration as well. When an antidepressant is prescribed, premature discontinuation is common. Elderly depressed patients are also less often seen for return visits, and they were seen less often by mental health professionals[196]. Although psychiatric hospitalization is associated with the highest increase in the relative risk of suicide, this event is only experienced by a small proportion of the elderly who commit suicide. Somatic hospitalization is the event experienced most frequently among older adults dying by suicide.

Among elderly persons, as many as 75% of those with probable depression receive no treatment for their depressive symptoms, and of those who do receive treatment, only 33% receive adequate treatment. Although research on risk factors continues to grow, there remains limited knowledge of the biologic changes that increase the risk for suicide, as well as limited information about contributing psychosocial processes that extend beyond demographic factors. No proven interventions are known at this time. Efforts are underway to test approaches that reach older adults who use primary care services. Continued efforts are needed to change attitudes about mental illness and treatment in order to reach older adults who do not use health care services[197].

Pharmacotherapy in the elderly requires special considerations. Frail elderly patients are more sensitive to side effects, and the adverse events they experience can be more severe. As a result, in these patients, treatment is often started at low doses to test tolerance. Yet older patients may be relatively treatment-resistant; as a result, full doses may be needed and longer duration of treatment may be required to achieve remission. Because of these considerations, the usual "start low" and "go slow" prescribing recommendations might be extended to include "keep going." Recent work suggests that with adequate dose, and duration, and in some cases with augmentation treatment, very good responses can be achieved in older patients[198]. Most studies of antidepressants have been performed in patients in the age range of 60–75 year old group. Recently, the larger studies are being completed in individuals with major depression who are 75 years and older[199].

Pharmacological treatment for late life depression includes considering co-morbid medical conditions, co-morbid dementia, and disabilities in hearing and vision, gait disturbance, nutrition, medical medications, and the potential for drug interaction.

Pharmacotherapy differences should be considered if the patient has bipolar depression or psychosis, since both groups of patients have more severe disorders and their treatment is more complicated; and they are at risk for more serious consequences.

During the past decade, the selective serotonin reuptake inhibitors (SSRIs) have become the medication most commonly used for the treatment of major depression in older people. Studies demonstrate that the full effects of antidepressants in older patients may require twelve weeks or more to be observed, rather than the usual four to six weeks. Since SSRIs have few adverse effects on the heart, they are much safer than the TCA in patients with heart disease. However, adverse effects of SSRIs in the elderly include hyponatremia, anorexia, and falling. The SSRI antidepressants can cause adverse effects in older patients. Special issues for elderly patients prescribed SSRIs include weight loss gait disturbance and falls, and hyponatremia. Fluvoxamine, citalopram, fluoxetine, paroxetine, and sertraline have been proven effective in placebo-controlled studies of SSRIs in geriatric depression.

Occurrence and course of suicidality during short-term treatment of late-life depression with antidepressant monotherapy notes that while suicidal ideation resolves rapidly, the resolution of thoughts about death is more gradual[200].

The following is an example of a case of major depressive disorder in an elderly patient at risk for suicide.

*SJ is a seventy-year-old, divorced, retired, male admitted to the psychiatric hospital for suicidal depression with a plan to hang himself. The patient has co morbid alcohol dependence and multiple medical problems. Despite decreasing his alcohol consumption, his depression has increased over the past several weeks. The depression is associated with hopelessness, low energy, poverty of thought, anhedonia, erratic sleeping, anxiety, increased physical symptoms, and suicidal thoughts, intentions and plans. There is no history of mania or psychosis. His medical problems include alcoholic cardiomyopathy, congestive heart failure, bilateral pitting pedal edema, macrocytic anemia, and nephritis. He has been non-compliant with his medical medications. Past psychiatric history shows one similar admission to a psychiatric hospital thirty years ago. He was prescribed a tricyclic antidepressant thirty years ago but stopped it. There is no history of treatment with any new antidepressant medications since then. Over the past twenty-five years, he has had five hospitalizations for alcohol dependence and complicated alcohol detoxifications. The patient's assets include having housing, financial income support of some neighbors, and an ex-wife.*

*On exam his appearance was disheveled. Moderate psychomotor retardation, flat affect, depressed mood, poor attention and concentration, doom and gloom thinking, anhedonia, erratic sleeping, anxiety were present, but there were no delusions. His insight and judgment was poor. He elaborated on his suicidal plan. He thought to hang himself with a rope in his shed in the backyard of his rural ranch.*

*The diagnosis of recurrent major depression, moderate without psychosi,s and alcohol dependence was made. The patient had a relatively uneventful hospital course. He did not exhibit any signs or symptoms of alcohol withdrawals. He was started on an SSRI, specifically citalopram, that was gradually titrated up to a therapeutic dose of 40 mg per day over a two-week period. The patient tolerated the medication well without side effects. Medical problems during the hospitalization included diagnosing intermittent atrial fibrillation as well as a urinary tract infection. He remained in the hospital for fifteen days. His mental status exam prior to discharge showed him to have better activities of daily living, good eye contact, brighter affect, and denied depression and suicidal ideations, intentions, and plans. His attention and concentration improved. There was no poverty of thought or speech. He was eating and sleeping well.*

*The patient was discharged from the hospital back home to his ranch. He was prescribed citalopram at 40 mg per day. He will follow up at the County Mental Health facility and with his primary care provider. The local county adult protective services were also notified of his disposition. Recommendations in the out patient setting included increasing the citalopram even more if the patient tolerates it, monitoring the patient carefully for non-compliance with the antidepressant, and discouragement of the resumption of alcohol use.*

Besides the SSRIs, second generation antidepressants include bupropion, venlafaxine, nefazodone and mirtazapine. The principle differences among these medications are their secondary effects. Bupropion or venlafaxine may be especially useful in apathetic patients or those already somewhat sedated. An advantage of nefazodone in late life depression is its beneficial effect on sleep. Since older depressed patients commonly experience weight loss and insomnia, mirtazapine may be of special benefit due to its secondary effects of weight gain and sedation. In general, all antidepressants are effective, but side effect profiles differ. In addition, elderly patients are more vulnerable to side effects and severe consequences, more resistant to treatment, and slower to respond. Typically, more than four to six weeks is needed with these antidepressants as well, to judge the full effect of the antidepressant in more severe elderly depressed patients.

Tricyclic antidepressants and benzodiazepines, in particular, should be prescribed with caution to the elderly with depression or at high risk of depression, since drug overdose is a common method of suicide. These medications in the elderly have been most commonly used in overdose. In one study of suicidal feelings, among patients with a mental disorder including depression in a sample of non-demented 85-year olds, suicidal feelings were associated with greater use of anxiolytics, but not of antidepressants[201]. Anxiolytics should not be prescribed to treat depression, rather antidepressants should. Many fatal suicide attempts involve the use of these benzodiazepene central nervous system depressants.

Finally, the potential for drug-drug interactions is a crucial issue in the treatment of depression in late life because, owing to medical illness, these patients are often receiving a variety of concurrent medications.

## Emergency, Trauma, and Surgery and Suicide

Beyond actual suicides, there are many more failed attempts. About a half-million Americans are treated in an emergency room each year after trying to kill themselves. For every person in the U.S. who dies by suicide, ten people attempt suicide and survive. Among older adolescents each suicide corresponds to 100–400 attempts of varying levels of lethality and intent. A suicide attempt itself indicates a severe risk of premature death and suicide is the main cause of excess deaths. There is excess mortality of suicide attempters[202]. The mortality from suicide, accident, homicide, and undetermined death is increased in the subsequent years, after a patient first presents to an emergency room with a suicide attempt. Not only is suicide a main cause of excess death, but a suicide attempt itself also indicates a severe risk of premature death from other unnatural and natural causes.

Suicidal patients may present to the emergency room with primary psychiatric disorders, substance related disorders, and general medical conditions. The suicidality may be intermixed with the appearance of fights, assaults, abuse, rape, alcohol intoxication, drowning, firearm accidents, homicidal ideations, or injuries related to motor vehicle accidents[203]. Despite advances in the treatment of depression and increasing awareness of mental illness, suicide remains a significant public health problem[204]. Although many suicides are preceded by recent contact with emergency departments due to non-fatal self-harm, there may be no contact with local mental health services. Suicide risk reduction in this setting might be enhanced if emergency departments, mental health services, and emergency medical services work closely together[205].

Since a careful history is expected along with direct examination in order to identify patients with true suicidal intent, emergency room physicians are frequently expected to evaluate and develop treatment plans for potentially suicidal patients. The struggle to prevent someone from self-injury while respecting their personal autonomy is frequently present in the emergency department and physicians must decide whether to intervene with a patient who does not seek treatment[206]. This problem faced by emergency room physicians when treating suicidal patients is highlighted in a recent review of emergency room protocols in Europe that showed the documentation of suicides and attempted suicides was unsatisfactory. Furthermore, underlying psychiatric disorders were scarcely recorded[207]. Some patients with emergency room visits due to self-poisonings and self-injury are medically hospitalized in a general hospital setting, and even less patients are hospitalized in a psychiatric hospital. Some do not even receive mental health evaluations. Nearly 20% leave before evaluation and disposition could be completed.

Trauma caused by all types of injury is the leading reason for visits to the emergency department, hospital admission, and death among adolescents in the US. Injuries are related to motor vehicle accidents, sports injury, homicide, drowning, firearm accidents, and suicide[208]. Types of injuries both fatal and non-fatal from suicidality include serious gunshot wounds, sharp stab wounds, blunt force trauma, poisoning, multiple general medical and surgical conditions with a variety of systemic and specific patterns of injury.

If a suicidal patient presents conscious, agitated and anxious in the local emergency department, avoiding the placement of the patient in a remote area is important since the patient needs continuous observation. The patient may require expedited care, quiet areas, and other measures to reduce risk of suicide. As the psychiatric patient's triage status may change, monitoring for worsening agitation or anxiety is important. Under psychiatric care, subsequent treatment may be provided for the suicidality.

Easy access to firearms increases the risk of suicide. Those who own a gun are 32 times more likely to commit suicide than those who do not own a gun. In one study, approximately 83% of fatal gunshot wounds are associated with suicides, compared with 7% for homicides committed by relatives, 3% for accidents, and only 2% for deaths involving strangers. In one study of children and adolescents in Alaska, suicide or suicide attempts was the leading cause of serious and fatal firearm injuries. They had unsupervised, easy access to firearms[209].

Close range shotgun and rifle injuries to the face are extremely difficult to treat and require experience in microsurgery and craniofacial surgery. Early aggressive surgery with immediate bone and soft tissue reconstruction is recommended for the management of extensive facial gunshot wounds. It is unusual for patients with self-inflicted gunshot injuries to the face to reattempt suicide[210].

Fatal self-inflicted stab wounds with a sharp instrument to the arms, neck, chest, and/or abdomen and most often associated with suicide in older individuals, men more than women, but there is a tendency for women to incise their wrists in particular. Hesitation marks and scarring of the writs from previous suicide attempts can be noted. Committing suicide by using sharp objects is a relatively uncommon[211].

Falling from a train or being hit by a train is a method of suicide in Europe/Turkey with a strikingly high mortality rate. Extremity fractures and lower extremity amputations are often encountered. The mortality rate was high in victims who were directly hit by the train[212].

Jumping that causes head and chest injuries are responsible for majority suicide completions. Pelvic, limb, and vertebral injuries predominate the pattern of injuries suffered by patients who survive a suicide attempt by jumping. Abdominal injuries are associated with a poor outcome, but survival might improve with immediate surgical exploration in hemo-dynamically unstable patients[213].

A comparison study with respect to the distribution of skeletal system injury between patients who committed suicide by jumping and falling showed patients who jumped had more severe injuries, higher death rate, and more fractures per person. Jumping caused more rib (particularly on the right), pelvic, and lower limb fractures but fewer skull fractures. Thus, jumping causes different injuries compared to falling from a height. It is proposed that patients who jump have a tendency to land feet-first and then try to break their falls on their dominant side, sustaining more right-sided rib fractures in the process. These types of patterns of skeletal system injury may be useful in evaluating whether a patient jumped from suicidal thoughts or fell by accident[214].

Open and closed head injuries, decapitation, dental damage, neck injuries incised and stab wounds to the neck, asphyxiation with ligature strangulation, cervical vertebrae dislocation, hyoid fractures, and upper airway obstruction are some common injuries to the head and neck in suicidal patients.

Penetrating head injury caused by an ice pick was described in a 39-year-old man, with a three year history of schizophrenia, who attempted suicide. Spinal cord injuries and shock caused by falling from the fifth floor of the building following this injury was also noted on admission. The CT scan revealed that the ice pick had deeply penetrated the posterior fossa from the forehead. No new neurological deficits or cerebrospinal fluid leakage appeared after admission. The ice pick was removed completely and without difficulty. Cerebral angiography was used to determine the extent of vascular injury to decide if surgery should be performed[215].

Complete decapitation of the head can occur in rare cases of a suicide attempt by hanging. A 47-year-old man committed suicide by hanging himself from a staircase banister of an apartment house. The man, weighing 144 kg, jumped with the noose of 2 cm thick and 2m long hemp rope around his neck, and he was completely decapitated. Death from a typical, normal suicidal hanging is usually due to cerebral ischemia caused by compression of the carotid and vertebral arteries. Except for bleeding at the clavicular insertions of the sternocleidomastoid muscles, there are only occasional injuries to the cervical soft parts or hyoid bone and or laryngeal cartilage. A fall with a noose around the neck, on the other hand, is associated with more frequent injuries to cervical structures through additional axial traction and radial shearing forces of the tightening noose. Thus, complete decapitation can occur in rare cases under extreme conditions such as heavy body weight, inelastic and/or thin rope material, and fall from a great height[216]. In another case report, a case of self-decapitation by suicidal hanging from a river bridge is described. The torso and the head of the victim were found about 500 meters apart in a river. At autopsy, torn ligaments of the cervical vertebrae between the atlas and axis, accompanied by fractures in the axis at the interarticular surface, were indicative of a traction force. This traction force, combined with anteroflexion of the head by falling from a height and the radial pressure due to a strong, single twisted nylon rope with a slip knot, was considered to have contributed considerably to the subsequent skin laceration with wavy marginal abrasions. This decapitation mechanism suggested head movement at the time of decapitation[217].

Cervical aerodigestive injuries to the neck from gunshot wounds, stab wounds, or blunt trauma can involve airway compromise and require surgical repair with or without a tracheostomy[218]. A patient with attempted suicide by hanging presented with severe subcutaneous facial, palpebral, and cervical emphysema, dysphonia, dysphasia, and respiratory difficulty. Fiber optic bronchoscopy revealed upper airway obstruction due to edema in an intact airway. CT scan gave evidence of hyoid fracture and laryngeocele, and pneumo-mediastinum. Esophageal tests revealed functional alteration of the upper esophageal sphincter. Suprasternal cervicotomy to drain the pneumo-mediastinum and laryngeal microsurgery to treat the laryngocele resolved the problem[219].

Corrosive injuries of the esophagus caused by acid consumption as suicidal intention have a high mortality even after surgical interventions such as esophagogastrectomy or total gastrectomy with esophageal exclusion as a primary surgery. Those who survived had secondary esophageal reconstruction with colon substitute complications of subsequent dysphasia and corrosive stricture development[220].

Penetrating knife injuries to the chest involving the heart or lungs can result in hemothorax, cardiac tamponade, and hemorrhagic effusions, as well as injuries to the vital organs themselves including the heart and lungs. The following case report is described.

*A 39-year-old man attempted to kill himself using a small knife by penetrating the left anterior chest wall because of trouble at work and with his girlfriend. On arrival to the emergency room, his consciousness was not clear, and his vital signs were unstable. The knife remained vertically located in the left anterior chest wall. A large left hemothorax was identified by x ray, and moderate cardiac tamponade was detected by echo-cardiography. Inserting a chest tube performed left sided chest drainage, and about 2500 ml of hemorrhagic effusion was drained. An emergency operation was performed to relieve the cardiac tamponade and repair the penetrating cardiac injury. Within an hour, a median sternotomy was performed in the operating room. The knife had injured the surface of the right ventricular outflow tract, the left lung, and the third intercostal artery and vein. Cardiopulmonary bypass was immediately prepared for the repair of the cardiac injury. The wounds were repaired with sutures. The postoperative course was uneventful, and the patient was discharged 9 days later[221].*

Similarly, abdominal stab wounds and injury can result in visceral organ injury, hemo-peritoneum, and exsanguation.

The plastic surgeon may occasionally be consulted by a patient who wishes to discuss what can be done for the scars of self-inflicted wounds on the forearms. These scars are popularly referred to as hesitation marks or suicide gestures. Unlike patients suffering from factitial ulcers or Munchhausen syndrome, these patients will admit to the physician that the scars are the result of self-inflicted wounds. These scars often consist of multiple, parallel, white lines extending up and down the forearms, usually on the volar surface, with more on the non-dominant side. Although the pattern of these scars is apparently what drives these patients to the plastic surgeon for relief, because even lay people identify these scars as self-inflicted suicide marks, proper surgical treatment of this condition can be offered[222].

Other patterns of injury include those caused by self-destructive burns. A 23-year-old, Oriental woman was inadvertently burned during an attempted suicide. After arguing with her boyfriend, she attempted suicide by using alcohol, benzodiazepene, and burning charcoal within her sealed bedroom. Burning charcoal in a sealed room is an emerging form of suicide in Asia. Her left leg fell over the edge of the bed while she was semiconscious, which resulted in direct contact with a hot pot causing a full thickness burn involving left tibialis anterior and other leg muscles. She was initially resuscitated with 100% oxygen and gastric lavage, and she was subsequently cared for at a burn unit. She had recurrent surgical debridement of the burn wound, skin grafts, and psychological support[223]. Suicide attempt by self-immolation was reported in Egypt. The total body surface area burned ranged between 15 and 95% with a mean of 45%, and the mortality rate was 73%. Kerosene was used by all the patients to ignite the fires[224].

Suffocation with a plastic bag has been a method used for suicide. This suicide by asphyxiation with a plastic bag placed over the head can include helium available at toy stores where it is sold in tanks for balloon inflation. It produces asphyxiation by the exclusion of oxygen in enclosed spaces. A report of seven fatalities throughout an eighteen-month period was reported in coincidence with a publication of an update to a popular right to die text in which this method is described, reflecting exposure to this information[225]. This rather uncommon method of suicide was reported in Canada to be more common in older women as compared with other methods of suicide. In 40% of the cases, the deceased was suffering from a serious illness. Autopsy findings were usually minimal, with facial, conjunctival and visceral petechiae present in a minority of cases. One or more drugs were detected in the blood in over 90% of cases where toxicological testing was performed. Benzodiazepines, diphenhydramine and antidepressants were the most common medication used with diphenhydramine the most common at an elevated concentration[226].

Drug overdoses and poison ingestions may be less violent, but they vary in their toxicity and lethality. Risk of a fatal outcome of a suicidal act is least with weak intent and the use of a method of low lethality methods, such as overdose involving a harmless medication. Highly lethal poisons with a low intent can also prove fatal. Paraquat poisoning is a significant means of suicide in Trinidad and Tobago, particularly among young East Indian persons[227]. Pesticide poisonings are an example of a non-violent method with a high lethality potential. Easy internet access to purchase a variety of pharmaceuticals and to access prescription medications, herbal products, and over-the-counter medications increases the patient's access to potentially lethal substances.

The following case illustrates a patient presenting with behavioral disturbances from a closed head injury caused by a head-on collision as the driver in a motor vehicle accident. It was finally determined that he attempted suicide by driving his car head on into another car going in the opposite direction.

*The patient is an eighteen-year-old, single white male. He was referred to the state psychiatric hospital due to an inability to care for himself. He had been involved in a motor vehicle accident in which he had sustained a closed head injury. He does not remember the incident that occurred several days prior. Following this motor vehicle accident, where he hit another car head on collision, he exhibited silent behavior and refused to speak until three days prior to admission when he attacked his mother. He was brought to the rural community hospital and given several doses of haloperidol for agitation prior to admission.*

*Upon admission to a psychiatric hospital, the patient was noted to have severe extra pyramidal side effects, which were described as a shuffling gait, drooling, difficulty swallowing, akinesia, and tremors. He was given benztropine at 2 mg intramuscular with good effect. When asked about the car accident he was unable to remember the incident. He stated he had been feeling weird, and he not been able to concentrate since the accident. However, he denied auditory or visual hallucinations. He reported some depressive symptoms, but he denied suicidal or homicidal ideations, intentions, or plans.*

*His past psychiatric history is unremarkable, with no history of inpatient or outpatient psychiatric care and no exposure to psychotropic medications. He reported a vague history of suicidal ideation several months ago, but he could not elaborate. The patient had been living with his mother, father and brother. He is unemployed, and he graduated from high school with a grade point average of 2.8 in the year 2002.*

*His medical history is remarkable for recent closed head injury secondary to a motor vehicle accident. He has no known allergies.*

*The mental status examination on admission revealed a disheveled young male. He displayed very poor eye contact and poor grooming. There appeared to be a slight drooping of the right side of his mouth. His attitude was one of cooperativeness in the beginning of the assessment, however, as the assessment was nearing completion, the patient appeared to not want to continue, and he walked out of the room. He rated his mood as five on a scale of one to ten. His affect was incongruent with this thought content. He appeared to be flat. He was only able to answer direct questions. Speech was slurred, soft, and incoherent most of the time. There was no flight of ideas or delusions. The patient's level of cognition changed; alert but lethargic at times, disoriented to place, date, time, and situation. He was only oriented to self. His attention and concentration was very poor, being unable to demonstrate digit span testing. Remote memory was difficult to assess, and his recent and immediate memory were impaired. He had concrete interpretation of proverbs. He scored only eight of thirty on the Folstein Mini-Mental Status examination.*

*The working diagnosis was Mood disorder, NOS, recent delirium secondary to closed head injury due to motor vehicle accident, and neuroleptic induced dyskinesia, with a global assessment of functioning (GAF) of 20.*

*The patient's four and one half month hospitalization was remarkable. He required over fifty incidents of seclusion and restraints. Both major and minor tranquilizers were ineffective in controlling is agitation. Trials of gabapentin, valproic acid, and phenotoin, lithium were not effective. Benzodiazepines disinhibited the patient even more, and neuroleptics induced neurological side effects such as parkinsonism. He had a chemical hepaitits, and most medications had to be discontinued. Neurology consultation suggested that his behavior was most likely due to his head injury. Finally, the patient required sodium phenobarbital intramuscular injections to relieve his agitation.*

*He was eventually discharged to a rehabilitation center for head injury patients out of state, and he was finally stabilized on the following medication: neurontin at 900 mg/day, haloperidol at 10mg/day, and benzotropine at 4 mg/day. Several years have passed since then and his quality of life as well as his prognosis remains extremely poor. All of this mental and physical suffering and an extremely poor quality of life are due to a suicide attempt.*

Finally, suicides can be masked as homicides. A case report of a 48-year old man who initially appeared to have died of a homicidal beating describes the pertinent autopsy findings consisted of blunt force closed head injury, combined with numerous cutaneous abrasions and contusions of the entire body. Further inquires confirmed a medical history of paranoid schizophrenia and a previous attempt at suicide. It was determined that this case was an extreme example of severe blunt force trauma sustained during fatal self-mutilation. Masquerading as a homicide, this apparent suicide underscores the importance of correlating a through background investigation with autopsy findings in determining the appropriate manner of death[228].

# CHAPTER 4 END NOTES

1) Pfeffer, H, Conte R, Plutchik, et al. Suicidal behavior in latency-age children. *American Academy of Child Psychiatry.* 1979; 679-692.

2) Wahl OF. Mental Illness Education on Campus: breaking down the barriers of stigma. *NAMI Advocate.* 2003; 31.

3) Goldman S, Beardslee WR. Suicide in children and adolescents. In: Jacobs D, ed. *Harvard Medical School Guide to Assessment and Intervention in Suicide.* San Francisco, Calif: Jossey-Bass; 1998: 417-442.

4) *The Twin Falls Times-News,* 2004, April 8,2004. Available at: http://www.magicvalley.com/news/world/nation/index.asp?StoryID=8178. Accessed April 8, 2004.

5) American Association of Suicidology. USA Suicide: 2002 Official Final Data. Available at: http://www.suicidology.org/index.html. Accessed 2/3/03.

6) Andrews JA, Lewinsohn PM. Suicidal attempts among older adolescents: prevalence and co-occurrence with psychiatric disorders. *J Am Acad Child Adolesc Psychiatry.* 1992; 31:655-662.

7) Center for Disease Control. National Center for Injury Prevention & Control. 2001. Available at: http://www.cdc.gov/ncipc/factsheets/suifacts.htm. Accessed 9/2/001.

8) Washoe County District Health Department. Chronic Disease & Injury Epi-letter. Suicides in Washoe County, 2002; 3:2-4.

9) Brent DA. Familial pathways to early-onset suicide attempt. Risk for suicidal behavior in offspring of mood-disordered suicide attempters. *Arch Gen Psychiatry.* 2002; 59:801-807.

10) Depression in Children and Adolescents: A Fact Sheet for Physicians. NIH Publication No. 00-4744. http://www.nimh.nih.gov/publicat/depchildresfact.cfm. Accessed 11/09/02.

11) Finzi R, Ram A, Shnit D, Har-Even D, et al. Depressive symptoms and suicidality in physically abused children. *Am J Orthopsychiatry.* 2001; 71:98-107

12) Alaimo K, Olson CM, Frongillo EA. Family food insufficiency, but not low family income, is positively associated with dysthymia and suicide symptoms in adolescents. *J Nutr.* 2002; 132:719-725.

13) Eynan R, Langley J, Tolomiczenko G, Rhodes AE, Links P, et al. The association between homelessness and suicidal ideation and behaviors: results of a cross-sectional survey. *Suicide Life Threat Behav.* 2002; 32:418-27.

14) Johnson JG, et al. Childhood adversities, interpersonal difficulties, and risk for suicide attempts during late adolescence and early adulthood. *Arch Gen Psychiatry. 2002; 59:741-749.*

15) Wunderlich U, Bronisch T, Wittchen HU, et al. Gender differences in adolescents and young adults with suicidal behavior. *Acta Psychiatr Scand.* 2001; 104:332-339.

16) Thompson KM, Wonderlich SA, Crosby RD, et al. The neglected link between eating disturbances and aggressive behavior in girls. *J Am Acad Child Adolesc Psychiatry.* 1999; 38:1277-84.

17) Psychiatric dispatches. *Primary Psychiatry.* 2003; 10:27-28. or In Columbia University's National Center

for Addiction and Substance abuse (CASA). Gender difference in substance abuse. at www.casacolumbia.org

18) Silverman JG, Raj A, Mucci LA, et al. Dating violence against adolescent girls and associated substance use unhealthy weight control, sexual risk behavior, pregnancy, and suicidality. *JAMA*. 2001; 286:572-9.

19) Freitas GV, Botega NJ. Prevalence of depression, anxiety and suicide ideation in pregnant adolescents. *Rev Assoc Med Bras*. 2002; 48:245-9.

20) Bearman PS, Moody J. Suicide and friendships among American adolescents. Am J Public Health. 2004; 94:89-95

21) Russell ST, Joyner K. Adolescent sexual orientation and suicide risk: evidence from a national study. *Am J Public Health*. 2001; 91:1276-81.

22) Goldberg J, True WR, Ramakrishnan V, et al. Sexual orientation and suicidality. *Arch Gen Psychiatry*. 1999; 56:867-874.

23) Grunbaum JA, Kann L, Kinchen SA, et al. Youth risk behavior surveillance—United States, 2001. *MMWR Surveill Summ*. 2002; 51:1-62.

24) Phillips DP, Carstensen LL. Clustering of teenage suicides after television news stories. *N Engl J Med*. 1986; 315:685-689.

25) Sonneck G, Etzersdorfer E, Nagel-Kuess S. Imitative suicide on the Viennese subway. *Soc Sci Med*. 1994; 38:453-457.

26) Jobes DA, Berman AL, O'CarrollPW, et al. The Kurt Cobain suicide crisis: perspectives from research, public health, and the news media. *Suicide Life-Threat Behav*. 1985; 15:43-50.

27) The American Foundation of Suicide Prevention, Recommendations to the media on how suicides should be reported. Available at: http://www.afsp.org/education/printrecommendations.htm. Accessed July 15, 2004

28) Bridge JA, et al. Major depressive disorder in teens and suicide. *J Am Acad Child Adolesc Psychiatry*. 2003; 42:1294-1300.

29) Enns MW, Cox BJ, Inayatulla M. Personality predictors of outcome for adolescents hospitalized for suicidal ideation. *J Am Acad Child Adolesc Psychiatry*. 2003; 42:720-727.

30) Lecomte D, Fornes P. Suicide among youth and young adults, 15 through 24 years of age. A report of 392 cases from Paris. *J Forensic Sci*. 1998; 43:964-8.

31) Pfeffer CR, Newcorn J, Kaplan G, et al. Suicidal behavior in adolescent psychiatric inpatients. *American Acadamy of Child and Adolescent Psychiatry*. 1988; 27:357-361.

32) Moscicki EK. Epidemiology of suicide. In: Jacobs D, ed. *Harvard Medical School Guide to Assessment and Intervention in Suicide*. San Francisco, Califo: Jossey-Bass; 1998: 40-51.

33) Tondo L, Baldessarini RJ, Hennen J, et al. Suicide attempts in major affective disorder patients with comorbid substance use disorders. *J Clin Psychiatry*. 1999; 60:63-69.

34) Light H. Suicidal and drug-related behaviors of rural seventh and eighth grade students. *Percept Mot Skills*. 2002; 94:1196-8.

35) Hardan A, Sahl R. Suicidal behavior in children and adolescents with developmental disorders. *Res Dev Disabil*. 1999; 20:287-96.

36) Gau SF, Soong WT. Psychiatric co-morbidity of adolescents with sleep terrors or sleepwalking: a case-control study. *Aust N Z J Psychiatry* 1999; 33:734-9

37) Pilowsky DJ, Li-Tzy W, Anthony JC. Panic attacks and suicide attempts in mid adolescence. *Am J Psychiatry*. 1999; 156:1545-1549.

38) Gould MS, Greenberg T, Velting DM, et al. Youth suicide risk and preventive interventions: a review of the past 10 years. J Am Acad Child Adolesc Psychiatry. 2003; 42:386-405.

39) Weissman MM, Wolk S, Goldstein RB, et al. Depressed adolescents grown up. *JAMA*. 1999; 281:1707-1713.

40) Diagnostic and Statistical Manual of Mental Disorders, 4th ed. Text Revision. Washington, DC: American Psychiatric Association; 2000: 382-401.

41) Harrington R, Bredenkamp D, Groothues C, et al. Adult outcomes of child and adolescent depression, III: Links with suicidal behaviors. J Child Psychol Psychiatry 1994; 35:1309-1319

42) Child and Adolescent Bipolar Disorder: An update from the National Institute of Mental Health. NIMH Pub. No. 00-477, 2000.

43) Geller B, Williams M, Zimerman B, et al. Prepubertal and early adolescent bipolarity differentiate from ADHD by manic symptoms, grandiose delusions, ultra-rapid or ultradian cycling. *J Affect Disord.* 1998; 51:81-91.

44) Geller B, Zimerman B, Williams M, et al. Diagnostic characteristics of 93 cases of a prepubertal and early adolescent bipolar disorder phenotype by gender, puberty and co-morbid attention deficit hyperactivity disorder. *J Child Adolesc Psychopharmacol.* 2000; 10:157-64.

45) Weller EB, Weller RA, Sanchez LE. Bipolar disorder in children and adolescents. In: Lewis M, ed. *Child and Adolescent Psychiatry.* 3rd ed. Philadelphia, PA: Lippincott Williams & Wilkins; 2002: 782-791.

46) West SA, Strakowski SM, Sax KW, et al. Phenomenology and co-morbidity of adolescents hospitalized for the treatment of acute mania. *Biol Psychiatry.* 1996; 39:458-460.

47) NIH Publication No. 00-4744. September 2000. Depression in Children and Adolescents. available at http://www.nimh.nih.gov/publicat/depchildresfact.cfm. Accessed 11/09/2002.

48) Article in CNS News, March 2003. In the column: The Stacks. Immediate outpatient suicide treatment effective [in *Psychiatric Services.* 2002: 53;1574-1579.] page 63.

49) Article in Clinical Psychiatry News. March 2003. In the column: Clinical Rounds. Twelve drugs identified for pediatric studies. page 62.

50) Article in CNS Spectrums, January 2003. In the column: CNS Reports. Fluoxetine receives FDA approval for depression in children and adolescents. page 24.

51) King RA, Riddle MA, Chappell PB, et al. Emergence of self-destructive phenomena in children and adolescents during fluoxetine treatment. *J Am Acad Child Adolesc Psychiatry* 1991; 30:179-186

52) Vorstman J, Lahuis B, Buitelaar JK. SSRIs associated with behavioral activation and suicidal ideation. *J Am Acad Child Adolesc Psychiatry* 2001; 40:1364-5.

53) Olfson M, Shaffer D, Marcus SC, et al. Relationship between antidepressant medication treatment and suicide in adolescents. *Arch Gen Psychiatry.* 2003; 60:978-982.

54) Sood BA, Weller E, Weller R. SSRIs in children and adolescents: where do we stand? Current Psychiatry. 2004; 3:83-89

54) Preskorn SH. Outpatient management of depression: a guide for the practitioner, 2nd ed. Caddo, OK: Professional Communications, 1999.

55) Weintrob N, Cohen D, Klipper-Aurbach Y, et al. Decreased growth during therapy with selective serotonin reuptake inhibitors. *Arch Pediatr Adolesc Med* 2002; 156:696-701

56) Axelson D, Perel J, Rudolph G, et al. Significant differences in pharmacokinetic/dynamics of citalopram between adolescents and adults: implications for clinical dosing (abstract). San Juan PR: American College of Neuropsychopharmacology annual meeting, 2000.

57) Sood B, Sood R. Depression in children and adolescents. In: Levenson JL (ed). *Depression: key diseases series.* Philadelphia: American College of Physicians, 2000: 244.

58) DelBello M, Schwiers M, Rosenberg H, Strakowski S. A double-blind, randomized, placebo-controlled study of quetiapine as adjunctive treatment for adolescent mania. *J Am Acad Child Adol Psychiatry.* 2002; 41:1216-23.

59) Heisel MJ, Flett GL, Hewitt PL. Social hopelessness and college student suicide ideation. *Archives of Suicide Research* 2003; 7:221-235.

60) Kessler RC, McGonagle KA, Zhao S, et al. Lifetime and 12-month prevalence of DSM-III-R psychiatric disorders in the United States: results from the National Co-morbidity Survey. *Arch Gen Psychiatry.* 1994; 51:8-19.

61) Burt VK, Stein K. Epidemiology of depression throughout the female life cycle. *J Clin Psychiatry* 2002; 63(suppl 7):9-15.

62) Kornstein SG, Schatzberg AF, Thase ME, et al. Gender differences in chronic major and double depression. *J Affect Disord.* 2000; 60:1-11.

63) Kornstein SG. The evaluation and management of depression in women across the life span. *J Clin Psychiatry.* 2002; 622(suppl 24):11-17.

64) Bebbington PE, Brugha T, MacCarthy B, et al. The Camberwell Collaborative Depression Study. I. Depressed probands: adversity and the form of depression. *Br J Psychiatry.* 1988; 152:754-765.

65) Leibenluft E, Hardin TA, Rosenthal NE. Gender differences in seasonal affective disorder. Depression 1995; 3:13-19.

66) Rapaport MH, Thompson PM, Kelsoe JR, Jr., et al. Gender differences in outpatient research subjects with affective disorders: a comparison of descriptive variables. *J Clin Psychiatry* 1995; 56:67-72.

67) Pajer K. New strategies in the treatment of depression in women. J Clin Psychiatry. 1995; 56(suppl2):30-37.

68) Hirschfeld RM, Russell JM. Assessment and treatment of suicidal patients. N Engl J Med 1997; 337:910-915.

69) Bisaga K, et al. Menstrual functioning and psychpathology in a county-wide population of high school girls. *J Am Acad Child Adolesc Psychiatry.* 2002; 41:1197-1204.

70) Baca-Garcia E, Diaz-Sastre C, de Leon J, Saiz-Ruiz J. The relationship between menstrual cycle phases and suicide attempts. *Psychosom Med.* 2000; 62:50-60.

71) Endicott J. History History, evolution, and diagnosis of premenstrual dysphoric disorder. J Clin Psychiatry 2000; 61(suppl 12):5-8.

72) Basoglu C, Cetin M, Semiz UB, Agargun MY, Ebrinc S. Premenstrual exacerbation and suicidal behavior in patients with panic disorder. *Comp Psychiatry.* 2000: 41:103-5.

73) O'Hara MW, Schlechte JA, Lewis DA, et al. Controlled prospective study of postpartum mood disorders: psychological, environmental, and hormonal variables. *J Abnorm Psychol* 1991; 100:63-73.

74) O'Hara MW. Social support, life events, and depression during pregnancy and the puerperium. *Arch Gen Psychiatry.* 1986; 43:569-573.

75) Cohen LS, Viguera AC, Lyster AK, et al. Prevalence and predictors of depression during pregnancy [abstract]. Presented at the 155th annual meeting of the American Psychiatric Association; May 2002; Philadelphia, PA.

76) Einarson A, Selby P, Koren G. Abrupt discontinuation of psychotropic drugs during pregnancy: fear of teratogenic risk and impact of counselling. *J Psychiatry Neurosci.* 2001; 26:44-8.

77) Green L, Ardron C, Catalan J. HIV, childbirth and suicidal behavior: a review. *Hosp Med.* 2000; 61:311-4.

78) Moylan PL, Jones HE, Haug NA, Kissin WB, Svikis DS. Clinical and psychosocial characteristics of substance-dependent pregnant women with and without PDST. *Addict Behav.* 2001; 26:469-74.

79) Khlat M, Ronsmans C. Deaths attributable to childbearing in Matlab, Bangladesh: indirect causes of maternal mortality questioned. *Am J Epidemiol.* 2000; 151:300-6.

80) Langer A. Unwanted pregnancy: impact on health and society in Latin America and the Caribbean. *Rev Panam Salud Publica.* 2002; 11:192-204.

81) Mitchison S. Suicides after pregnancy. Study did not show association between induced abortion and suicide. *BMJ.* 1997; 314:902-3.

82) Frautschi S, Cerulli A, Maine D. Suicide during pregnancy and its neglect as a component of maternal mortality. *Int J Gynaecol Obstet.* 1994; 47:275-84.

83) Granja AC, Zacarias E, Bergstrom S. Violent deaths: the hidden face of maternal mortality. *BJOG* 2002; 109:5-8.

84) Pastuszak A, Schick-Boschetto B, Zuber C, et al. Pregnancy outcome following first-trimester exposure to fluoxetine (Prozac). *JAMA* 1993; 269:2246-2248.

85) Evans J, Heron J, Francomb H, et al. Cohort study of depressed mood during pregnancy and after childbirth. *Br Med J.* 2001; 323:257-260.

86) Nonacs R, Cohen LS. Postpartum mood disorders: diagnosis and treatment guidelines. *J Clin Psychiatry.*

1998; 59(suppl 2):34-40.

87) Davidson J, Robertson E. A follow-up study of post partum illness, 1946-1978. *Acta Psychiatr Scand.* 1985; 71:451-457.

88 ) Lyons-Ruth K, Wolfe R, Lyubchik A. Depression and the parenting of young children: making the case for early preventive mental health services. *Harv Rev Psychiatry.* 2000; 8:148-153.

89) Murray L, Fiori-Cowley A, Hooper R, et al. The impact of postnatal depression and associated adversity on early mother-infant interactions and later infant outcome. *Child Dev.* 1996; 67:2512-2526.

90) Appleby L, Warner R, Whitton A, et al. A controlled study of fluoxetine and cognitive-behavioral counselling in the treatment of postnatal depression. *Br Med J.* 1997; 314:932-936.

91) Stowe ZN, Cassarella J, Landry J, et al. Sertraline in the treatment of women with postpartum major depression. *Depression.* 1995; 3:49-55.

92) Cohen LS, Viguera AC, Bouffard SM, et al. Venlafaxine in the treatment of postpartum depression. *J Clin Psychiatry.* 2001; 62:592-596.

93) Kendell RE, Chalmers JC, Platz C. Epidemiology of puerperal psychoses. *Br J Psychiatry.* 1987; 150:662-673.

94) Reich T, Winokur G. Postpartum psychoses in patients with manic depressive disease. *J Nerv Ment Dis.* 1970; 151:60-68.

95) Pfuhlmann B, Stoeber G, Beckmann H. Postpartum psychoses: prognosis, risk factors, and treatment. *Curr Psychiatry Rep.* 2002; 4:185-90.

96) Harlow BL, Cohen LS, Otto MW, et al. Prevalence and predictors of depressive symptoms in older pre-menopausal women: the Harvard Study of Moods and Cycles. *Arch Gen Psychiatry.* 1999; 56:418-424.

97) Cohen LS. Gender-specific considerations in the treatment of mood disorders in women across the life cycle. J Clin *Psychiatry.* 2003; 64(suppl 15):18-29.

98) Muyrphy SL. Deaths: final data for 1998. *Natl Vital State Rep.* 2000; 48: 1-100.

99) Fu Q. Heath AC, Bucholz KK, Nelson EC, Glowinski Al, et al. A twin study of genetic and environmental influences on suicidality in men., *Psychol Med.* 2002; 32:11-24

100) Stone G. *Suicide and attempted suicide.* New York, NY: Carroll and Graf; 1999.

101) O'Carroll PW, Berman AL, Maris RW, Moscicki EK, Tanneyt BL, et al. Beyond the tower of Baberl: a nomenclature of suicidology. *Suicide Life-Threat behav.* 1996; 26:237-252.

102) Russell D, Judd F. Why are men killing themselves? A look at the evidence. Aust Fam Physician. 1999; 28:791-795.

103) Bradvik L, Berglund M. Seasonal distribution of suicide in alcoholism. *Acta Psychiatr Scand.* 2002; 106:299-302.

104) Conner KR, Duberstein PR, Conwell Y. Domestic violence, separation, and suicide in young men with early onset alcoholism: reanalyses of Murphy's data. *Suicide Life Threat Behav.* 2000; 30:354-9.

105) Murphy GE. Why women are less likely than men to commit suicide. *Compr Psychiatry.* 1998; 39:165-175.

106) Moller-Leimkuhler AM. The gender gap in suicide and premature death or: why are men so vulnerable? *Eur Arch Psychiatry Clin Neurosci.* 2003; 253:1-8.

107) Gustavsson G, Traskman-Bendz L, Higley JD, Westrin A. CSF testosterone in 43 male suicide attempters. *Eur Neuropsychopharmacol.* 2003; 13:105-9.

108) Luoma JB, Martin CE, Pearson JL. Contact with mental health and primary care providers before suicide: a review of the evidence. *Am J Psychiatry.* 2002; 159:909-16.

109) National Institutes of Health. Public Health Service. Depression and suicide facts for older adults. OM-99-4207. www.nimh.nih.gov.

110) Hamilton NG. Suicide prevention in primary care. Careful questioning, prompt treatment can save lives. *Postgrad Med.* 2000; 108:81-4.

111) Druss B. Pincus H. Suicidal ideation and suicide attempts in general medical illnesses. *Arch Intern Med.* 2000; 160:1522-6.

112) Arciniegas DB, Anderson CA. Suicide in neurologic illness. *Curr Teat Options Neurol.* 2002; 4:457-468.

113) Lindesay J. Validity of the general health questionnaire (GHQ) in detecting psychiatric disturbance in amputees with phantom pain. *J Psychosom Res.* 1986; 30:277-281.

114) Breslau N, Davis GC. Migraine, major depression and panic disorder: a prospective epidemiologic study of young adults. *Cephalalgia.* 1992; 12:85-92.

115) Korszun A. Facial pain, depression and stress-connections and directions. *J Oral Pathol Med.* 2002; 31:615-619.

116) Krishnan KR, France RD, Pelto S, McCann UD, Davidson J, et al. Chronic pain and depression: I. Classification of depression in chronic low-back pain patients. *Pain.* 1985; 22:279-285.

117) Yap AU, Tan KB, Chua EK, Tan HH. Depression and somatization patients with temporomandibular disorders. *J Prosthetic Dentistry.* 2002; 88:479-484.

118) Cohen H, Neumann L, Haiman Y, Matar MA, Press J, et al. Prevalence of post-traumatic stress disorder in fibromyalgia patients: overlapping syndromes or post-traumatic fibromyalgia syndrome? *Semin Arthritis Rheum.* 2002; 32:38-50.

119) Walker EA, Boy-Byrne PP, Katon WJ, Li L, Amos D, et al. Psychiatric illness and irritable bowel syndrome: a comparison with inflammatory bowel disease. *Am J Psychiatry.* 1999; 147:1656-1661.

120) Fisher BJ, Haythornthwaite, JA, Heinberg LJ, Clark M, Reed J. Suicidal intent in patients with chronic pain. *Pain.* 2001; 89:199-206.

121) Nilsson L, Ahlbom A, Farahmand BY, Asberg M, Tomson T. Risk factors for suicide in epilepsy: a case control study. *Epilepsia.* 2002; 43:644-51.

122) Robins TB, Backman L, Lundin A, Haegermark A, Winblad B, et al. High suicidal ideation in persons testing for Huntington's disease. *Acta Neurol Scand.* 2000; 102:150-61.

123) Chwastiak L, et al. Depressive symptoms and severity of illness in multiple sclerosis: Epidemiologic study of a large community sample. *Am J Psychiatry.* 2002; 159:1862-1868.

124) Feinstein A. An examination of suicidal intent in patients with multiple sclerosis. *Neurology.* 2002; 59:674-8.

125) Pohjasvaara T, Vataja R, Leppavuori A, Kaste M, Erkinjuntti T. Suicidal ideas in stroke patients 3 and 15 months after stroke. *Cerebrovasc Dis.* 2001; 12:21-6.

126) Teasdale TW, Engberg AW. Suicide after a stroke: a population study. *J Epidemiol Community Health.* 2001; 55:863-6.

127) Lovett JK, Rothwell PM. Suicide in a patient with symptomatic carotid occlusion. *J R Soc Med.* 2002; 95:93-4.

128) DeLeo D, Hickey PA, Meneghel G, Cantor CH. Blindness, fear of sight loss and suicide. *Psychosomatics.* 1999; 40:339-344.

129) Popelova J, Slavik Z, Skovranek J. Are cyanosed adults with congenital cardiac malformations depressed? *Cardiol Young.* 2001; 11:379-84.

130) Wulsin LR, Singal BM. Do depressive symptoms increase the risk for the onset of coronary disease? A systematic quantitative review. *Psychosom Med.* 2003; 5:201-10.

131) Penninx BW, Beekman AT, Honig A, Deeg DJ, Schoevers RA, et al. Depression and cardiac mortality: results from a community-based longitudinal study. *Arch Gen Psychiatry.* 2001; 58:221-7.

132) Ziegelstein RC, Fauerbach JA, Stevens SS, Romanelli J, Richter DP, et al. Patients with depression are less likely to follow recommendations to reduce cardiac risk during recovery from a myocardial infarction. *Arch Intern Med.* 2000; 160:1818-23.

133) Havranek EP, Ware MG, Lowes BD. Prevalence of depression in congestive heart failure. *Am J Cardiol.* 1999; 84:348-50.

134) Westin L, Carlsson R, Erhardt L, Cantor-Graae E, McNeil T. Differences in quality of life in men and women with ischemic heart disease. A prospective controlled study. *Scand Cardiovasc J.* 1999; 33:160-5.

135) Malhotra S, Tesar GE, Franco K. The relationship between depression and cardiovascular disorders. *Curr Psychiatry Rep.* 2000; 2:241-6.

136) Goodwin RD, Olfson M, Shea S, Lantigua RA, Carrasquilo O, et al. Asthma and mental disorders in pri-

mary care. *Gen Hosp Psychiatry.* 2003; 25:479-83.

137) Druss B, Pincus H. Suicidal ideation and suicide attempts in general medical illnesses. *Arch Intern Med.* 2000; 160:1522-6.

138) Carpenter KM, Hasin DS, Allison DB, Faith MS. Relationships between obesity and DSM-IV major depressive disorder, suicide ideation, and suicide attempts: results from a general population study. *Am J Public Health.* 2000; 90:251-7.

139) Fagiolini A, Kupfer DJ, Rucci P, Stat D, Scott JA, et al. Suicide attempts and ideation in patients with bipolar I disorder. J Clin Psychiatry 2004; 65:509-514.

140) Banaschak S, Bajanowski T, Brinkmann B. Suicide of a diabetic by inducing hyperglycemic coma. *Int J Legal Med.* 2000; 113:162-3.

141) Koller EA, Doraiswamy PM. Olanzapine-associated diabetes mellitus. Pharmacotherapy. 2002; 22:841-852.

142) Allison DB, Fontaine KR, Heo M, et al. The distribution of body mass index among individuals with and without schizophrenia. *J Clin Psychiatry.* 1999; 60:215-220.

143) Meyer JM. A retrospective comparison of weight, lipid, and glucose changes between risperidone and olanzapine-treated inpatients: metabolic outcomes after 1 year. *J Clin Psychiatry.* 2002; 63:425-433.

144) van Heeringen K, Audenaert K, Van de Wiele L, Verstraete A. Cortisol in volent suicidal behaviour: association with personality and monoaminergic activity. *J Affect Disord.* 2000; 60:181-9.

145) Gmitrowicz A, Kolodziej-Maciejewska H. Dysfunction of the hypothalamic-pituitary-adrenal axis in adolescents after a suicide attempt. *Psychiatr Pol.* 2001; 35:803-818.

146) Levin TR, Terrell TR, Stoudemire A. Organic mood disorder associated with the HAIR-AN syndrome. *J Neuropsychiatry Clin Neurosci.* 1992; 4:51-4.

147) Levy NB. Psychiatric considerations in the primary medical care of the patient with renal failure. *Adv Ren Replac Ther.* 2000; 7:231-8.

148) Ishikura R, Morimoto N, Tanaka K, Kinukawa N, Yoshizawa S, et al. Factors associated with anxiety, depression and suicide ideation in female outpatients with SLE in Japan. *Clin Rheumatol.* 2002; 20:394-400.

149) Karassa FB, Magliano M, Isenberg DA. Suicide attempts in patients with systemic lupus erythematosus. *Ann Rheum Dis.* 2003; 62:58-60.

150) Lesser R, Walters JL, Pebenito R, Klee S, Khan R. Improvement of neuropsychiatric lupus with addition of SSRI antidepressant/antipsychotic therapy. *J Clin Rheumatol.* 1997; 3:294-298.

151) Dickens C, Jackson J, Tomenson B, Hay E, Creed F. Association of depression and rheumatoid arthritis. *Psychosomatics.* 2003; 44:209-15.

152) Timonen M, Viilo K, Hakko H, Sarkioja T, Ylikulju M, et al. Suicides in persons suffering from rheumatoid arthritis. *Rheumatology.* 2003; 42:287-91.

153) Slaughter JR, Parker JC, Martens MP, Smarr KL, Hewett JE. Clinical outcomes following a trial of sertraline in rheumatoid arthritis. *Psychosomatics.* 2002; 43:36-41.

154) Rohde P, Noell J, Ochs L, Seeley JR. Depression, suicidal ideation and STD-related risk in homeless older adolescents. *J Adolesc.* 2002; 24:447-460.

155) Yager J. Which HIV-positive patients attempt suicide? *Psychiatry Journal Watch.* 2003; 3:24.

156) Roy A. Characteristics of HIV patients who attempt suicide. *Acta Psychiatr Scand.* 2003; 107:41-4.

157) Kalichman SC, Heckman T, Kochman A, Sikkema K, Bergholte J. Depression and thoughts of suicide among middle-aged and older persons living with HIV-AIDS. *Psychiatr Serv.* 2003; 51:903-907.

158) Iannaccone R, Sue YJ, Avner JR. Suicidal psychosis secondary to isoniazid. *Pediatr Emerg Care.* 2002; 18:25-7.

159) Friedlander AH, Mahler ME. Major depressive disorder. Psychopathology, medical management and dental implications. *J Am Dent Assoc.* 2001; 132:629-38.

160) Goodwin RD, Stein MB. Generalized anxiety disorder and peptic ulcer disease among adults in the United States. *Psychosom Med.* 2002; 64:682-6.

161) Centers for Disease Control and Prevention. Recommendations for the prevention and control of hepatitis C virus (HCV) infection and HCV-related chronic disease. MMWR. October 16, 1998. Available at: www.cdc.gov/mmwr/preview/mmwrhtml/00055154.htm. Accessed December 10, 2003.

162) Rosenberg P. Hepatitis C: a hepatologist's approach to an infectious disease. *Clin Infect Dis*. 2001; 33:1728-1732.

163) Ademmer K, Beutel M, Bretzel R, et al. Suicidal ideation with IFN-alfa and ribavirin in a patient with hepatitis. *Psychosomatics*. 2001; 42:365-367.

164) Drugs that cause psychiatric symptoms. *Med Lett*. 2002; 44:1134.

165) Guthrie E, Jackson J, Shaffer J, Thompson D, Tomenson B, et al. Psychological disorder and severity of inflammatory bowel disease predict health-related quality of life in ulcerative colitis and Chron's disease. *Am J Gastroenterol*. 2002; 97:1994-9.

166) Hjerl K. Depression as a prognostic factor for breast cancer mortality. *Psychosomatics*. 2003; 44:24-30.

167) Filiberti A, Ripamonti C. Suicide and suicidal thoughts in cancer patients. *Tumori*. 2002; 88:193-9.

168) Chochinov HM, Wilson KG, Enns M, Lander S. Depression, hopelessness , and suicidal ideation in the terminally ill. *Psychosomatics*. 1998; 39:366-370.

169) Tanaka H, Tsukuma H, Masaoka T, Ajiki W, Koyama Y, et al. Suicide risk among cancer patients: experience at one medical center in Japan, 1978-1994. *Jpn J Cancer Res*. 1999; 90:812-17.

170) Cullivan R, Crown J, Walsh N. the use of psychotropic medication in patients referred to a psycho-oncology service. *Psychooncology*. 1998; 7;301-6

171) Kochanck KD, Murphy SL, Andersonm RN, et al. (2004). Deaths: Final data for 2002. Nartional Vital Statistcs Reprots, 53 (5). Hyattsville, MD: National Center for Health Satistics. DHHS Publication No. (PHS) 2005-1120.

172) Robins Ln, Helzer JE, Weissman MM, et al. Lifetime prevalence of specific psychiatric disorders in three sites. *Arch Gen Psychiatry*. 1984; 41:949-958.

173) Fitten LJ, Morley JE, Gross PL et al. Depression. *J Am Geriatr Soc*. 1989; 37:459-472.

174) Conwell Y, Duberstein PR, Cox C, et al. Relationships of age and axis I diagnoses in victims of completed suicide: a psychological autopsy study. *Am J Psychiatry*. 1996; 53:1001-1008.

175) Szanto K, Mulsant BH, Houck P, et al. Occurrence and course of suicidality during short-term treatment of late-life depression. *Arch Gen Psychiatry*. 2003; 60:610-617.

176) Duberstein PR, Conwell Y, Caine ED. Age differences in the personality characteristics of suicide completers: preliminary findings from a psychological autopsy study. *Psychiatry*. 1994; 57:213-224.

177) Wilson DR, Widmer RB, Cadoret RJ. Judiesch K. Somatic symptoms: a major feature of depression in a family practice. *J Affect Disord*. 1983; 5:199-207.

178) Harman JS, Brown EL, Have T, Mulsant BH, Brown G, et al. Primary car physicians' attitude toward diagnosis and treatment of late-life depression. *CNS Spectrums*. 2002; 7:784-790.

179) Conwell, Y. Suicide in elderly patients. In: Schneider, LS, Reynolds CF III, Lebowitz BD, Friedhoff AJ, eds. *Diagnosis and treatment of depression in late life*. Washington, DC: American Psychiatric Press, 1994; 397-418.

180) Harman JS, Schulberg HC, Mulsant BH, Reynolds CF. Effect of patient and visit characteristics on diagnosis of depression in primary care. *J Fam Prac*. 2001; 50:1068.

181) Unutzer J, Simon G, Berlin TR, Datt M, Kanton W, et al. Care for depression in HMO patients age 65 and older. *J Am Geriatr Soc*. 2000; 48:871-878.

182) Clark DC, vonAmmon Cavanaugh S, Gibbons RD. The core symptoms of depression in medical and psychiatric patients. *J Nerv Ment Dis*. 1983; 171:705-713.

183) Waern M, Beskow J, Runeson B, Skoog I. Suicidal feelings in the last year of life in elderly people who commit suicide. *Lancet*. 1999. 354:917-918 [letter].

184) Musselman DL, Evans DL, Nemeroff CB. The relationship of depression to cardiovascular disease: epidemiology, biology, and treatment. *Arch Gen Psychiatry*. 1998; 55:580-592.

185) Frazure-Smith N, Lesperance F, Talajic M. Depression following myocardial infarction. Impact on 6-month

survival. *JAMA.* 1993; 270:1819-1825.

186) Koenig HG, Blazer DG. Minor depression in late life. *Am J Geriatr Psychiatry.* 1996; 4:514-521.

187) Turvey CL, Conwell Y, Jones M, Phillips C, Simonsick E, et al. Risk factors for late life suicide. *Am J Geriatr Psychiatry.* 2002; 10:398-406.

188) Duberstein PR, Conwell Y, Cox C. Suicide in widowed persons: a psychological autopsy comparison of recently and remotely bereaved older subjects. *Am J Geriatr Psychiatry.* 1998; 6:328-334.

189) Byrne GJ, Raphael B. Depressive symptoms and depressive episodes in recently widowed older men. *Int Psychogeriatr.* 1999; 11:67-74.

190) Heisel MJ, Flett GL, Besser A. Cognitive functioning and geriatric suicide ideation: testing a mediational model. *Am J Geriatr Psychiatry* 2002; 10:428-436

191) Rubenowitz E, Waern M, Wihelmson K, Allebeck P. Life events and psychosocial factors in elderly suicides—a case-control study. *Psychol Med.* 2001; 31:1193-1202.

192) Conwell Y, Duberstein PR, Cox C, Herrmann J, Forbes, et al. Age differences in behaviors leading to completed suicide. *Am J Geriatr Psychiatry.* 1998; 6:122-126.

193) Conwell Y Duberstein PR. Suicide in Elders. *Ann N.Y. Acad Sci.* 2001; 932:132-150.

194) Langa KM, Valenstein MA, Fendrick MA, et al. Extent and cost of informal care giving for older Americans with symptoms of depression. *Am J Psychiatry.* 161:857-863.

195) Katon W, von Korff M, Lin E. Adequacy and duration of antidepressant treatment in primary care. *Medical Care.* 1992; 30:67-76.

196) Unutzer J, Katon W, Russo J, et al. Patterns of care for depressed older adults in a large-staff model HMO. *Am J Geriatr Psychiatry.* 1999; 7:235-243.

197) Pearson JL. Recent research on suicide in the elderly. *Cur Psychiatry Rep.* 2002; 4:59-63.

198) Nelson JC. Diagnosing and treating depression in the elderly. J Clin Psychiatry. 2001; 62(suppl 24):18-22.

199) Roose S. Presented at the 15th Annual Meeting of the American Association for Geriatric Psychiatry; Feb 24-27,2002; Orlando, Fla.

200) Szanto K, Mulsant BH, Houck P, Dew MA, Reynolds CF. Occurrence and course of suicidality during short term treatment of late-life depression. *Arch Gen Psychiatry.* 2002; 60:610-7.

201) Skoog I, Aevarsson O, Beskow J, Larsson L, Palsson S., et al. Suicidal feelings in a population sample of nondemented 85-year-olds. *Am J Psychiatry.* 1996; 153:1015-1020.

202) Ostamo A, Lonnqvist J. Excess mortality of suicide attempters. *Soc Psychiatry Psychiatr Epidemiol.* 2001; 36:29-35.

203) Gofin R, Avitzour M, Haklai Z, Jellin N. Intentional injuries among the young: presentation to emergency rooms, hospitalization, and death in Israel. *J Adolesc Health.* 2000; 27:434-442.

204) Rives W. Emergency department assessment of suicidal patients. *Psychiatr Clin North Am.* 1999; 22:779-787.

205) Gairin I, House A, Owens D. Attendance at the accident and emergency department in the year before suicide: retrospective study. *Br J Psychiatry.* 2003; 183:28-33.

206) Schmidt TA, Zechnich AD. Suicidal patients in the ED: ethical issues. *Emerg Med Clin North Am.* 1999; 17:371-383.

207) Pajonk FG, Gruenberg KA, MOecke H, Naber D. Suicides and suicide attempts in emergency medicine. *Crisis.* 2002; 23:68-73.

208) Schwarz D. Adolescent Trauma: epidemiologic approach. *Adolesc Med.* 1993; 4:11-22.

209) Johnson MS, Moore M, Mitchell P, Owen P, Pilby J. Serious and fatal firearm injuries among children and adolescents in Alaska: 1991-1997. *Alaska Med.* 2000; 42:3-10.

210) Duominen E, Tukiainen E. Close-range shotgun and rifle injuries to the face. *Clin Plast Surg.* 2001; 28:323-337.

211) Byard RW, Klitte A, Gilbert JD, James RA. Clinicopathologic features of fatal self-inflicted incised and stab wounds: a 20-year study. *Am J Forensic Med Pathol.* 2002; 23:25-18.

212) Agalar F, Cakmakci M, Kunt MM. Train-pedestrian accidents. *Eur J Emerg Med.* 2000; 7:131-3.

213) Beale JP, Wyatt JP, Beard D, Busuttil A, Graham CA. A five year study of high falls in Edinburgh. *Injury.* 2000; 31:503-8.

214) Teh J, Firth M, Sharma A, Wilson A, Reznek R. et al. Jumpers and fallers: a comparison of the distribution of skeletal injury. *Clin Radiol.* 2003; 58:482-6.

215) Onizuka M, Kaminogo M, Fujita H, Irie N, Shibata S. Penetrating head injury caused by an ice pick. *No Shinkei Geka.* 2001; 29:1101-5.

216) Rothschild MA, Schneider V. Decapitation as a result of suicidal hanging. *Forensic Sci Int.* 1999; 106:55-62.

217) Zhu B, Quan L, Ishida K, Oritani S, Taniguchi M, et al. Decapitation in suicidal hanging—a case report with a review of the literature. *Leg Med (Tokyo).* 2000; 2:159-62.

218) Vassiliu P, Baker J, Henderson S, Alo K, Velmahos G, et al. Aerodigestive injuries of the neck. *Am Surg.* 2001; 67:75-9.

219) Canizares MA, Arnau A, Fortea A, Zarzuela V, Martinez-Vallina P, et al. Hyoid fracture and traumatic subcutaneous cervical emphysema from an attempted hanging. *Arch Bronconeumol.* 2000;36:52-4.

220) Vereczkei a, Varga G, Poto L, Horvath OP. Management of corrosive injuries of the esophagus. *Acta Chir Hung.* 1999; 38:119-22.

221) Furukawa H, Tsuchiya K, Ogata K, Kabuto Y, Iida Y. Penetrating knife injury to the heart. *Jpn J Thorac Cardiovac Surg.* 2000; 48:142-4.

222) Welch JD, Meriwether K, Trautman R. Stigmata: part I. Shame, guilt, and anger. *Plast Reconstr Surg.* 1999; 104:65-71.

223) Ying SY, Ho WS. Contact burn by charcoal in an attempted suicide. *Burns.* 2001; 27:512-4.

224) Mabrouk AR, Omar M, Massoud K, Sherif M, El Sayed N.. Suicide by burns: a tragic end. *Burns.* 1999; 25:337-9.

225) Gilson T, Parks BO, Portefield CM. Suicide with inert gases: addendum to final exit. *Am J Forensic Med Pathol.* 2003; 24:306-8.

226) Bullock MJ, Diniz D. Suffocation using plastic bags: a retrospective study of suicides in Ontario, Canada. *J Forensic Sci.* 2000; 45:608-13.

227) Hutchinson G, Daisley H, Simeon D, Simmonds V, Shetty M, et al. High rates of paraquat-induced suicide in southern Trinidad. *Suicide Life Threat Behav.* 1999; 29:186-91.

228) Hunsaker DM, Thorne LB. Suicide by blunt force trauma. *Am J Forensic Med Pathol.* 2002; 23:355-9.